FOREVER STRUGGLE

FOREVER STRUGGLE

ACTIVISM, IDENTITY, & SURVIVAL IN BOSTON'S CHINATOWN, 1880–2018

MICHAEL LIU

UNIVERSITY OF MASSACHUSETTS PRESS

Amherst and Boston

ISBN 978-1-62534-546-2 (paper); 545-5 (hardcover)

Designed by Deste Roosa
Set in DIN Schrift and Minion Pro
Printed and bound by Books International, Inc.

Cover design by 4eyes Design
Cover photo by Douglass Brugge, *Elderly with Megaphone.*
Courtesy of the Chinese Progressive Association.

Library of Congress Cataloging-in-Publication Data

Names: Liu, Michael, 1948– author.
Title: Forever struggle : activism, identity, and survival in Boston's
Chinatown, 1880–2018 / Michael Liu.
Other titles: Activism, identity, and survival in Boston's Chinatown,
1880–2018
Description: Amherst : University of Massachusetts Press, [2020] | Includes
bibliographical references and index. |
Identifiers: LCCN 2020019276 | ISBN 9781625345462 (paper) | ISBN
9781625345455 (hardcover) | ISBN 9781613767917 (ebook) | ISBN
9781613767924 (ebook)
Subjects: LCSH: Chinatown (Boston, Mass.)—History. | Boston
(Mass.)—History. | Chinese Americans—Massachusetts—Boston—History. |
Chinese Americans—Massachusetts—Boston—Social conditions. | Chinese
Americans—Political activity—Massachusetts—Boston—History. |
Community activists—Massachusetts—Boston—History. | Community
organization—Massachusetts—Boston—History. |
Immigrants—Massachusetts—Boston—History.
Classification: LCC F73.9.C5 L58 2020 | DDC 974.4/610951073—dc23
LC record available at https://lccn.loc.gov/2020019276

British Library Cataloguing-in-Publication Data
A catalog record for this book is available from the British Library.

For the Liu and Louie extended families,
whom Chinatowns nurtured,
and in memory of Tunney Lee, Louse Liu,
Gim Kang Wong Louie, and Gan Toy Lee.

CONTENTS

CONTENTS

PREFACE & ACKNOWLEDGMENTS

I have had a long-standing need to write about Boston Chinatown, my birth neighborhood, not only because of its extraordinary history but also because it will soon change beyond recognition. Within a city overwhelmed by the forces of development, it has somehow survived, but not without wounds or change. Examining the history of Boston Chinatown offers complicated answers to questions about place, particularly as they affect low-income communities of color in new Boston's post-industrial identity. This book explores Chinatown's journey and its struggle to survive via strategies such as compliance, negotiation, massive protests, multiple mobilizations, self-reliance, and community planning. In the end, this is a story of struggle against a structure that privileges development for maximum profit above all other values.

My commitment to uncovering, telling, and continuing this story stems from my love for Chinatown and its people, a love that grew from a childhood spent on its streets. The early immigrant workers I describe were much like my own garment- and restaurant-worker parents. I was among the young activists who challenged traditional control and institutional encroachment, formed new grassroots democratic groups, and organized to retain and nurture our beloved community. I also worked in the local public school and university systems, directly engaging with the Asian American community. Chinatown has been a focus of my activism for more than five decades.

This book is a history of a community's activism. Where my role influenced that activism, I noted it, but this is a collective history. I've chosen to tell this narrative through the voices and eyes of others in order to reflect as thoroughly and fairly as I can the reality through which the community lived. My role as a participant-observer was crucial in establishing relationships and grounding an understanding of the dynamics of neighborhood mobilization. At the same time, however, it may have limited my access to neighborhood stakeholders who took differing positions on community issues.

In the course of writing and researching this book, I was fortunate to receive help and support from many people. Tunney Lee, Shauna Lo, Suzanne Lee, and Stephanie Fan offered their perspectives on the community and sometimes argued with me about them. Lorrayne Shen shared her work on Boston busing, which included many interviews. Karen Chen of the Chinese Progressive Association and Carolyn Chou of the Asian American Resource Workshop opened their organizations to me. Tom Chen's doctoral dissertation served as a guide for various sections of the book, particularly the development of T-NEMC's urban renewal plans, the events and mobilization around the Merchants Building, and the organizing around Boston busing. My life partner, May Louie, edited the manuscript, made perceptive suggestions, and, most importantly, helped me significantly rewrite sections about which she had direct knowledge. Any remaining faults and failings rest with me.

Many family members, colleagues, and friends encouraged me when the work became difficult. They include Callie Watkins Liu, Claire Andrade-Watkins, Mark Liu, Sharon Cho, Lawrence Cheng, Wayne Yeh, Carolyn Wong, and Myrna Morales; members of community groups such as Activist Training and the Asian American Resource Workshop; and my long-time fellow travelers in "the dinner group." I thank Lydia Lowe, Star Wang, and especially Ashley Shen, who offered to look at and proofread drafts.

Brian Halley, my editor at the University of Massachusetts Press, has endured this long trek with me. His urgings and suggestions and those of his colleagues, Rachael DeShano and Dawn Potter, have made my manuscript a much better book. My work at the Institute for Asian American Studies at the University of Massachusetts Boston has made crucial contributions, and I'm grateful for Paul Watanabe's and Shauna Lo's tolerance and support.

Finally, I thank the informants and interviewees who shared their time and insights about a complicated neighborhood. Richard Chin, Zenobia Lai, David Moy, Mary Yee, Howard Wong, Angie Liou, Caroline Chang, Mah Wah, and many others have given Chinatown their passion, energy, and ideas. Their engagement has shaped and sustained the community into what it is today—this place that has given me a story to tell.

ABBREVIATIONS

AACA   Asian American Civic Association (formerly CACA)
AAU   Asian Americans United
ABN   Alliance of Boston Neighborhoods
ABCD   Action for Boston Community Development
ACDC   Asian Community Development Corporation
BCNC   Boston Chinatown Neighborhood Center (formerly QSCC)
BCPA   Boston Chinese Parents Association
BPS   Boston Public Schools
BRA   Boston Redevelopment Authority (later Boston Planning and Development Authority)
CACA   Chinese American Civic Association (later AACA)
CCBA   Chinese Consolidated Benevolent Association
CCC   Chinatown Community Center
CCCNE   Chinese Christian Church of New England
CDC   Community Development Corporation
CEDC   Chinese Economic Development Council
CETOC   Chinatown Employment and Training Opportunity Coalition
CNC   Chinatown Neighborhood Council
CPA   Chinese Progressive Association (founded as the Chinatown People's Progressive Association)
CPC   Campaign to Protect Chinatown
CPPA   Chinese Progressive Political Action
CRA   Chinatown Resident Association
DSNI   Dudley Street Neighborhood Initiative
GBLS   Greater Boston Legal Services
ILGWU   International Ladies' Garment Workers' Union
MDEP   Massachusetts Department of Environmental Protection
PCCOS   Philadelphia Chinatown Coalition to Oppose the Stadium
PCDC   Philadelphia Chinatown Development Corporation
RTTC   Right to the City Coalition

ABBREVIATIONS

QSCC	Quincy School Community Council (later BCNC)
TCC	The Chinatown Coalition
T-NEMC	Tufts–New England Medical Center
UDAG	Urban Development Action Grant
USDA	U.S. Department of Agriculture
YES	Boston Chinese Youth Essential Service (later Boston Asian Youth Essential Service)

FOREVER STRUGGLE

INTRODUCTION

A CHINATOWN WALK

On a stroll down Boston Chinatown's main thoroughfare, Beach Street, the sense of an ethnic neighborhood is palpable. The area's dense street patterns feel too narrow for the numbers of people coursing through them; the brick and stone buildings seem to be rooted in a forgotten era; the residents are speaking many different languages. The Chinese restaurants, grocery stores, street vendors, gift shops are stacked chock-a-block, pressing on you.

The commercial face of Chinatown is unmistakable, but where do its 5,000 residents live? That is less obvious. Many live on back streets or above hectic storefronts, overshadowed by the towering edifices of the Tufts–New England Medical Center (T-NEMC). The medical center dominates the neighborhood: you have to walk south past Kneeland Street through T-NEMC buildings to find Chinatown's residential core. But this sense of invisibility is nothing new. For most of the community's tenure, local media have limited their coverage, producing occasional profiles of Chinatown's people to titillate readers or reporting on municipal drives to punish residents. Only in the past few decades have newspapers, magazines, and broadcast media covered this hardscrabble, 140-year-old neighborhood with any depth.

Despite Chinatown's popularity as a tourist destination, few visitors are aware that a neighborhood exists here. Even fewer know that its poverty rate is more than 30 percent higher and its density more than five times the city's average.[1] Since the end of World War II, continuous development pressure on this immigrant enclave has forced many of its inhabitants into corners, basements, isolated patches, or housing developments. Yet despite being seen as a passive and powerless community, Chinatown has survived and reshaped its identity by challenging outside claims on its land and buildings. Drawing on cultural and social networks and building on neighborhood attachments and symbols of ethnic and neighborhood solidarity, its residents have, over course of fifty years, created new leadership structures and adopted a variety of mobilization methods to assert more control over their community. Its leaders have organized the growing Chinese and Asian communities in the Boston area, demanding that they have a place in the city. In so doing, Chinatown has transformed its relationship to Boston.

WHY CHINATOWN MATTERS

Sociologists have seen low-income areas as settings for *ethnic succession,* a pattern in which a recent migrant group replaces a more established migrant group as the latter rises economically and moves out to wealthier neighborhoods.[2] Since the 1950s, however, many people have pointed out the limitations of this concept, noting the obstacles to social mobility faced by people of color. The persistence of certain Chinatowns and their issues illustrate these obstacles.[3] These racial hurdles may also underlie the intensity with which inhabitants have historically defended their communities.

Chinatown is one of several ethnic neighborhoods that established itself in post–World War II Boston, and it illustrates the sustained effort such neighborhoods have made to survive the city's urban transformation. As one former resident put it, "this is a forever struggle. . . . Chinatown can never rest."[4] Other ethnic neighborhoods in the city have either literally or virtually dissipated. While newer enclaves further from the downtown development pressures have established themselves, Chinatown's story has much to teach us about the prospects of immigrant and low-income neighborhoods in a growing city.

Given Boston's multi-decade development boom, questions about inclusivity and tolerance in local elites' growth plans are critical. When development plans target low-income communities, what treatment can the residents expect? These inhabitants have the fewest resources to adapt to the demands of rising land and housing values. Will low- and middle-income neighborhoods have a place in growing knowledge-based cities, or will such cities become simply the province of wealthier residents? The tenure of working people, people of color, and immigrants in metropolises such as Boston has become increasingly tenuous as developers' attraction to them intensifies.

Boston Chinatown has fought for more than half a century to keep its place, slowly ceding ground but over time gaining a more prominent voice. Its experiences illustrate a struggle that continues to envelop urban America as low-income, immigrant communities, which lack money and power, exercise their available agency against dominant local elites. By confronting decisions broadly beyond their control, residents and organizations in Chinatown have gained some voice in discussions about their community's fate, influencing subsequent phases of neighborhood development and the surrounding cityscape. Yet these gains often mask deeply rooted internal conflicts as residents grapple with contested identities and visions for the future. Boston Chinatown's history shows that marginalized identities and positions can become more fully formed when stakeholders challenge the broader society's intolerance, exploitation, or antagonism—an evolution that may lead to urban social movement building. Though Boston's Chinese community is relatively small, studying its experiences adds new dimensions to our understanding of public life and offers a unique vantage point from which to examine the city's historical and geographical development. Through their courage, resilience, and ingenuity, residents of this low-income immigrant neighborhood of color, as well as their allies, have earned a place in our urban narratives.

THE NEIGHBORHOOD OUTLINED

Chinatown is a small, irregular neighborhood, comprised of about forty square blocks and housing 5,000 residents, that rubs against Boston's downtown financial and retail districts. Its working-class brick rowhouses and concrete housing developments are dwarfed by iridescent towers—the Ink Block, Troy Boston, and 345 Harrison developments to the south; Millennium Place, the State Street Financial Center, and the Kensington to the north. Tufts–New England Medical Center dominates Chinatown's western flank, and the neighborhood backs against Interstate 93 and the Massachusetts Turnpike Extension to the east. Development and institutions encircle the neighborhood and seem to overwhelm it.

Today, the growth of outlying enclaves is challenging Chinatown's centrality among the region's Asian American communities. It nevertheless remains the locus of much of the political, institutional, and social life of Chinese and other Asian Americans. Chinatown remains at the heart of these communities, thanks to its social attachments, historical roots, and the arteries of the city's mass transit system, four of which converge near the neighborhood. Nonresident community members shop, work, mobilize, socialize, and run businesses in the neighborhood. The concentration of social service agencies, social and cultural associations, political organizations (averaging nearly three per block), and ethnic businesses makes the neighborhood a center for Chinese Americans and Asian Americans who live well beyond its geographic boundaries.[5]

Historically, Boston Chinatown has had a tenuous trajectory compared to prominent, expansive ethnic communities in other parts of the country such as Little Havana in Miami, Koreatown in Los Angeles, and Chinatown in New York. Amplified by a swell of new immigrants, those neighborhoods have spread outward from their initial borders to become undeniable ethnic enclaves. Boston Chinatown, along with Philadelphia's, is one of the few survivors among a group of smaller enclaves, and its existence remains fragile. Most of this group—Chinatowns in Baltimore, Providence, Cleveland, Detroit, New Orleans, and Phoenix; Little Manilas in Stockton and San Francisco; Japantowns in Marysville and Sacramento—have disappeared.[6]

Kneeland Street, which demarcates commercial Chinatown from residential Chinatown, reveals the garment industry's mark on the neighborhood. The fourteen-story art deco Hudson Building once housed a hundred garment businesses and serves as a historical record of the way in which garment lofts migrated into the area, planting a line of structures along Kneeland and displacing much of the housing.[7] Walking

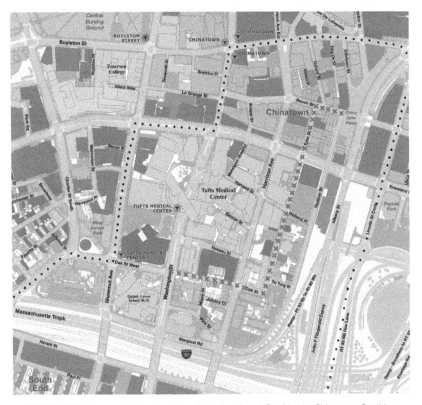

FIGURE 1. Chinatown walk, showing the neighborhood as defined by the Chinatown Coalition. Adapted from a Boston Redevelopment Authority map.

one short block south of Kneeland, down Tyler Street, brings you to the back of T-NEMC's buildings and its staff parking lot. Here, you'll also find three- and four-story working-class brownstones built in the 1850s after a local corporation filled the cove under the Chinatown area. Gaze east, and you'll see the twenty-first century, mixed-income One Greenway development, one of several high-rise towers that now house most of Chinatown's residents.

Further down Tyler, the old Maryknoll Center sits abandoned, no longer an outpost for Christian proselytism. In front of the next building, a small statue of Confucius marks the stone-stepped entrance to the Chinese Consolidated Benevolent Association (CCBA) complex, which occupies the original Josiah Quincy School, the first graded elementary school in the United States. It is a three-story steel-doored brick edifice built in 1847 ringed with an asphalt playground now converted into a parking area.

The battles fought over the future of the neighborhood can still be seen in Chinatown's physical landscape. Before the construction of One Greenway, observers looking through the CCBA complex, across the former school playground, saw a gray wall supporting the Interstate 93 ramp.[8] Highway construction to the east and medical center expansion from the west has separated Chinatown's commercial area from its residential areas. The resulting constriction of the neighborhood at Kneeland Street has left the remaining rowhouses on a block-wide strip along Hudson and Tyler streets backed against each other. The odd-numbered Hudson Street rowhouses face I-93; their even-numbered brethren were destroyed during highway construction. The even-numbered Tyler Street rowhouses, whose backyards look onto Hudson Street's, face T-NEMC's Posner Hall. I-93 meets the Massachusetts Turnpike two and a half blocks to the south, creating a hard border along the southern side of residential Chinatown. As a result of this construction, the neighborhood has eighteen times more people for its open space than the next most paved neighborhood in central Boston does.[9] A visitor strains to find any significant green space where resident children can play.

Continuing along Tyler Street and looking up, you can see the four- to fifteen-story buildings of Tai Tung Village, Chinatown's largest housing project, pressing against the I-93/Mass Pike intersection. Tai Tung is one of a handful of muted tan and brown concrete projects built for Chinatown's residents. The others appear as you turn right to the west, before the turnpike, and walk down Oak Street. Multistory projects named Oak Terrace, Quincy Towers, and Mass Pike Towers come into view. Along Oak Street, they flank the local elementary school and the Wang YMCA.

Most of Chinatown's residents live in buildings like Tai Tung. A 2007 survey found that 34 percent of the neighborhood's units are overcrowded, with more than one person for each room in an apartment.[10] In 2010, three-quarters of the neighborhood's population was Chinese American, two-thirds of whom were immigrants.[11] Despite decades of surrounding development, the residents remain poor and disadvantaged. Census data for 2014–18 reported a median household income of less than $25,280 or less than 40 percent of the citywide median; the unemployment rate was 44 percent, higher than the city average.[12]

The community's 2010 master plan noted that the working population is employed in "the lowest paying industry sectors: food service, accommodations, retailing, manufacturing, or education." Small businesses occupy the ground floors of every housing project and many of the brownstones. Chinatown's economic life revolves around an ethnic ecosystem with food at its center. Numerous other small businesses—hair salons, groceries, travel agencies, and massage parlors—are also evident. Local business directories list more than two hundred enterprises, but most have fewer than ten employees. They employ Chinese American workers, often paying them low wages, putting them into difficult or dangerous conditions, and denying them sick leave and holidays.[13]

A visitor approaching Chinatown's edges can view the pressures on the community. Development forces have repeatedly tested this centrally located area: even during a period of slow growth linked to the Great Recession of 2008, they besieged Chinatown. Community builders have developed a few modest, affordable housing projects, but they are overwhelmed by the massive luxury projects on the perimeters. The Ink Block mixed-use developments, for example, house three hundred so-called "lifestyle apartments" in three buildings, a Whole Foods store, a yoga and cycling fitness center, and three restaurants. The Ink Block is just one of several large new developments—Troy Boston, 345 Harrison, the Lucas, the Quinn, 321 Harrison, 100 Shawmut—just over the Harrison Avenue overpass in the South End, draped with huge banners encouraging people to buy into the modern urban lifestyle. The city and the state are now contemplating a "gateway to Boston" development area to the east. Clearly, ongoing gentrification has had a dramatic impact on the physical and demographic landscape of New England's oldest Chinese American community.

NEIGHBORHOOD POLITICAL DYNAMICS

To appreciate Chinatown's intricate political dynamics, colored by traditional relationships of obligation, patriarchy, hierarchy, and status, an observer must take a different route. Decades of social change and developmental threats have created profound differences in strategy and priorities, straining the neighborhood's political and social fabric. One way to conceptualize them is to focus on four basic dimensions: Chinatown's working-class residents, its community leadership, its relationship with greater Boston, and the city's changing demographics.

First, working-class residents are at the heart of Chinatown politics. Within the predominately immigrant population, they are the majority. One-third are noncitizens, and they are reluctant to mobilize. According to Suzanne Lee, who has served as an organizer in the neighborhood for forty years, "the Chinese-speaking sector feels like they are nobody."[14] Historically, they have ceded their voice to a few community leaders, and competition for their trust and loyalty is a primary element of Chinatown politics. Over the years, this contest has involved fierce community elections, lawsuits, and organizational intrigue. Today, however, the community's culture has become more democratic and is now highly mobilized toward community action. New organizing methods, including protest politics, lobbying, electoral activism, and more collective leadership, have given voice to previously unheard residents.

Second, a wide variety of community groups and organizations compete for leadership and limited resources and influence. The CCBA is one of many social service agencies, social and cultural associations, and political organizations that have deep and diverse roots in Chinatown. In the late nineteenth century, the CCBA evolved as the umbrella organization for the neighborhood's more traditional groups, which had formed in China along extended family and geographic relationships and primarily represented the community's Chinese-speaking, immigrant, and business-oriented cohorts. They tended to be male-dominated and hierarchical. In contrast, modern social service agencies and smaller activist groups more closely mirror the community-based organizations found in other Boston neighborhoods. They draw their leadership from immigrant workers or college-educated professionals and are more often female-led.

The neighborhood's various interest groups have a volatile history, often competing for neighborhood leadership in intense, raucous contests or coming together in episodic collaborations to address common interests. Since the 1970s, traditional organizations such as CCBA have seen a steady decline in their influence and have undergone debilitating internal battles. Nonetheless, they still exert a great deal of power in Chinatown, even though social service agencies and activist groups pose a significant and growing challenge to their dominance. As a result, business groups, agencies, organizations, and individual elites seem to be engaged in a constant dance, endlessly shifting their loyalties among candidates, projects, and campaigns.

Third, the business sector's advantageous relationships with the broader Boston community have had a significant effect on Chinatown, partly because of the sector's ties to mainstream institutions such as City Hall and major developers. For instance, the Chin brothers, Frank and Billy, had been pivotal in the neighborhood's modern history, successfully nurturing relationships with the city's political elites over the course of four decades. Today, other cohorts, including social service agencies and activist groups, are also fiercely competing for these relationships even as they build alternative ties and vie for influence with officeholders. Since the 1980s, the community, primarily through its activist organizations, has also been developing relationships with other neighborhoods: both in communities of color such as Roxbury and Jamaica Plain and in predominately white communities facing development pressures such as the Back Bay and Brighton. At the same time, service agencies, community development associations, and faith organizations have been constructing their own networks among residents and power groups.

Finally, Chinatown has reflected Boston's larger demographic and political changes. In 2000, Boston became a majority-minority city, making it one of the last major urban areas in the country to make this transition. For much of the first half of the twentieth century, the city's political, social, and economic dynamics were shaped by a struggle between Yankees (led by the Boston Brahmins, the established Protestant elites) and Irish Catholic immigrants.[15] By the 1960s, the restive communities of color had assumed a more significant role; and since then, they have consistently pressed for greater influence and more positions in decision-making venues. The city's rapidly growing Asian American population, with Chinatown as its most politically active and visible center, has been integral to this change. Once an isolated neighborhood,

Chinatown has emerged as a leading voice in urban affairs, transforming its relationships with city government, universities, foundations, and institutions to redefine its role in twenty-first-century Boston. It has been a long-standing and integral local actor in a popular upsurge in the cities, which the sociologist John Mollenkopf calls a "neighborhood movement" and Manuel Castells an "urban movement."[16]

The interaction of government planning, commerce, development, and community agency has contributed to Chinatown's physical configuration—a place whose character is unresolved.[17] It is, in one former resident's words, a "compromise area," seemingly caught between competing forces.[18] The community's strengths have helped it navigate more than a century in a city that has often tested the neighborhood.

ABOUT THIS BOOK

Chapter 1 explores the settlement of Chinatown on the margins of a changing Boston and its evolution from a refuge to a viable community with a local economy and organizational infrastructure. Chapter 2 describes the transformational changes in Boston and Chinatown in the three decades after World War II. The next few chapters consider how Chinatown fashioned its responses to succeeding decades of encroaching development and changing circumstances. Chapter 3 covers Mayor Kevin White's administration (1974–83), when commercial development, institutional expansion, and urban planning challenged the neighborhood's borders and Chinatown's often-overlooked organizing around the controversial school busing initiative presaged the emergence of a new, popular force in the community. Chapters 4 and 5, covering 1983–89, describe how Chinatown joined the neighborhood movement against downtown interests, how local activism contributed to the election of a populist mayor, and how the neighborhood made limited gains under a more sympathetic regime.

Chapters 6 and 7 focus on how a campaign against a proposed garage propelled the activist sector in Chinatown to a prominent position in the city. Chapter 8, covering 1999–2007, describes how renewed development pressures led activists to search for new community strategies.

Chapter 9, covering 2008 to the present day, follows the city's recovery from a severe economic downturn and shows how, in an ever more intense development environment, Chinatown evolved to embrace other communities and plan its own destiny. Chapter 10 places the neighborhood's evolution within a broader mosaic of immigrant enclaves and East Coast Chinatowns. Finally, chapter 11 assesses Boston Chinatown's future, its role in the city, and its strengths and weaknesses amid the current political and demographic environment.

While I open this book with a discussion of Boston Chinatown's origins, I am primarily focused on its activist history since the 1960s, when the neighborhood started mobilizing around urban policies and the impacts of growth. My sources include numerous documents, archival records, in-depth interviews, film and other media, and direct and participant observation. I consulted letters, pamphlets, meeting minutes, census data, city government reports, city directories, public planning documents, redevelopment proposals, maps, newspapers, magazines and other periodicals, and photographs. I also examined parallel documents on the community level, including multiple media sources and oral histories, as well as student research work (theses, dissertations, and group projects), a number of which involved interviews with neighborhood leaders and residents.

For much of its history, Chinatown has received little institutional attention, meaning that documentation of its early years is relatively scarce. The U.S. Census population schedules from 1870 to 1930 are an essential window into young Chinatown. City directories supplement this picture, as does the research of Rhoads Murphey, Xiao-Huang Yin, Arthur Krim, Neil Larson and Kathryn Grover, and a few others. The voices of settlement workers and storytellers, notably through the *Chinatown Banquet* video project, fill in many details. Public records, particularly around urban renewal, produced profiles of the neighborhood over time. Boston's many early newspapers provided occasional, if jaundiced, insights into the original community. Their articles also described various projects and initiatives and occasionally summarized urban plans and the performance of city administrations.

After the establishment of several modern community organizations, community-based studies became the critical records of the neighborhood. The most comprehensive are community-planning documents: Chinatown has issued three master plan studies since 1990. The area is fortunate to have had a community newspaper, *Sampan*, since 1971, as well a series of community videos produced in the 1970s and 1980s by the Asian American Resource Workshop. The recent work of the urban planners Tunney Lee and David Chang on the *Chinatown Atlas* website is a guide to other primary sources.

Primary materials from the neighborhood include community groups' newsletters, annual meeting reports and booklets, obituaries, grant proposals and reports, community-produced films and videos, membership lists, flyers, meeting minutes and notes, photographs, brochures, and neighborhood directories. The Chinese Historical Society of New England, a relatively new organization, is a useful source for primary materials and a few monographs. It produced an insightful photographic book but still lacks finding aids for its collection. The Northeastern Library Boston History Collections hold the archives of some organizations prominently mentioned in this book, though they are only partially indexed. I also conducted dozens of personal interviews with community residents and neighborhood leaders. Unless otherwise noted, any cited newsletters, letters, fliers, and other ephemera are in my own personal collection.

I have written the book for a general audience, especially for those engaged in similar struggles. I have included some timelines and short summaries in later chapters to help readers navigate the many intersecting events and players.

CHAPTER 1

BANDS OF BROTHERS BUILD COMMUNITY, 1880–1941

The South Cove area, where Boston Chinese built their Chinatown, was created on a landfill in the 1830s. Once, a narrow neck along present-day Washington Street had been the only connection from the Shawmut Peninsula, where the city stood, to outlying communities to the south such as Roxbury and Dorchester. In 1833, investors created a corporation, the South Cove Company, in 1833 to develop the tidal flats around "the Neck." The company launched an ambitious plan to replace fifty-five acres of wharves and flats in South Cove with mud and gravel fill from South Bay, Roxbury, and later Brighton. By 1839, the company had added about thirteen feet of fill to attract investments from railroad interests. This filled land became today's Leather District, Chinatown, and part of the South End neighborhood. The remains of the cove became known as Fort Point Channel, which borders Chinatown today.

In the 1840s, the Boston and Worcester Railroad built railyards that they promoted as the "largest merchandize depot" in the world.[1] The depot was one of seven railway terminals in Boston and occupied the half of South Cove that lies east from Interstate 93 and the John Fitzgerald Surface Road in present-day Chinatown.[2] The yards attracted leather and shoe manufacturers and then garment makers, all of whom had been displaced from the older part of the city by rising rents.

The garment manufacturers, most of them Jewish, built many of the large factory lofts along Essex, Beach, Harrison, and Kneeland streets to the west of Dover Street. Their industrial activity soon made Boston the largest manufacturing center in the country, and they continued to expand in the area until the 1940s.

Drawn by these industries, immigrants began moving into the South Cove area. Its rowhouses were densely packed, on lots sixty to seventy feet deep and twenty to twenty-five feet wide. The first appeared on Front Street (renamed Harrison Avenue in 1841). Most of these buildings were cheaply constructed, wood-framed Greek revival–style homes.[3] In 1837, a nationwide economic panic precipitated a fall in land values, forcing the South Cove Company to sell lots to shareholders. The new owners continued to build housing, initially for native-born Bostonians, then largely for the Irish immigrants who began to arrive in the 1850s.[4]

South Cove was not an attractive area. Many believed that its low-lying land harbored disease, and the neighborhood's dual role as Boston's industrial core and entry point for new immigrants kept rents low. It didn't help that raw sewage from the city had flowed into the tidal flats before their reclamation and later continued to flow into the channel and South Bay. At the same time, an emerging middle class and the availability of new modes of transportation were influencing ideas about urban living. By the second half of the nineteenth century, a rural ideal was becoming fashionable. Taking advantage of newly built streetcar lines, which tripled the distance that commuters could travel for work, Boston's middle classes began moving to suburban areas such as Brighton, West Roxbury, and Dorchester. During this period, Boston annexed these towns and connected them to the city's modern sewage and water system. This made it easier for those with means to abandon central city areas, long considered artificial, immoral, and unhealthy.[5]

Like most urban enclaves in the nineteenth century, South Cove experienced waves of ethnic succession as newer immigrants began to occupy the homes and alleyways vacated by earlier arrivals. Waves of Irish, Jewish, and Italian immigrants moved into the area, followed by Syrian and Lebanese immigrants—the immediate predecessors of the Chinese. The geographer Rhoads Murphey tied the physical decline of the area to its "succeeding immigrant waves," which gradually brought in people who had "a lower and lower status in American eyes," who were "progressively more foreign."[6]

Over the years, South Cove was home to a few immigrants who later became prominent. The Lebanese poet Kahlil Gibran, author of the bestseller *The Prophet,* lived with his family on Oliver Place and at 76 Tyler Street. The Chinese revolutionary Sun Yat-Sen met with his supporters at 12 Tyler Street and at the Hankow Restaurant on Essex Street, where they plotted the overthrow of the Qing dynasty. The North Vietnamese revolutionary Ho Chi Minh reportedly worked at Boston's venerable Parker House Hotel in his formative years and may have lived in Chinatown.[7]

South Cove's long history as a space for Boston's immigrant working class established it as a locus of social and political activism. The downtrodden immigrants who lived and worked there attracted evangelists and philanthropists looking to improve conditions for urban poor. In 1892, the College Settlement House Association established Denison House at 93 Tyler Street to serve Syrian, Lebanese, and Italian women. Denison House later expanded to offer numerous services to the Chinese population, including English classes, recreational activities, and a dormitory. It brought in women activists such as Amelia Earhart, who worked alongside the suffragette Mary Kenney O'Sullivan during the late 1920s. Earhart's attention was particularly focused on the children, and her conclusion, rather exceptional in those times, was that the "Chinese are an adorable people."[8]

In 1901, the Atlantic Avenue elevated streetcar line opened in South Cove. The line turned west at Beach Street and proceeded south down Harrison Avenue through the length of present-day Chinatown to Castle Square in the South End. The new line, known as the El, darkened, dirtied, and rattled the adjoining streets. The sound of the train's screeching wheels lowered land values everywhere they could be heard; the sharp turn at the corner of Beach Street and Harrison Street produced a particularly loud shriek.[9]

CHINATOWN CHINESE

Chinese workers began settling in Boston in large numbers in the late nineteenth century. According to the 1880 census, a few hundred resided in the city at that time. Many of them were fleeing the anti-Chinese vio-lence then sweeping through the western United States and the nativist-inspired hostility that eventually precipitated the 1882 Chinese Exclusion Act. According to the historian Mae Ngai, the Chinese were the only group to be excluded by name from immigration into the United States. This made them, in a sense, "permanent foreigners."[10]

During the last decades of the century, the Chinese population in the eastern United States multiplied. These migrants traveled east using the transcontinental rail system, whose United Pacific leg had been largely constructed by Chinese laborers. They were part of a wave of migrants churning through Boston, one component of a throng of motivated immigrants from various countries as well as lower-income natives.[11]

Though the 1880 census indicates that 121 Chinese were living in a six-block area north of Kneeland Street, a recognizable "Chinese quarter" or "Chinatown" did not coalesce until a few years later. The researcher Shauna Lo traces the first reference to Chinatown to an 1884 *Boston Globe* article.[12] Despite a long-standing neighborhood account that the first Chinese lived around Ping On Alley (at the time, Oliver Place), evidence suggests that the original center of the community was more likely the eastern side of upper Harrison Avenue, which intersected with Beach Street.[13] For decades, a Chinese-influenced balcony and tile doorstep, now removed, marked the location of the Hong Far Low Restaurant with the caption "Established 1879" below the name at 36–38 Harrison Avenue. In 1886, the *Boston Herald* identified Chinatown as 32, 34, 36, 38, and 38½ Harrison Avenue. Businesses typically occupied the first floors and often the basements, while the upper floors served as boardinghouses, family living spaces, or gathering areas. The alley behind Harrison, known as Oxford Place, became almost exclusively Chinese by the end of the century. The buildings were unadorned except for dormers at the top and granite steps leading to recessed doorways. While Harrison Avenue was a wide, heavily trafficked commercial thoroughfare, Oxford Place was narrow and dark. As a journalist reported in 1893, "Chinatown lies huddled and congested. Remember if you will, the crowded conditions of the avenue at this point, filled with heavy teams and a constant stream of electrics en route to the depots and South Boston." He reported on a city council investigation, whose chairman testified,

The sanitary conditions are very poor and inadequate for such a large mass of people crowded together. In many places . . . we found water closets in a very filthy condition, in some cases without any outside ventilation. . . . Many of the surroundings of this locality are also in a poor sanitary condition. Such I found to be the case in Oxford pl., where the mud was some six to eight inches deep, and, although a cold night at the time of our visit, many foul odors arose on all sides.[14]

The Chinese community was homogenous. The vast majority of individuals had their roots in the Sze Yap (four counties) area of the Pearl River delta on the southeastern coast of China, particularly Toisan (modern-day Taishan), on the western side of Canton (Guangzhou). The Sze Yap people were mostly poor and very nationalistic, the peasant cousins of the Cantonese. Him Mark Lai, a scholar of Chinese American history, has characterized them as enterprising, adventurous, and open to new ideas due to their exposure to outside influences.[15] While Sze Yap workers often adopted a cautious approach toward American society, other Chinese considered them loud, contentious, and uncultured.

Sze Zap immigrants maintained deep group connections built on ethnic networks and family relationships. According to Peter Kwong, a New York Chinatown scholar, southern Chinese build these robust networks as a practical survival strategy.[16] These were parochially loyal, often aligning with specific geographic or family networks. To insulate themselves against a hostile mainstream society, they often isolated themselves. Significantly, their loyalties based on Chinese place origins led to amplified conflicts among community organizations that were active in Chinatown.

Chinese enclaves in Boston were overwhelmingly male and often quite young. The Pearl River delta, suffering from decades of war, poor harvests, and burdens imposed by western imperialist countries and the importation of opium, had become a difficult place to survive. In the delta region, young men were considered adults at age fifteen. Families thus sent many of the area's young males overseas at about this age to earn income for the family. Many went first to California, where gold had been discovered. The first large group to come to Massachusetts arrived in 1870 to work in shoe factories in North Adams. Of that group of seventy-five, more than half were sixteen years old or younger.[17]

Like many other immigrants, the southern Chinese who settled in Boston were persistent, hardworking, and frugal. Many had worked on the transcontinental railroad, where they demonstrated these characteristics. Chinese workers on the Central Pacific line won the speed record for laying railroad track against a team of larger white workers on the Union Pacific line. In winter, they labored and died excavating tunnels in the Sierra Mountains, when many other workers declined to work. They displayed their inventiveness, learning to work with newly invented nitroglycerine explosives and drilling into rock cliffs while hanging from baskets.[18] They were also contracted as groups to work in the expanding factories, mines, and railroads of the American West. In the 1870s, half of San Francisco's factory workers were Chinese. They were critical in building the levee network in the Sacramento and San Joaquin river deltas, a project that made California the nation's agricultural center.[19]

The first Chinese in Massachusetts worked in diverse occupations, serving as factory and farmworkers, servants, and "pedlars."[20] Until the 1940s, Massachusetts state law prohibited Chinese from working in more than twenty occupations, most of them professional jobs. Other laws restricted municipal and state government employment to citizens, a status for which they were rarely eligible. Union membership in Boston—necessary for jobs in most skilled trades—was barred to them based on their race.[21]

Following patterns in other Chinatowns, the population began to specialize in certain occupations to avoid competition with an increasingly hostile white labor force. Through both exclusion and choice, laundry work became the occupation of more than 95 percent of the population. According to the 1875 *Boston Directory,* the city's first documented businesses in Chinatown were laundries located on Beach Street and Harrison Avenue. The 1880 *Boston Directory* listed half of the city's ninety laundries as Chinese-owned. By 1892, Chinese laundries were recorded in a separate section and numbered nearly 250.[22] The 1900 census listed three laundry agents in Boston, including one on Harrison Avenue, and the treasurer of a "laundry union," indicating the pervasiveness of the occupation in the area. While Chinatown was the center of the community, laundries spread throughout every county in Massachusetts that year, following the expansion of new streetcar and railroad lines. The *Boston Globe* reported robberies or other issues involving Chinese laundries in various sections of Boston and in towns as distant as Milford and Haverhill.

Laundry had the stigma of being considered a female occupation; it was also isolating and physically demanding. The business was both low status and low paying. According to descriptions of that life, frugal laundrymen saved money by sleeping and cooking meals of white rice in their tiny shops, only occasionally allowing themselves vegetables and meat. Neil Chin, a laundry worker in the 1920s, recalled,

> When you go to work in the laundry, you would stay in that laundry all week long. You ate there, you worked there, you slept there. . . . You would have to get up around 6 o'clock in the morning, possibly start work at about 6:30 and you wouldn't stop until 12 o'clock midnight. And the only break that you would get was for lunch and for supper. That's about eighteen hours a day for at least five and a half days a week. . . . If you were lucky or if you were a fast worker and you were able to get through your week's work by Saturday afternoon, you would then have the luxury of coming up to Boston or back to Chinatown, and you would get the rest of Saturday and Sunday off.[23]

Laundries were not a path to social mobility in Boston. In the nineteenth century, that tended to be limited to "men of old native stock." As the historian Stephan Thernstrom has shown, ethnic differences had a significant influence on an individual's life chances. Looking at the major ethnic groups, he found a descending hierarchy of social mobility. While long-tenured natives could improve their stations over time, Jewish immigrants and the American-born children of English parents faced more significant constraints. It was more difficult still for those of Irish and Italian descent, who moved ahead only "sluggishly and erratically." The "Negroes" were a dismal case who lacked any progress at all. Although Thernstrom did not examine the Chinese in this period, their status was arguably closer to the situation of African Americans than to the Irish and the Italians.[24]

Under both the Chinese Exclusion Act of 1882 and subsequent legislation, the United States essentially banned Chinese immigration. The only Chinese females allowed entry were those who were the spouses of merchants or American-born Chinese. In the 1900 census, nearly half of Chinese residents in the United States reported married status, but many of their weddings had occurred before immigration or when they had returned for once-in-a-decade visits. Their wives remained in China. The ban against wives, intended to preclude Chinese family growth in the United States, was maintained until after World War II. According to the historian Sucheng Chan, the percentage of females in the U.S. Chinese population fluctuated between 4 and 7 percent in the nineteenth century and rose very slowly in the first half of the twentieth century.[25]

This distorted gender balance fostered the formation of a primarily working-age, male-dominated society in Chinese communities throughout America. The situation was particularly dramatic in Massachusetts. In the 1870 census, eighty-seven of the eighty-nine Chinese residents in Massachusetts were male. In 1883, a local newspaper referred to the sixteen-year-old wife of the merchant Sam Wah Kee as the "only pureblooded Chinese woman in Boston."[26] By the 1900 census, the commonwealth's Chinese population was still 99 percent male. Of the 254 Chinese listed as residents of Boston Chinatown, eleven were female. Ninety-six percent of the population were either single males or husbands living apart from their spouses in China.[27]

But Chinatown continued to grow. As the neighborhood evolved into the cultural, social, and political center of the region's Chinese population, it became a popular destination for Chinese laundry workers throughout New England, who often went there on their limited days off. They found little support or comfort in mainstream society, but Chinatown provided refuge, services, and community. The area had grocery stores and eating establishments, where people could socialize, congregate, and purchase familiar foods. It offered Chinese newspapers, translators, baths, a place to send and receive mail, as well as people who could read those letters and write return ones to families back in China.

Entertainments such as gambling and opium smoking were available. As the scholar Angelo Ancheta writes, "the reason that the Chinatowns existed and came into being was that simply Chinese could not gain access to business, to services, to any kind of commerce that other folks could . . . so that if you wanted to get a meal, if you wanted to stay in a hotel, if you wanted a place to live, you were basically not allowed to live with whites so that the Chinatowns became the segregated areas that they were at the time."[28]

CHINATOWN INSTITUTIONS

Soon after arriving in the United States, Chinese immigrants quickly formed associations, *huiguans,* to provide essential services, mediate disputes, and assure payment of debts.[29] These associations might be organized according to ties of geography, by kinship, or even by routes of passage to the United States. There were associations of people from particular districts in China, associations of people with the Chin surname, associations of Chinese who had passed through South America. These small organizations interconnected to form national and international networks. Associations linked with individual families predominated in different cities. In Boston, the Chin and Wong surnames became the most numerous, and these families exercised their influence through the Gee How Oak Tin and Wong associations. By the 1910s and 1920s, most of the major Boston huiguan associations had established themselves. Yet even though they performed some useful functions, the associations exacerbated existing conflicts among Chinese immigrants, who often became fiercely loyal to one group over others.[30]

In response to the growth of anti-Chinese sentiment in America, and with the encouragement of the Chinese government, the Chinese population in the United States began forming umbrella groups to intervene more actively with U.S. institutions and outside society. In 1882, the Chinese Consolidated Benevolent Association (CCBA) established itself in San Francisco. In other cities, it went by the name of Six Companies or Chong Wa Benevolent Association. In Boston Chinatown, it was organized during the early decades of the twentieth century as the Chinese Consolidated Benevolent Association of New England (also CCBA).[31]

Compared to the laborers, the merchants were more literate and better resourced. Thus, in Boston and elsewhere, the merchant class and the larger families dominated the associations, including the CCBA, whose presidency rotated among the larger traditional associations—the ones with the greatest voting power. The associations' primary internal function was to maintain the status quo through social control of the laborers, who formed the overwhelming majority of Chinese immigrants. They also regulated commerce, such as the geographic distribution of hand laundries and other Chinese-run businesses, to ensure sufficient customer bases for these services. Businesses of the same type were required to maintain minimum distances between locations. The CCBA heard and settled disputes, resorting to force if necessary. All Chinese were required to pay dues and fees to their respective associations for various transactions. By controlling business, lending, and employment through social and, at times, physical coercion, the associations were able to enforce their decisions.

Typically, the associations would meet and temporarily host new arrivals to the city, maintain the Chinese cemetery, and pay the burial expenses of the poor. They also provided a meeting place for members who had traveled into the city from their outlying laundry shops. Yet because the associations were informally run, their effectiveness in serving their members varied widely. In the early 1880s, the Chinese consul general criticized this inconsistency and complained about the limited services that the associations provided to their constituents, given the level of resources they drew from fees and dues.[32]

In addition to the associations, political and fraternal societies known as tongs developed. The tongs were influential members of CCBA, and their social, political, fraternal, and, at times, criminal activities overlapped. In 1903, Boston's On Leung and Hip Sing tongs engaged in violent and often fatal conflicts that led to police actions and scores of deportations. A former resident remembers a gangster named Two-Gun Cohen, who worked for On Leung, driving the tong's laundrymen members back to their shops on Sunday night, a way of providing protection from rival factions. Eventually, a division of territory between the nation's two largest tongs, On Leung and Hip Sing, gave On Leung dominance on the East Coast and lessened the conflict.[33]

Although it did engage in criminal activity, On Leung tong, known in English as the Chinese Merchants Association, also supported civic institutions and services—for instance, by funding the Kwong Kow Chinese school. Like many associations and tongs, it maintained links with brother organizations in China. Into the late twentieth century, the tongs made a significant amount of money from neighborhood gambling activities. But as state-sanctioned lotteries and casinos took hold, their influence declined.[34]

Politically, the tongs and associations were closely associated with the Tongmenghui, which became the Kuomingtang, the ruling political party of the 1911 Chinese Republic and later of Taiwan. Over time, many of the more important associations and tongs in the United States became officially affiliated with the Kuomingtang. The leaders would be awarded honorific positions in the Kuomingtang-led government.

Tongs and associations created a partially self-regulating community capable of settling disputes and providing essential services. As the scholar Bernard Wong writes, they "selected a strategy of peaceful coexistence with the dominant society and other ethnic groups as well. In dealing with the dominant society, they [were] careful to isolate its influence on the community." These groups engaged with outside power only when this influence was threatened, and the CCBA was Boston Chinatown's sole voice to the larger society.[35] City officials, in turn, largely ignored many of the community's needs, intervening only when events involved white individuals or exploded into tong wars. Thus insulated, the community's elites were left to administer affairs and control the population. The situation also preserved certain traditional cultural norms in the neighborhood that persisted long after homeland Chinese had adopted other, more modern practices.

CHINATOWN'S RELATION TO THE CITY

Chinese migrants established Chinatown during a time of large-scale immigration into Boston. Between 1830 and the 1920s, three successive immigrant waves came to the United States: the first from the British Isles and Germany, the next from northern and western Europe, the last from southern and eastern Europe. As I have mentioned, the massive migration of poor Irish Catholics triggered a decades-long struggle for power between these new arrivals and the region's native-born Yankees, who tended to be Protestant and Anglo-Saxon. By the late nineteenth century, however, demographics were beginning to shift in favor of the Irish. By 1887, Boston's mayor, the president of its board of aldermen, the president of its common council, and its city clerk were all Irish Americans.

In the meantime, immigration was increasing. Enormous transatlantic ships—the "ocean greyhounds" run by the Cunard shipping line—could now carry thousands of people instead of hundreds and could cross the Atlantic in days rather than weeks. By 1847, 37,000 Irish, Italians, Jews, and southern and eastern Europeans entered through Boston's port annually.[36] From 1820 to 1890, the city's population of first- or second-generation immigrants rose from 22 to 68 percent. It continued increasing until at least 1920.[37] Tens of thousands of newcomers filled Boston's West End, North End, and East Boston before moving on to other neighborhoods. The Irish soon dominated the South Cove area. Compared to them, and to the "swarthy Italians, black-bearded Jews . . . and a motley collection of Poles, Lithuanians, Greeks, and Syrians," the neighborhood's Chinese community was relatively insignificant. In the northern section of South Cove, where the Chinese had sunk their roots on Harrison Avenue and Oxford Place, Syrians and Lebanese were living on nearby Oliver Place, and Armenians were living on Kneeland and Beach streets.[38]

In the eyes of established citizens, these new residents spoke incomprehensible languages, practiced unfamiliar customs, and ate strange foods. Nativist organizations such as the American Protective Society formed chapters in Boston. In 1894, three Brahmin intellectuals founded the Immigration Restriction League, advocating for a literacy test as a requirement for immigration. Their efforts culminated in the successful passage of both that requirement (in 1917) and the National Origins Act (in 1924), which set restrictive immigration quotas based on whether or not 2 percent of a country's foreign-born population had resided in the United States in 1890. The act effectively favored those from western and northern Europe; and along with the literacy test, it significantly reduced immigration.[39]

In the midst of this demographic uproar, Boston often left Chinatown to itself. A survey of newspaper articles from the 1890s shows that Irish and Italians were mentioned two to five times more often than Chinese were. City authorities had many groups and interactions to monitor. There were tensions between Yankees and Irish; skilled Irish and Canadian immigrants resented the new unskilled immigrants; Irish fought Italians and Jews in the neighborhoods; Irish residents were at the forefront of anti-Chinese and anti-Black agitation.[40] Some of the authorities' tolerance toward Chinatown may have been linked to the city's long-standing and profitable trade with China during the last half of the nineteenth century. This business relationship, involving items such as American otter pelts and Turkish opium, had built vast fortunes for families like the Darbys, the Forbes, the Cabots, and the Heards.

Chinatown may have been largely isolated from mainstream social and political intrusions, but it was an area of concern for Christian evangelists. Beginning in 1876, they established settlement houses there and as many as eighteen Chinese Sunday schools. The Baptists founded a permanent mission on Oxford Street in 1896. A settlement house writer observed that "the Chinaman is perhaps most attractive in his capacity of Sunday-scholar, though his responsiveness to missionary effort merely reflects his strong desire for some knowledge of the vernacular."[41]

Within the larger urban setting, Chinese were tolerated—after a fashion—but most were nevertheless permanent foreigners. Even those who attained citizenship were, in Mae Ngai's words, "alien citizens."[42] The settlement house writer noted that the Chinese "can never be in any real sense American."[43] Disdain colored this marginalization. As a contemporary reporter wrote, "it may not be that all Chinamen in the city are alike, but the greater number of them are gamblers, the devoted slaves of the opium pipe, and immoral to the last degree." One long-time resident recalled that a Chinese person walking on a sidewalk had to step into the gutter to let white persons pass by.[44]

After ignoring the Chinese for so many years, Boston eventually took notice of their enclave. When authorities decided to widen upper Harrison Avenue in 1893 to improve the flow of railway cars and commercial traffic, the city took possession of the eastern half of the street, where the Chinese businesses were, and spared the non-Chinese businesses on the western side. One newspaper saw this as a way to let Boston "be rid" of Chinatown. The Chinese, however, persisted, rebuilding on the same sites in foreshortened buildings.[45]

This "improvement" was the first of several such initiatives to take control of Chinatown. Racially motivated inspections and raids were common. In 1895, for instance, there were at least a half-dozen police raids, supposedly to control issues involving gambling, liquor, "sparrow fighting," and opium. State and city governments passed specific laws and regulations burdening Chinese businesses. In 1903, using a tong conflict as a precipitating event, police launched a massive sweep of Chinatown,

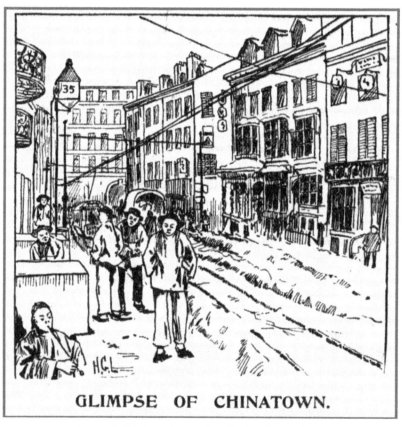

GLIMPSE OF CHINATOWN.

FIGURE 2. Chinatown, looking down Harrison Avenue, 1893.
Courtesy of the *Boston Globe.*

with the intent of limiting the growth of the Chinese population and deporting and dispersing many of its residents. In its wake, a significant number of Chinese left or were forced out of the city.[46]

On the whole, however, the city remained preoccupied with other immigrant groups. This, along with Chinatown's strategy for avoiding conflict and its cultivation of relations with certain respected white Bostonians, gave the enclave the space to develop. During the 1903 police sweep, for instance, the community was able to leverage its relationships with the broader population to organize a rally in which hundreds of people came out in support of the neighborhood. Participants included well-known abolitionists such as William Lloyd Garrison and Reverend John Galbraith, and "a goodly sprinkling of women, some of whom were Sunday school teachers," publicly denounced the raid.[47]

The community also developed spontaneous connections with other segments of the city's working population. When the women operators at the telephone exchange at 2–8 Harrison Avenue and Oxford Place (primarily Irish Americans) went on strike in 1919, Chinatown residents supported them with food. Rose Norwood, one of the strikers, remembered, "The Chinese were wonderful during the strike. The[y] . . . put a long table against the door so that the company couldn't bring strike-breakers in through the back entrance. They said, 'We keep scabs out.'"[48]

There were also occasional interracial marriages, primarily involving Yankee or Irish women. Public alarm arose about female Sunday school teachers' relations with their male Chinese students, a few of which resulted in marriage.[49] The historians Shauna Lo and Laura Ng have identified 136 interracial marriages, almost exclusively between Chinese men and white women, in the forty-five years between 1886 and 1930.[50] Successful Chinese laundries also began hiring white women to scrub clothes. The Chinese saw these women as poor workers and restricted them to the simplest and lowest-paying jobs; the ironing and starching tasks went to the Chinese. Because such job relationships remained problematic, both the white employees and the Chinese proprietors kept their roles quiet.[51] Relationships between the Chinese community and mainstream society, notwithstanding individual or rare exceptions, remained unequal and controlled.

BEGINNINGS OF CHANGE

As I have mentioned, restaurants began establishing themselves in Chinatown as early as 1879. They initially served a primarily Chinese clientele and were often located on upper floors in multipurpose rooms, with bunkbeds and gambling available in different corners. By 1889, six Chinese restaurants were reportedly in business, including Hong Far Low and Moy Auk, on Harrison Avenue. The food could be expensive and frequently featured locally grown Chinese vegetables. A missionary who worked closely with Chinese in the neighborhood said, "[They] are extremely fond of good living, and pay well for it."[52]

Two factors broadened the restaurants' customer base. First, during the 1890s, a social practice known as slumming introduced white visitors to "exotic" Chinatown and its many restaurants. According to the *Boston Globe* and the *Boston Herald,* such visitors included the state's lieutenant governor and other public officials; police chiefs; members of the Folk-Lore Society and the Boston Press Cycle Club; convention-goers; and ministers. Charles Hoyt's popular play *A Trip to Chinatown* (1896) illustrates the pervasiveness of this practice, and it was staged at the Tremont, Park, Columbia, and Castle Square theaters during that decade.[53]

Second, Jewish patrons, who dominated the expanding garment industry in Chinatown, also became regular customers. One resident commented, "The Chinese should always be grateful to the Jewish people because if it weren't for the[m] . . . the Chinese restaurants would have folded up years ago. Nobody ate Chinese food except for the Jews. In the beginning, anytime you wanted to open up a restaurant, first of all, they ask[ed], 'How many Jews there?'"[54] Over time, family dining at Chinese restaurants became a popular cultural tradition in the Jewish community.

By the 1920s, Chinese restaurants were easy to find. The 1931 Chinese Business Directory of New England lists thirty-four in Boston, fifteen of them in Chinatown. In the neighborhood, they were available along Beach Street and Oxford Place and down Hudson and Tyler streets, where patrons could avoid the noise of the El. Large nightclub-style Chinese restaurants began operating in other parts of the city. These catered to a non-Chinese clientele and featured dancing, big band music, and cabaret. Ruby Foo's Den was reportedly the first Chinatown restaurant to successfully pursue this customer base. During the Prohibition era, many Chinese engaged in bootlegging to serve these establishments.[55]

As technological advances such as washing machines and steam presses began to undermine the laundry business, food service became one of the few viable occupations open to Chinese, particularly during the Great Depression. Although they tried to branch into other occupations, such as importing Chinese lace and selling antiques, laundries and restaurants dominated and endured.[56] Soon Chinatown's restaurants began spawning related food-industry businesses—groceries, butcher shops, noodle makers, bean-sprout growers, and bakeries. These small businesses, unlike the laundries, allowed their owners to move up into merchant status, which in turn allowed their wives to immigrate and a visible family presence to develop in the neighborhood. During the 1890s, the first Chinese babies were born in Boston.[57]

Such gender diversification occurred more quickly in the country's larger Chinatowns, where it rapidly stimulated economic growth. But even Boston's smaller Chinatown showed significant change in the early decades of the twentieth century. According to the researcher Xiao-huang Yin, census figures for the city show that the ratio of men to women improved from 26 to 1 in 1910 to 3.7 to 1 in 1940. The 1910 census identified only twenty-five families among Chinatown's five hundred residents. Of these families, only two-thirds included Chinese wives, and only two-thirds had children. The 1930 census records a total population of more than 950 Chinese residents, and the number of families had nearly tripled, with about fifty of them listing children.

These families were often large, with seven, nine, ten, and even thirteen children crowded into the small tenements on Harrison Avenue. The presence of Chinese children and their mothers became increasingly evident in the community, and families began to exert influence over the social and economic life of Chinatown. By the early 1900s, Chinese students were attending the Josiah Quincy Elementary School.[58] In 1916, the community founded the Kwong Kow Chinese language school for local children. A 1931 photograph shows about a hundred Kwong Kow students.

In 1932, the Chinese Young Men's Christian Association opened on Tyler Street. During that decade, residents of Boston Chinatown also sponsored a Cantonese music club and a national nine-man volleyball tournament, institutions that continue to this day.[59] The Chinese American Citizens Alliance, a national association of young American-born Chinese outside of the traditional huiguan network, briefly opened a chapter in Boston in 1921. (Though it had a building on Harrison Avenue, there is no evidence that it had any lasting effect in the city.)[60]

Since the Chinese had first settled in Boston, newspapers, magazines, and "Yellow Peril" novels had caricatured them as filthy, inferior, and undesirable as well as dangerous and threatening. As Chen notes, "contemporary news coverage fixated on sensational stories that emphasized murder, drugs, and other illicit activities. Between 1912 and 1923, Boston papers devoted 1257 column inches to coverage of 104 murders involving Chinese tongs around the country."[61] The publisher Horace Greeley observed that the typical Chinese man was "an inveterate gambler, an opium smoker, a habitual rum drinker, and a devotee of every sensual vice," while the few Chinese women were "utterly shameless and abandoned."[62] He and others visualized Chinatown as a maze of alleys and dens—sometimes amusing, sometimes dangerous.

But in the 1920s and 1930s, its image began to morph slowly from a place of sin, temptation, and vice to an exotic yet approachable destination for entertainment. Political and physical changes in Boston were the impetus for this shift. In South Cove, a third of the neighborhood's housing was destroyed, thanks to economic fallout from the Great Depression and the continuing expansion of the garment industry. Landlords took to demolishing their buildings to reduce property values, and the construction of fifteen-story garment factories and commercial buildings on Kneeland Street cleared out tenements and houses.[63] Some Chinese began moving south into neighboring Syriantown. The area, located between Kneeland and Curve streets, was home to many Syrians and Lebanese and had grocery stores, a few churches, bakeries, public showers, and other residential features.[64] But it, too, was undergoing change as the immigrant population aged and the second generation moved out of South Cove into other neighborhoods. Venturesome Chinese found housing increasingly available in this area, and their own growing population precipitated the enclave's geographical expansion and the development of residential Chinatown.

In 1938, service ceased on the Atlantic El line, and by the early 1940s the city dismantled the tracks along Beach Street and down Harrison

Avenue, using it as scrap metal to serve America's war effort. Removal of the El brightened the area and relieved congestion and noise. It also made land in Chinatown more desirable and protected property values from the Depression era declines experienced in other areas of the city.

By 1941, Chinatown occupied about seven city blocks crowded with residential, commercial, and industrial units crammed beside and on top of one another. Its merchants were gradually reshaping the physical and cultural landscape of neighborhood, both as individual entrepreneurs and through their traditional associations. Some remodeled and upgraded existing commercial spaces in ways that promoted the area's cultural identity. This was a common strategy in Chinatowns around the nation. As the scholar Kathryn Wilson writes, these enclaves were the "first urban landscapes to be identified and commodified as ethnic."[65] In Boston, the merchants took advantage of Chinatown's location adjacent to the city's brightly illuminated theater district. The neighborhood was also close to "movie row" along Washington Street and to a newly established retail area that would soon be a tourist destination. Immediately north and east lay Boston's central business district, home to a number of insurance and finance companies.[66]

Changes in Boston Chinatown were also significantly influenced by political and social turmoil in China at the turn of the twentieth century. As early as 1909, a new Chinese political organization known as the Tongmenghui (later renamed the Kuomingtang party) established a Boston chapter. To support the creation of the Chinese Republic, the Tongmenghui was extending its reach globally, and overseas Chinese were a ready audience. Many supported the removal of the debilitated Ching dynasty, which had long been helpless against European occupation of Chinese territory in Tientsin, Tsingtao, Shanghai, Hong Kong, and down the coast. They were eager to back the Tongmenghui, who successfully overthrew the dynasty and established the republic in 1911.[67]

But it was Japan's incursions into China in the 1930s that triggered Boston Chinatown's greatest activism and changed the neighborhood's civic dynamics. As the Japanese took control of ever-larger areas of China, overseas Chinese mustered to support resistance efforts. Street demonstrations, parades, and fundraisers became commonplace. Marchers would carry a giant Chinese flag through the streets of Chinatown, collecting coins and bills from residents. An activist coalition known as the United Chinese Association raised hundreds of thousands of dollars for the war effort and organized boycotts of Japanese goods.[68] Ordinary Chinese residents found themselves becoming more engaged, taking on new roles, and thinking of themselves differently. They began to see themselves as a united bloc of Chinese rather than as members of localized clans or groups, and this growing nationalism began to undermine the basis of the CCBA and the huiguan system.

As stories of Japanese abuses circulated in the press, the broader population became more sympathetic to the concerns of Chinatown and its residents. The neighborhood's declining crime rate, its residents' anti-Japan campaigns, and the accumulated good will that had developed as the neighborhood became a recognized community enclave strengthened that empathy, which increased yet again after the Japanese bombing of Pearl Harbor.

On the eve of World War II, Boston Chinatown was at a tipping point. Its population had climbed to 1,300 and included increasing numbers of families. Residents were becoming more publicly active. A few American-born Chinese had even started to filter into mainstream jobs: the 1930 census listed an occasional interpreter for the courts and the federal government, a hotel waiter, a nurse, and an office clerk, although employment linked to restaurants and laundries still dominated. Nevertheless, the process of ethnic succession in South Cove had stalled with the Chinese. Thanks to immigration restrictions, housing discrimination, and other racial barriers, Boston's Chinese population had been confined primarily to the Chinatown area for sixty years—for roughly three generations. Despite improvements in their socioeconomic status, they were geographically circumscribed. In this enclave, the merchant class, through the CCBA and huiguan organizations, still exerted control, and the city and the community continued to hold each other at arm's length in terms of both public oversight and community services. Yet change was taking root. The shifting demographics of Chinatown and the nation's postwar policies would upset this long-standing mutual arrangement of benign neglect.

A NEIGHBORHOOD MOVES THROUGH UNFAMILIAR TIMES, 1942–1974

Between 1930 and 1960, Boston's story was one of economic decay. Numerous factors contributed to its stagnation. One factor was a lack of private investment and the flight of manufacturing firms that had undermined the city's economic base. By the 1920s, the textile and leather industries, which had once made Boston a national industrial center, had begun moving their operations to suburban and rural areas, most often in the South, to avoid high taxes, regulations, and unions and gain cheaper land, labor, and raw materials.[1] At the same time Boston's role as a transportation hub had lessened. The port's cargo volume and value dropped steadily during these years, though passenger traffic rose modestly. On the railroads, heavily backed by Boston investments, both passenger volume and freight traffic declined.

Though World War II provided a temporary stimulus for the city, wartime demand did not remedy Boston's underlying problems. The effects of the Great Depression persisted. After the war, the city's machine shops, shipyards, and the South Boston army base slowed their activities and production, but there were no new postwar industries to replace them. What remained of the city's economic activity circled around trade, finance, insurance, real estate, and services.[2]

As automobiles and trucking increasingly dominated transportation, industries became more metropolitan in scope. City businessmen who had profited during the war now established firms in the suburbs. New computer, electronics, banking, and development businesses clustered along the fabled Route 128 highway belt that encircled the city. Within Boston, cars eliminated the need for streetcars but generated unmanageable congestion. Traffic problems became an abiding concern of the city's business interests.

The Boston planning board estimated that, because of traffic congestion, from 1925 to 1930, the value of downtown real estate fell by $34 million while, in other parts of the city, real estate valuations rose by more than $100 million.

The conflict between the Irish and the Yankee populations, particularly during Mayor James Michael Curley's administrations, became another reason to divest from the city. Curley, whose four intermittent terms began in the late 1910s and ended in 1950, dominated the city in those years. Although he was a Democrat, he had a conflicted relationship with President Franklin Roosevelt, and he regularly battled with Republican governors and the often Republican-controlled state legislature. He fought with city councilors and was in continuous contention with the Yankee business establishment. These tensions delayed New Deal spending on public programs during the Depression, limited state aid to the city, and essentially halted significant private investment.

While raising assessments on commercial property, Curley also shifted municipal spending to focus on the neighborhoods. He built parks, health clinics, and beaches while eschewing investments in the downtown and in infrastructure, improvements that might have attracted business. Thirty years after the beginning of the Great Depression, Boston had only two new buildings in its skyline: the ten-story New England Life and the twenty-six-story John Hancock.[3] The Yankees who dominated state government limited Boston's governance; and, through state legislation, it lost control over its police department, port, transit system, and water and sewer system construction. It also no longer had auditing power over city finances. According to the historian John H. Mollenkopf, Massachusetts extended its "authority over everything from the city's towing fees to its liquor licenses, to what it spen[t] on library books."

Boston even lost control of local zoning; its only remaining power was its ability to set property tax rates.[4]

As industrial production in the region declined, so did the number of wage earners and the total wages paid by manufacturing activity. From 1950 to 1960, Boston employment dropped nearly 8 percent, from 312,000 to 288,000.[5] The city's population, which had reached its high point in 1950, declined steadily until the 1980s. The white populace abandoned Boston: between 1950 and 1960, their numbers fell sharply, from 758,700 to 622,746. By 1970, only 524,000 white residents lived in the city—a startling loss of nearly a quarter-million people in just two decades. This outmigration coincided with an influx of people of color, particularly Blacks; suburban residency was often an opportunity denied to them. By the late 1950s, Boston's tax base had shrunk to 75 percent of what it had possessed in 1929. As a result of these years of economic disinvestment, Moody's investor service demoted Boston to the lowest bond rating of all U.S. cities with a population of more than 500,000.[6] In sum, between the end of World War II and 1960, Boston was dealing with, as Mollenkopf writes, "rapid suburban growth, declining central-city population and employment, stagnant central-city real estate values, and an influx of minorities, particularly Blacks, into central-city neighborhoods."[7]

NEW FACES IN CHINATOWN

World War II brought only fleeting improvement for the city as a whole, but it transformed Chinatown's bachelor-dominated society. As it did for other marginalized citizens, the war created new opportunities for residents. Many young Chinese men (and a few young women) entered the armed forces, one of the few integrated institutions in the United States at the time. Those who stayed home found new lines of employment, often manufacturing war supplies at the Hingham and Boston naval shipyards, the South Boston naval yard annex, and the Watertown arsenal. In undertaking these roles, they left behind the old Chinatown and began to integrate into the larger society.[8] When they returned to the enclave, they brought back different views of and aspirations for Chinatown's place in the city.

The war effort mobilized all sectors of the population, and this was another catalyst for change in the community. As discussed in chapter 1, even before America entered the war, women, workers, and children were marching in the streets against Japanese incursions into China. Now China's position as a wartime ally of the United States legitimized a new Chinese American boldness. Mei-ling Soong, the wife of China's president Chiang Kai-shek, was a Wellesley College alumna, and she played a significant role in building ties between the allies. She inspired Chinese American women to become even more active. When she visited Boston during the war, thousands waited for her at South Station, and her public statements were nationally broadcast. Her entourage drove through Chinatown, which was festooned with hundreds of Chinese flags. Soong influenced the establishment of organizations such as the New England Chinese Women's New Life Association.[9] Returning veterans also affected the neighborhood culture—among them, Neil Chin, a Navy veteran, who brought a decidedly mainstream organization, an American Legion post, into Chinatown. He would later contribute to building several modern service organizations in the community.[10] Such activism fostered new roles for residents who had previously allowed traditional Chinatown elites to speak and act for them.

As the war continued, the Chinese Exclusion Act began spurring domestic protests, and the Japanese began using it as propaganda fodder on their radio broadcasts. In 1943, the federal government formally repealed the act and its related legislation, which had become increasingly embarrassing policies, given that China was a wartime ally. Although Congress continued to limit Chinese immigration to a tiny annual quota of 105 people, the 1945 War Brides Act permitted servicemen to bring overseas wives into the United States, and this opened an important loophole in the quota system. It allowed large numbers of Chinese women to enter the country along with returning Chinese American war veterans. A 1946 law further loosened the immigration quota by removing restrictions on the overseas wives of Chinese American citizens.[11]

Thanks to these measures, Chinatown's population ballooned to nearly 3,000 residents by 1950, and its once bachelor-heavy society was transformed into a neighborhood of families. For them, Chinatown was a familiar but spartan home. Families were packed into crowded rowhouses that landlords had long ago subdivided into tiny apartments. Heating systems and hot water were unusual luxuries.[12] Recreation facilities were limited to "two small tot lots, a blacktop play area, and the Quincy school yard."[13] Former Quincy School students recalled that a white teacher referred to her students by number because she had difficulty pronouncing Chinese names and would dry out paper towels on the radiator for them to reuse.[14]

The neighborhood itself became an extension of both home and playground. Children and teenagers played handball against the blank brick wall adjoining the Quincy School playground, stickball in parking lots, basketball at the YMCA. They got involved in occasional fights and

FIGURE 3. My family, 1956. Courtesy of the author.

constantly roamed the streets, watched over by adults who knew their families. Vibrant social interactions occurred on apartment stoops, where whole families might congregate. One resident recalled, "It was like growing up in a small village. So a lot of the kids grew up like brother and sister. So it was like having a large extended family."[15]

In the early 1960s, a limited number of refugees fleeing Communist China were allowed to enter the United States. By that time, American-born Chinese formed a large percentage of both Chinatown's population and that of the extended Chinese community in greater Boston.[16] Now Chinese women were beginning to enter the labor market in large numbers to support their growing families. They found jobs in local garment and leather factories, working alongside Italian female immigrants; and, over time, they became the primary workforce for more than three dozen garment shops in the Chinatown area.[17] The growing number of families also created a new housing demand, but the ever-expanding New England Medical Center facilities on the neighborhood's western flank limited these options. So the Chinese population pushed further along the eastern side of the neighborhood into the Syrian and Lebanese area south of Kneeland, and by 1960 that area, too, was predominantly Chinese.

THE DEVELOPMENT OF BOSTON'S GROWTH COALITION

In the postwar period, the federal government enacted a number of new policies targeting poor neighborhoods, with the intent of reviving American cities. New Deal–era highway and urban redevelopment programs sharply accelerated, and the 1949 Housing Act established a flow of federal funds that lasted for decades. Federal initiatives in roadway construction, such as the Federal Highway Act of 1956, had a particularly dramatic effect on the urban landscape. But while the goal was to give suburban residents better access to the cities, these projects in fact accelerated white flight from urban areas, and newly erected highway infrastructure physically isolated many poor neighborhoods from the social, cultural, and economic life of the rest of the city. These policies significantly threatened urban Chinatowns and other communities of color in the United States.

The sociologists John Logan and Harvey Molotch, in their historical analysis of postwar urban development, have identified national trends among urban decisionmakers to refashion cities through intensified land use. These "growth coalitions"—alliances between local political and business leaders—often saw poor neighborhoods and their residents as obstacles to unfettered economic and physical growth.[18] In Boston, power-ful political and business interests coalesced to take advantage of the new urban development opportunities and, in so doing, began erasing historical divisions between the Irish political machine and the primarily Yankee business community. During a succession of mayorships, beginning with John Hynes's in 1947, new institutions facilitated pro-growth policies.[19] They included the Boston College Citizens Seminars, the Boston Redevelopment Authority (BRA), and the Boston Coordinating Committee. This last organization, often referred to as "the Vault," was comprised of financial and business leaders who periodically consulted together at the offices of the Boston Safe Deposit and Trust Company. The coalition of groups and leaders was determined to remake Boston as a "headquarters city."[20] The result of this mobilization was a series of studies, culminating in the 1950 "General Plan for Boston."[21] Outlining what many saw as a crisis in the city, the studies called for bold action to remove blight and rebuild infrastructure, and they catalyzed an era of urban renewal.

According to urban planner Charles Abrams, this generation of U.S. urban renewal policies "deflected from [their] original social reform course and pointed toward ousting minorities." Moreover, because they were dependent on private developers to implement change, cities made decisions that anticipated the needs of those developers, considering investment capital rather than the best interest of residents. Between 1950 and 1970, four low-income units were destroyed in America's urban areas for every one that was built.[22] With a comparatively small popula-tion of people of color, Boston's urban renewal initiative, the largest per capita program in the country, focused primarily on class distinctions: "[The city's] planning in the 1950's became notorious for its insensitivity toward poor residents."[23]

During the mid-1950s, the demolition of an area known as the New York Streets, a working-class, multiracial neighborhood in Boston's South End, signaled how the new renewal fervor was likely to affect poor residents. Mel King, who grew up and later organized in that area, recalled its previous vitality:

> Let me tell you what I remember about the New York streets from my childhood. Up and down Harrison Avenue there were shops and stores of all descriptions and families who lived over them in apartments upstairs. On the corner of Seneca and Harrison, there was an Armenian store with olives in barrels out front, and a fish market next door. The next block down on the corner of Oneida was Leo Giuffre's bakery, I think. There was a synagogue on Oswego. Bikofsky's bakery was on the corner of Lovering and Harrison, and Saroka's Drug Store a block down on Davis Street. The only liquor store in the neighborhood was on the corner of Gloucester, Golden Liquors. On Dover Street the popcorn man would set up business. Across the street were Green-Freedman Bakery Co. and Derzowitz's Deli.... On Seneca Street, where I lived with my parents, there were also Irish, Portug[u]ese, Albanians, Greeks, Lithuanians, Armenians, Jews, Filipinos, Chinese, and a few (very few) Yankees. Across the tracks were Syrians and Lebanese and a larger number of Chinese.[24]

The city cleared the New York Streets with the goal of creating a vacant area for development, but developers showed no interest in the area until the *Boston Herald* decided to locate its new newspaper plant there. As King's book makes clear, the urban renewal that he lived through was not a neighborhood program but a high-magnitude, business-driven revitalization effort in support of downtown interests.[25]

Other large-scale renewal efforts followed. In 1959, the city wreaked similar destruction on the West End, and the researcher Herbert Gans has famously documented the fate of the neighborhood and its white ethnic population in his study *The Urban Villagers*. The West End's working-class Italian, Jewish, and Polish residents were unable to mobilize an effective opposition to the redevelopment effort, but their resentment endured for a lifetime. By 1975, a local writer observed, "The transition here is nearly complete. From a neighborhood once predominately made up of blocks of closely packed, walk-up three-to-five story brick tenements inhabited by mixed ethnic groups of low- and middle-income families, the West End is now an enclave for more affluent residents and for office, medical and retail tenants."[26] The "new" West End was now home to luxury and market-rate housing at Charles River Park and numerous parking garages.

John Collins, who succeeded Hynes as mayor in 1960, confronted furious neighborhood opposition to redevelopment projects, particularly in the West End. With Edward Logue, the new director of the BRA, he responded by modifying the policy of wholesale clearance of housing and began conducting consultations with neighborhood leaders. Yet these consultations largely took place with homeowners, business owners, and church leaders; they did not involve the majority of neighborhood residents, who were renters. Alongside these efforts to increase transparency and consensus, development intensified: a new city hall was built in the cleared West End, the Prudential Center replaced old railroad yards in Back Bay, luxury apartments appeared on the waterfront, and market-rate housing went up in the South End and Charlestown. Mollenkopf estimates that Collins and Logue "demolished 9,718 low-rent units while constructing only 3,504 new units, of which only 982 were federally subsidized."[27]

Neighborhood fury increased. In the early 1960s, predominately white, working-class neighborhoods such as Charlestown, South Boston, and Allston-Brighton organized against development plans. Residents in mostly Roman Catholic Allston disrupted community meetings around development plans for a section of the neighborhood known as Barry's Corner. They were particularly irate at one regular attendee, Monsignor Francis Lally, the editor of a church publication called the *Pilot* and chair of the BRA board. In Charlestown, fifty Boston police officers, armed with mace and truncheons, were called in to maintain order at community meetings involving thousands of residents and organizers. Opposition was equally intense in neighborhoods of color. In the South End, where there were more than a hundred meetings between the BRA and the community, residents led by Mel King organized blockades, a tent city, effigy burnings, and picket lines to protest renewal plans.

They elected an alternative urban renewal committee and forced local agencies to sever contracts with the BRA. Their activism directly challenged urban renewal policies that, in their view, focused on moving poor people and renters to make room for middle-class homeowners. In the end, the residents did achieve some success, winning control of a parcel in the South End.[28]

Despite fiery neighborhood opposition throughout the city, Collins and Logue were able to meet many of the growth coalition's goals and continued to prioritize the needs of business. During their tenure in leadership, renewal plans affected a quarter of the city's land area and half of the city's residents, and they brought in $2 billion in public and private capital.[29] "Meanwhile," as J. Anthony Lukas writes, "Collins reduced property taxes five of his eight years in office. As a result, while downtown gorged on plump new developments, the working-class neighborhoods were systematically starved. Few new schools, playgrounds, parks, or community centers were built during the Collins years."[30]

DEVELOPMENT HITS CHINATOWN

Chinatown was just another disposable neighborhood in the "New Boston." As a 1970 anti-poverty agency report noted, the enclave faced multiple, imposing, institutional intrusions on its land: "Since the early 1960's, residential Chinatown, adjacent to the Central Business District, has been the object of competition for its prime space by the Boston Redevelopment Authority (BRA) for the South Cove Renewal Project, Tufts–New England Medical Center, the Massachusetts Turnpike Authority, and the Department of Public Works."[31] Central artery construction in the area had begun in 1954, leveling a portion of eastern Chinatown. The project wiped out part of the newly built Chinese Merchants Building as well as residential and industrial buildings on Albany Street—among them the Better-Maid Sportswear Shop, Yee Yee Noodle, Serval Slide Fasteners, Pete's Lunch, Boston Paperboard, and Chee Yee—as well as the Tyler Street library reading room and other municipal buildings. In the words of one former resident, the highway destroyed "the soul of Chinatown."[32] The original plan for the artery, publicized in the early 1950s, was so egregious that an article in the *Boston Traveler* observed, "The most important and compelling reason [for the opposition] . . . is that such destruction appears to be totally unnecessary. . . . The result of running the highway through Chinatown would be that thousands of Chinese would not only lose their homes, but their jobs. The state plan would also wipe out three churches, two schools, a playground, a 14-story garment building, and other valuable property."[33]

In 1963, construction of the Massachusetts Turnpike extension wiped out more housing on the southern and eastern ends of Chinatown and amplified the effects of the central artery construction. Road construction demolished sixty buildings and one flank of Hudson Street. Gone were the Busy Corner Spa, Saint John of Damascus Orthodox Church, and the Kin Company Grocery. Gone, too, were the residents, including Albert Woo, who had lived above the grocery; Salma Hadaya, one of the last surviving Syrian Lebanese residents; and Bak Moy and Hee Wong, who had lived at 34 Hudson. An urban planner recalled:

> They told everyone that they had to sell, they had to move, and that was it. . . . They took all of Chinatown. They took Albany Street, Hudson Street. That was half the Chinese community originally. That's what forced the Lebanese out, the Syrians out, and the Chinese out. . . . The residents and businesses would be served with a notice, a piece of paper either tacked to the door or handed to the resident or business person, giving them sixty days to vacate the premises.[34]

Highway construction, done primarily to serve suburban commuters, destroyed one-third of Chinatown's housing stock. This demolition left the remaining odd-numbered buildings on Hudson Street with a view of a grim, concrete wall partitioning the street from the new turnpike extension. A Harvard University report described the wall as "a visual and acoustic blight on the community. No effort has been made . . . to alleviate these effects through landscaping or other means."[35] The construction also isolated the neighborhood: the central artery cut Chinatown off from the city to the east; the turnpike extension separated the neighborhood

FIGURE 4. View of the Massachusetts Turnpike going east. Chinatown is at the upper left. Courtesy of Northeastern University Libraries, Archives and Special Collections.

from the South End. For those living next to leveled homes and stores, for the children playing in the rubble of friends' houses, the sense of loss was haunting.

As I have discussed, the Second World War loosened constraints on the Chinese; and now, with their enclave in peril, they were able to slowly broaden their residential reach. Many of the residents displaced by highway construction moved to the South End, staying close to their wounded but still interconnected community. Others moved further away to areas such as Allston-Brighton, Forest Hills, and Brookline, resettling near public transit lines so that they could maintain their connection to Chinatown, where they continued to work, shop, socialize, and operate businesses. As David Moy remembers,

> When we moved to J.P. [Jamaica Plain], we were like the third or fourth Chinese family there, and so it was not a good place to hang out when you're Chinese. So, basically,

in terms of social life, for all intents and purposes, my whole family came back to Chinatown to work, to hang out, to play, to do whatever. So even though we weren't physically in Chinatown, we were, in the sense . . . [that] where we lived was right off the Orange Line. So you walk to the station, you get on the train, and you're in Chinatown in fifteen minutes. So geographically, though our beds were four miles away, socially, we were in Chinatown.[36]

The highways were only the beginning of a long series of efforts to appropriate Chinatown's increasingly vulnerable land. The main instrument in this campaign was the 1965 South Cove Urban Renewal Plan, designed by the BRA in cooperation with Tufts Medical School and New England Medical Center (NEMC). According to the plan, the city would take housing and factories by eminent domain to support new development and the broader agenda of the city's growth coalition. The medical center area, located in the western part of the neighborhood, grew out of a series of mergers based around the Boston Dispensary on Bennett Street, long present in the community. In 1950, Tufts University moved its distressed medical and dental schools from Huntington Avenue to this neighborhood—a significant step in the medical center's development plans. For a period of time, Tufts Medical School and NEMC merged and then disassociated, but eventually they eventually recombined as T-NEMC.[37]

During the Cold War, a sharp increase in federal spending on science and medical research reinforced the ties between T-NEMC's institutional expansion and Boston's renewal program. By the 1960s, merging these federal spending streams with urban renewal funding had strengthened the power of universities and hospitals in urban politics. Already, in 1955, T-NEMC had commissioned "New England Medical Center in the South Cove," a study by the planner Kevin Lynch of the Massachusetts Institute of Technology. It called for T-NEMC's complete takeover of "its neighborhood," including residential Chinatown south of Kneeland Street, thus quadrupling the medical center's total land area. The report served as a blueprint for what eventually evolved into the BRA's South Cove Urban Renewal Plan.[38]

Cuts in federal spending had delayed redevelopment efforts, but by 1965 the newly formed BRA was designating Chinatown as "a blighted community." This classification allowed the agency, under the 1949 Housing Act, to make it a renewal area—in other words, it sanctioned the demolition of much of the remaining neighborhood. To prevent T-NEMC from taking the gentrifying Bay Village neighborhood to the immediate west, the BRA instead promised the medical center three acres of land within Chinatown. The agency's decision reflected a continuing bias in planners' attitudes toward low-income communities—their discounting of working-class culture and society.[39] Compounding it may have been a subtle opportunistic racism. According to the scholars Zenobia Lai, Andrew Leong, and Chi Chi Wu, "the BRA thought the Chinese Americans would not complain about the different treatment because they were 'reticent,' 'close-knit,' and 'self-contained.'"[40] That is, the agency believed that redevelopment projects would be less troublesome in Chinatown.

These incursions transformed the core of a formerly close-knit neighborhood. Highways and ten-story institutional and residential buildings replaced the three- and four-story brick rowhouses that had defined the area. It was harder to find corner and basement stores selling snacks, bean sprouts, and groceries. Along with half of Hudson Street, the South Cove section of Broadway, Albany, and Warrenton streets was demolished. Curve, Ohio, Corning, and Naonet streets disappeared. The commercial heart of Chinatown familiar to the tourists was still evident, but the established routines of a lived-in neighborhood were damaged.

In the face of this upheaval, the community showed somewhat less reticence than the BRA had expected. During the 1950s, Chinatown's traditional leaders had strongly protested and organized against a proposal that had initially routed the central artery through the middle of the neighborhood's business area, further up Hudson Street, threatening numerous garment and leather manufacturers. The route would have demolished many Chinatown businesses as well as the apartments above them. That plan had also called for the demolition of the symbolic Chinese Merchants Association building, just completed in 1951. Protests, including petitions taken on the steps of the Merchants building, joined the lobbying efforts of the garment industry, the leather and shoe industry, and the International Ladies Garment Workers Union. Their combined efforts successfully pushed the route slightly east, preserving the businesses and housing north of Kneeland. The revised plan halved rather than demolished the ornate Merchants building, and today that once-grand and now cleaved auditorium ironically greets commuters arriving off the new expressway to Chinatown with a neon sign on its roofline: "Welcome to Chinatown."[41]

Yet the enclave's elites did not replicate their mobilization when the Massachusetts Turnpike extension went through the residential portion of the community south of Kneeland. Reggie Wong, who grew up in the neighborhood and later became president of the CCBA, said, "Back then, we were very passive. We were too busy going to school, too busy going to work, or didn't have the foresight of what was going to happen in the years to come."[42] Nonetheless, there was growing anger against urban renewal after the brutal clearance of the New York Streets and the West End neighborhoods. As a way to assuage the residents of Chinatown, the city signed memorandums of understanding with the CCBA in 1963 and 1970. These agreements recognized fifteen blocks as the neighborhood's official boundary. In the residential area, this effectively preserved Tyler Street and the odd-numbered side of Hudson Street from further T-NEMC encroachment.[43]

However, these agreements did not stop additional land grabs in Chinatown, particularly after 1965. According to the Harvard report, T-NEMC, the BRA, and other institutions owned the majority of the land within Chinatown's boundaries by the end of the decade. By 1970, redevelopment had destroyed 418 buildings, 1,200 housing units, 4 restaurants, and 10 leather and garment shops. Consequently, much of the remaining population had to squeeze into the fissures and cracks of the community, often above and behind restaurants and groceries. Others were moved into tall new housing developments such as Tai Tung Village and Mass Pike Towers, a pair of two-hundred-unit subsidized housing complexes overlooking the three-story rowhouses. The buildings had been constructed in 1970 to house a fraction of the people displaced by urban development. In the view of planner Tunney Lee, these low-income developments would sustain a base of working-class Chinese who would anchor the Chinatown community.[44]

It was during this period that the neighborhood achieved its present, peculiar configuration: a shape like an ancient key, wide at the top (where restaurants and businesses were concentrated) and at the tip (where the housing projects were), with the ends connected by a thin shaft of rowhouses along Tyler and Hudson streets. Metaphorically, this key-shaped area, forged by highways and institutional encroachment, seems to suggest that the neighborhood is still trying to unlock a way into a future. Yet Chinatown's challenges have not been unique, either in Boston or in the country as a whole. Institutional expansion from the city's many hospitals, universities, and highways have affected other Boston neighborhoods, particularly Roxbury, Jamaica Plain, and Roslindale, which were in the path of the Southwest Expressway.[45] As I will discuss in chapter 10, mid-twentieth-century urban redevelopment projects threatened or demolished nearly every Chinatown in the Midwest and the Northeast.

NEW IMMIGRATION AND NEW VOICES

The Immigration and Nationality Act of 1965 eliminated the national quotas that had restricted immigration from most of the non-European world, particularly from China. The new law also gave immigration preference to those who were highly educated or possessed skills in high demand. By 1970, between 200 and 250 new Chinese immigrants were arriving in Boston each year.[46] These newcomers were predominately female and, unlike previous generations of immigrants, most were not from Toisan. Instead, the majority came from Hong Kong, Canton (now Guangzhou), and Taiwan. About a quarter of them, primarily those from Taiwan, were highly educated and relatively well off, and they tended to settle outside of Chinatown. But working- and middle-class Chinese from Hong Kong and mainland China still gravitated to Chinatown. Even though they often had professional or managerial backgrounds, these new arrivals faced social, cultural, linguistic, and other barriers that drove most of them, at least initially, into the food and declining garment industries.[47]

The new immigrants differed from the resident Sze Yap population. According to Zenobia Lai, a Hong Kong native and a long-time community lawyer, Chinatown's village mentality conflicted with the newcomers' and stymied their efforts to transcend ethnic borders and integrate more fully into greater Boston. Whereas the older generation of traditional leaders and city authorities were comfortable with established relationships and structures, newer immigrants, particularly women and young activists, strove to assimilate and find work in industries other than restaurants and the garment factories.[48]

The development upheaval in Chinatown contributed to their struggle. The new arrivals faced housing competition for a dwindling number of rowhouses and new housing projects, limited asphalt recreational space, and an encroaching medical center. They discovered that their community was poorer than other Boston neighborhoods and was dominated by small businesses. A 1972 community conference study counted twenty-one restaurants; twenty-six trading companies, grocery stores, and gift shops; four barbershops or hairdressers; three travel agents; two Chinese laundries; two Chinese printing companies; two bookstores; and one tailor in the area. Although the number of families had increased, three hundred residents—15 percent of Chinatown's population—were single older men, a clinging vestige of the once-dominant bachelor society.[49]

In a 1970 report, Boston's primary anti-poverty agency, Action for Boston Community Development (ABCD), identified a specific litany of challenges for new immigrants in Chinatown (see table 1). It found that the neighborhood's median family income of $5,170 was the lowest in the city, 9 percent lower than Boston's next-lowest income target area. Eighty-two percent of the neighborhood's heads of household worked in service industries, 6 percent in blue-collar employment. In the available housing, there was "a large concentration of elderly men living in overcrowded conditions." Seventy-eight percent of the neighborhood's units had more than one person per room, as compared to 8 percent in the rest of the city. Seventy-two percent of the housing was deemed deteriorating or dilapidated. Furthermore, "despite the magnitude of these problems, there are no social services directly available to the community. Chinatown itself is not included in any anti-poverty target area."[50]

TABLE 1. Socioeconomic Indicators among Antipoverty Target Areas, Chinatown and Boston, 1970

		Chinatown	Boston
Median family income		$5,170 (12th out of 12 areas)	$7,543
Occupation (%)	White collar	12	46
	Blue collar	6	39
	Service	82	15
Housing (%)	Sound	28	86
	Deteriorating or dilapidated	72	14
	Overcrowded	78	7
Educational attainment, heads of household (%)	8th grade or less	69	22
	High school graduate	12	29
	College graduate or above	3	14
Infant mortality (number per 1,000 births)		66.7 (1st out of 12 areas)	25.6

SOURCE: Data adapted from Charles Sullivan and Kathlyn Hatch, *The Chinese in Boston, 1970* (Boston: Action for Boston Community Development, 1970), 44, 57, 61, 65, 68.

The occupation numbers for heads of household excluded employed Chinese American women who worked in the garment factories in the area. However, most of the newly arrived women found jobs, which were an important supplement to family income.[51] The International Ladies Garment Workers Union represented these women; and while it didn't always advocate aggressively for them, its unionized jobs provided health insurance for workers' families, a significant void in the restaurant and laundry industries.[52] Though the garment industry was in the midst of long-term decline, the ethos of worker solidarity fostered by the union was important in mobilizing women in later struggles to overcome dislocations in the industry and organize around community issues.[53]

With both parents working, children often had to fend for themselves. They streamed through the neighborhood, finding diversions in the narrow streets and changing landscape, and took on responsibilities like care of their younger siblings and dinner preparation. The ABCD report cited rising dropout rates, truancy, runaways, and unwed pregnancies. Street gangs became increasingly prevalent, subject to the influence of the neighborhood's widespread gambling enterprises and associated tongs.

The ABCD report noted that new immigrants in Chinatown found a "society and system of values that, in many respects, would have been anachronistic even in mainland China. The social control exercised by elders is more rigorous and extensive than in Hong Kong."[54] Amid many challenges and few remedies, the new population was confronting old systems of social support and control. In response, they began to form a new social ecosystem of diverse constituencies whose alliances were open and in flux. As a result, the politics of Chinatown changed, as evidenced by a series of increasingly well organized neighborhood protests about land-use issues. One neighborhood youth articulated their grievances:

> "Slice, Slice, Slice," the young Chinese man said angrily, emphasizing each word with an imaginary knife stroke, the ball of his right hand slamming into the palm of his left. "That's how Tufts cut up our community. Those mother fuckers really sneak. They buy up the land—or the BRA takes it from the people and gives it to Tufts under the table. . . . They own land around here we don't even know about. They say they have a deficit; they say they can't afford a free health clinic for the Chinese, but if a guy buys a house and then buys another, he doesn't have a deficit."[55]

Young activists and community youth, eventually followed by elderly and displaced tenants, began carrying placards around the streets; they shouted bilingual slogans and marched uninvited into development sites and official events. These new tactics mirrored community actions in the South End and elsewhere in the city, and they were a dramatic change from the traditional leadership's compliant approach.

As I have discussed, early Chinatown residents, who were low-income workers and immigrants, had built a neighborhood within a city that, at best, was indifferent and, at worst, hostile to them. The community had developed a network of institutions to defend itself; its merchant-class

leaders had preferred strategies of self-reliance and had avoided conflict and attention. Now, however, many in Chinatown had begun to
reevaluate this pattern. They wondered if their traditional leaders had
the ability to meet the needs of working families and a more diverse
population in a less restrictive society.

Few service agencies had addressed the needs of the neighborhood's
bachelor society. So as the Chinese community expanded and became
more family-oriented, there were only a handful of them active in
Chinatown. Saint James Catholic Church on Harrison Avenue, originally
built for the Irish, Italians, and Syrians, remained in the community
when the neighborhood became predominantly Chinese but provided
little support beyond religious services and instruction. The Chinatown
YMCA on Tyler Street did offer some recreational youth programs, but
it was severely hampered by the lack of a permanent facility: for decades,
its activities took place in an inflated fabric structure that residents
affectionately called "the bubble." The Maryknoll Center, also on Tyler
Street, had established itself in the early 1960s as a transitional training
center for young nuns who would eventually go overseas for missionary
work. Rotating groups of nuns each spent a few years in the community, organizing events for new families and English classes for women.
Eventually, a nondenominational Chinese Christian church opened and
became Saint James's rival for Chinese American souls. Peter Shih, a
graduate of the Hartford Theological Seminary, ran a mission founded
by Baptists and Episcopalians that offered some day-care services and
summer programs for youth.

The new immigrants were not alone in chafing at the traditional
structure's inadequacy. Beginning in the 1960s, many native-born community members, most of whom had grown up in the enclave in the
1930s and early 1940s, began voicing criticism of Chinatown's feudalistic
and outmoded traditional organizations. To address ongoing pressures
from both inside and outside the community, they started founding
new types of organizations modeled after mainstream American ones.
Great Society legislation under President Lyndon Johnson was providing
much-needed funding to expand programs for poor and immigrant
communities in urban America. While Chinatown's more moderate
activists did not share the anger of other protest movements, they did
want to alleviate the deprivation they saw in their community.

The founders of the Chinese American Civic Association (CACA) included people such as Warren Eng, an electrician; Caroline Chang, a scientist; and Neil Chin, a state worker. All had grown up around Chinatown, had experienced its limitations, and wanted to improve the neighborhood. Initially organized in 1967 for social purposes, CACA soon began to concern itself with service provision and eventually opened an important multiservice center to serve the new immigrant population. It also became part of ABCD. Several CACA committees spurred the creation of other service agencies, including what is known today as the South Cove Community Health Center, the largest community-based organization in the neighborhood.

Just a year earlier, a group of idealistic white and Chinese activists had advocated for community input into plans for a new elementary school in Chinatown. Their efforts, which were part of a nationwide push toward community-controlled local institutions, led to the formation of the Quincy School Community Council (QSCC). By the time the new Josiah Quincy Elementary School opened in 1976, QSCC was offering various services as part of the city's children, youth, and families programming. The council, later known as the Boston Chinatown Neighborhood Center, expanded to become Chinatown's largest multiservice provider. Together with CACA, it offered youth programs, English classes, job training, employment counseling, and service referrals. The creation of full-time service agencies had become a major trend in Chinatown, and the new providers were actively meeting sorely neglected needs.[56]

In the late 1960s and early 1970s, other young Asian Americans in Boston and around the nation coalesced into more confrontational activist organizations.[57] They tended to be ethnically ecumenical, adopting a new Asian American political identity rather than a strictly nationalist one. Across the country, young Chinese united with Japanese, Koreans, and Filipinos, finding commonalities in their histories and in current circumstances of exclusion and discrimination. The founders of Boston Chinatown's activist groups were primarily the postwar children of the Toisanese population, but they, too, incorporated non-Chinese individuals into their organizations.

Together these Asian Americans began to define a distinctive path. Building on the energy and spirit capturing much of the nation's youth, they increasingly questioned the value of existing institutions and agitated for immediate justice. Similar groups emerged in the large Asian American communities of New York City, San Francisco, and Los Angeles. In Boston, activism had spread among people of color in other parts of the city, giving rise to the Southwest Corridor Coalition in Roxbury, CAUSE in the South End, and new citywide tenants' groups. The civil rights and Black power movements, along with China's Communist experiment, informed their vision and methods. Directly and idealistically, they strove to address their communities' problems.

Heeding the call to "serve the people," some of these organizations provided free public services. Operating from the old Quincy School building, volunteers such as Albert Lau, a Massachusetts Institute of Technology student from New York's Chinatown, and York Liao, a cerebral student from Hong Kong, organized English language classes for the flow of new immigrants. Hundreds of students attended each week. Another group opened a free health clinic in the basement of the Golden Age Center on Harrison Avenue. Volunteers included Ramsay and Joan Liem, a Korean American couple who taught at local universities, and Frank and Pat Breslin, white medical students at Tufts.

Other organizations practiced civic engagement through protest politics. In 1971, the Free Chinatown Committee (FCC), comprised of young high school and college students, organized the first public demonstrations in the community in decades. I was involved myself. Along with Richard Gong, a VISTA worker from California, and Phil Ng, a high school student who lived on Tyler Street, we represented various groups who participated in the protest. Our target was T-NEMC: we pointed out its broken promise to retain "all Chinese housing units, increasing the housing stock." Instead, we said, the BRA had given T-NEMC "first preference in the development of over 15 parcels of land, while the Chinese had one parcel." Our fliers charged, "This self-interest-seeking institution, in alliance with the city, has stripped us of our land and has destroyed at least 650 of our homes. . . . We demand of T-NEMC 1) An end to all and any further T-NEMC expansion . . . 2) Minority hiring and training programs . . . 3) Adequate and free health care . . . 4) The establishment of adequate recreational and service facilities for the youth of Chinatown."[58]

Responding to the unexpected agitation, T-NEMC sent an open letter of apology for "[not being as] sensitive as we should have been to the needs of our neighbors."[59] The CCBA, horrified by the demonstration, apologized in return to T-NEMC and formed a "Seven-Man Committee" to conduct negotiations with the medical center. The committee excluded the FCC, which had brought attention to this unequal relationship.

Organizational inexperience caused the FCC to disband soon thereafter, but other grassroots organizations followed in its place. The Chinese Progressive Association flourished and grew increasingly active in community issues. The Pacific Asian Coalition (later the Asian American Resource Workshop) helped publicize and financially support tenants' advocacy and youth programs. Members of the Chinatown Housing and Land Development Task Force became active in a community-development to assert more local control over land-use decisions.[60]

There was a third new axis in Chinatown's shifting social and political landscape: the athletic, cultural, and social clubs that had traditionally avoided politics. The Knights Athletic Club, founded in 1961, primarily by second-generation Chinese American men, exemplified these groups. While their focus was on athletic and social activities, the Knights and similar organizations became an enduring part of the community, and their members played essential roles in the neighborhood.

The number of Chinatown volunteer and activist organizations, including both formal nonprofits and groups that eschewed government recognition, rose sharply in the 1960s and the following decades. Both the service agencies and the action organizations were challenges to the methods and legitimacy of the established community structure. At the same time, many of these agencies collaborated with traditional groups: the CACA, for instance, became a member organization of the CCBA. Still, many activist groups' stances were openly oppositional. At Chinatown's first community planning conference in 1971, organized by CACA, they bitterly criticized CCBA for its passivity and support of gambling and gangs. Traditional forces, in turn, routinely charged that many of these organizations were "Communists" and often worked with the FBI to identify radical elements in the community.[61]

Chinatown's new organizations did not yet pose a meaningful threat to CCBA and other more established groups. The social networks of traditional organizations—family and district associations and businesses—were still intact and extensive. During this era, those groups also expanded their activities, providing more direct services to meet the needs of residents. The CCBA's Billy Chin and his older brother, Frank, had maintained and solidified the neighborhood's only channel to city decisionmakers. Billy had served in the Korean War with Bill Bulger, who subsequently became the long-serving and powerful president of the Massachusetts State Senate, and after war the two maintained their relationship. The Chin brothers also significantly increased the neighborhood's voter base. Frank, sociable among his friends and severe toward those who opposed him, was appointed purchasing agent for the city in the 1970s. From this position, he developed significant influence and claimed that the Chins' political faction influenced 90 percent of the Chinatown vote. Billy ran the China Pearl Restaurant, which often hosted fundraisers for the state's Democratic party and candidates. China Pearl banquets raised more than $30,000 for Mayor Kevin White in 1975 and thousands of dollars for U.S. senators Ted Kennedy and John Kerry. In time, the Chins became the largest fundraisers for the state Democratic party, adapting a modern political tool for use within Chinatown's traditional social structure.[62]

The postwar period was a crossroads for the neighborhood. Beset by urban renewal destruction and institutional encroachment, residents nonetheless found a new freedom of movement. General outmigration would have probably allowed the city's urban planning scheme to destroy the neighborhood. Chinatown, however, had begun as a defensive refuge for a dispersed and unwelcome male population. That history continued to hold community meaning in the face of racial discrimination. Without a half-century of immigration exclusion laws, Chinatown residents would not have witnessed the loss of their first opportunity to establish a family-based neighborhood in a redeveloping city. Memories of that loss created a deep sense of grievance, one that paralleled the experiences of West Enders.

The neighborhood had also developed other functions. It had begun to operate, as Min Zhou has described in a study of New York's Chinatown, as an enclave economy that gave some residents more social mobility than would otherwise have been possible. Social networks, a pool of low wage labor, and access to capital underlay this economy.[63] Meanwhile, some stakeholders sensed the potential to organize voice and agency in the neighborhood. The appearance of machine politics and street protests were manifestations of that potential. Critically, the influx of immigration from China, Taiwan, and Hong Kong included a stream of working- and lower-middle-class populations that relied on the neighborhood and that the neighborhood, in turn, could support.

This confluence of factors led many neighborhood actors to decide to fight for Chinatown. But as they moved toward challenging urban elites, residents understood that they were disadvantaged, threatened, and politically weak. Despite the Chins' growing influence, discernible, positive effects from those connections were not yet evident in the neighborhood. According to a Harvard University urban field study, "even though the Chinese population of greater Boston and its surrounding cities has nearly doubled within the last decade [1960–70], the Chinese population in Boston Chinatown has actually decreased by 25%." The number of Chinese restaurants also dropped by 45 percent in the same period.[64] Chinatown needed to mobilize differently to face the new environment. Within its mixture of community constituents, different cohorts held and promoted diverse views about how to react.

In social movement terms, Chinatown entered the early 1970s with robust social networks and cultural symbols to sustain its ability to mobilize against development. These networks were rooted in committed leaders within the broader Chinese American community and a dense organizational structure. But despite its many organizations, the community had scarce and untested resources, and new arrivals' short tenure in the area constrained them. Still, activists found symbols around which to organize, ones that stressed Chinese American identity and the neighborhood's history of humiliating treatment, even though they lacked a unifying vision, an interpretive frame for moving forward, and the necessary mobilizing tactics to counter the pressures of Boston's growth coalition.

Chinatown had inherited relations designed for a bachelor society of laborers and a stagnant urban elite practicing benign neglect toward its community. Those neighborhood tools were ineffectual against a dynamic political and business coalition determined to change the physical base of the city. Boston's civic institutions and political and business elites were equally inept at dealing inclusively with the community, despite its long history in the city. These barriers became increasingly significant as Chinatown endured intense development pressures in the coming decades. To Boston's growth coalition, the neighborhood sounded like many voices singing different tunes. It seemed to be a cipher.

CHAPTER 3

THE NEIGHBORHOOD IN A WORLD-CLASS CITY, 1974–1983

In 1968, Kevin White was elected Boston's mayor on a platform that included a promise to reverse previous administrations' neglect of the neighborhoods. In the first years of his tenure, White made moves that seemed to keep that promise. He recruited innovative new actors from the communities and the middle class, including East Boston's Fred Salvucci, who later became the state's secretary of transportation, as well as future U.S. congressional representative Barney Frank. He supported progressive urban policies such as rent control. To engage local communities, he created satellites known as "little city halls" and neighborhood planning districts.

Eventually, however, his interest in community-centered politics began to wane. During White's first two administrations, he battled constantly with the neighborhoods, particularly over development. That turmoil only increased during the city's contentious and chaotic school desegregation process. Perhaps more significantly, both the Carter and Reagan administrations began restricting the urban renewal funds that had been the primary support behind policies of neighborhood transformation. Without these resources, White found dealing with the neighborhoods less appealing, and ongoing conflicts eroded his interest in engaging with their issues as well as his faith in his liberal allies. He soon jettisoned the reforms that had brought neighborhood partners into city planning and increasingly aligned himself with business and development interests.[1]

By 1975, the White administration had turned its focus to downtown development. The mayor supported a phaseout of Boston's rent-control program through "vacancy decontrol," allowing the market to determine rents in units that became vacant.[2] Like his predecessors Hynes and Collins, he began courting developers and promoting grand growth plans to reenergize the city's growth coalition. White's new goal was to transform Boston into "a world-class city." His shift in political focus was so striking that political commentators began calling his administration "Kevin II" and "Richard Daley East" (after the long-time iron-fisted mayor of Chicago).[3]

Meanwhile, the curtailment of federal funds at the end of the 1970s exacerbated Boston's systemic fiscal problems. For many years, Boston had levied higher property-tax rates on companies; and in 1978, a statewide referendum legalized differential property-tax rates for businesses and residences. But in 1979, in *Tregor v. Board of Assessors of Boston*, the state's highest court ruled that the unequal rates predating the referendum had been unconstitutional. Even more damaging, the ruling required the city to compensate businesses for decades of higher taxes. This decision placed the city under a huge debt burden. The following year, Proposition 2½, a statewide referendum, successfully capped overall tax rates throughout the state, limiting the city's income streams. Within a few years, city property-tax revenues, Boston's primary source of income, had dropped by one-third.[4]

Yet even though the city's coffers were severely constrained, conditions for development were healthy. Private developers were beginning to find Boston attractive. The growth coalition had successfully remade the city into a command center for regional capital, drawing thousands of businesses involved in global management and corporate services. Building on this improving reputation, the White administration increased its efforts to intensify downtown land use. Over the course of ten years, beginning in 1973, private developers built fourteen new office towers in the city. Public entities contributed to the demand by spending heavily on public administrative and office buildings. Together, federal, state, and city governments invested nearly $2 billion.[5] The new urban economy attracted young professionals and empty nesters to the city, creating a healthy housing market and raised concerns about gentrification. During these years, White played the role of "a business-oriented professional who could be depended on to keep the process of urban renewal rolling."[6]

During the 1970s, the availability of private capital for growth combined with the scarcity of public urban development funds allowed Boston's growth coalition to evolve. White's alliance with the developer Mort Zuckerman to create the Park Plaza project illustrated this shift. It was the first urban renewal project in Boston to depend solely on private investment, and it signaled how White would operate to continue the growth agenda. He creatively used chapter 121A of the Massachusetts General Laws to exempt projects from zoning controls and to restrict tax levies on developers. Within these new relationships, touted as public-private partnerships, public authorities would act to limit regulations and levies while the private sector would provide the capital needed for growth. The scholar Lawrence Kennedy has noted the contradictions in White's actions as mayor. Writing of Boston development in this era, he says, "In many ways planning during the Kevin White years was more democratic than at any time in the past, while in others it was less democratic."[7] By *democratic*, he refers to White's support of the neighborhoods during his early administrations; by *less democratic*, he points to the authoritarian management of the downtown district, where White always limited decision making to himself and developers.

KEVIN WHITE AND CHANGES IN CHINATOWN

The transition from urban renewal programs to public-private partnerships had many implications for Boston's neighborhoods, but its effect on Chinatown was particularly powerful. Whereas neighborhoods that were more distant from downtown suffered either a lack of growth or disinvestment, hundreds of millions of dollars in hospital, commercial, and office tower construction occurred in Chinatown between 1975 and 1989.[8] At the same time, during White's tenure as mayor, immigration into the neighborhood continued to increase demand for public services that would address housing, education, and family needs. By the mid-1970s, an estimated 2,000 people lived in Chinatown proper and many more in the abutting portion of the South End, especially in Castle Square Apartments, a project subsidized with urban renewal funds.[9] Despite such new residential projects, however, inadequate housing remained a critical problem for the community.

Numerous new service agencies sprang up in Chinatown—including, for a time, one of White's little city halls. Caroline Chang, who had a long history of community service in the area, became its first manager in 1970 and viewed it as the neighborhood's first full-time social welfare agency. In 1976, the Quincy School Community Council (QSCC) opened the new Josiah Quincy Elementary School on Washington Street and began providing various services, including recreational activities. The Chinese American Civic Association's (CACA) multiservice center continued to grow, and other agencies spun off from it, including the Chinese Economic Development Council (Chinatown's first community development corporation) and the South Cove Community Health Center. The health center flourished, establishing a clinic in the new Quincy Elementary School complex.[10] Jane Leung started Chinese Youth Essential Service (YES), a program for at-risk youth, in a room on Harrison Avenue.

Activist organizations also continued to sink roots into the community. In 1975, I Wor Kuen, the Asian equivalent of the Black Panther party, began publicly organizing in the neighborhood. By the late 1970s, it, along with the Chinatown Progressive Association (CPA), the Chinatown Housing and Land Development Task Force, and the Pacific Asian Coalition, were mobilizing in Chinatown around issues of land use, art and culture, peace, and workers' rights. I Wor Kuen and the CPA openly supported the People's Republic of China (PRC), the mainland Communist government that the traditional organizations vehemently opposed. They organized celebrations on the anniversary of the founding of the PRC, showed films, and shared literature about China. They also sought to build relations with other communities of color in Boston. Members of I Wor Kuen supported the Third World Jobs Clearinghouse that organized to open construction jobs to minority workers.[11]

The 1979 establishment of diplomatic relations between the United States and the People's Republic of China encouraged the activist groups. During the previous forty years, Chinatown factions had supported either the People's Republic or the Republic of China (Taiwan). For the Chinese Progressive Association (CPA), the neighborhood's largest activist group and the primary community voice for normalization of relations, and its supporters in the community, the change in U.S. policy provided a sense that they were part of the rising tide of history. For the traditional organizations, closely allied with the government in Taiwan, it was a stunning reversal.[12]

It was an exciting and turbulent moment. Creating full-time service agencies had become a major new trend in Chinatown and was fulfilling sorely neglected needs. The activist groups were publicizing a panoply of issues facing the community and beginning to mobilize long-quiescent sectors of the population. In their view, conditions were urgent and required intense activity. As Neil Chin has observed, students were the primary triggers of activism in Chinatown.[13]

Faced with this changing community, Mayor White revealed the limitations of his relationship with Chinatown. In a March 1975 meeting with the neighborhood's leadership, he appeared with representatives from a range of traditional and service organizations, including the Chinese Consolidated Benevolent Association (CCBA), CACA, the Golden Age Center, the YMCA, and the little city hall manager. Chinatown's activist groups were not present. White was unprepared for the meeting. According to a Sampan reporter, "[he] floundered at times, because here and there his background on Chinatown, his knowledge of the progress or lack of it of various projects, was shady."[14]

Given the city's long-standing links with the CCBA, it was no surprise that this organization's agenda dominated the discussion. CCBA representatives requested control of the old Josiah Quincy School building on Tyler Street and asked for public funds to renovate it. They also wanted funds for a Chinese foot patrol and affirmed that the CCBA could organize the patrol members itself, even though similar patrols had recently failed in the city's African American community. Despite this evidence, White supported the idea, claiming that the CCBA's attitude of self-reliance would work in Chinatown.[15] His shallow engagement with the neighborhood was not new. In a 1971 interview, he had observed that "those that are trying to provide vitality without disruption are not heard, it's the squeaky wheel that gets the grease. . . . It has been the Chinese community's greatest contribution, and, in a way, its greatest liability."[16] Thanks to the CCBA, the community rarely squeaked. Thus, White was able to continue the city's pattern of willful blindness to Chinatown's complexities and choose the more comfortable route of working through traditional neighborhood powers.

Early in the decade, Frank Chin had become chair of a community task force, and in 1974 the city employed him as its purchasing agent. He fit well into White's political machine. Despite his reformist image, the mayor was a skilled practitioner of patronage. He explicitly supported Chinatown's existing power structure and allowed traditional organizations and service organizations that deferred to them to manage neighborhood needs. As new development projects squeezed the community, this arrangement had significant repercussions. Boston Globe reporter Steve Bailey wrote that the Chin brothers "provided ready support for City Hall and almost any developer with a plan for Chinatown."[17]

Despite the traditional organizations' outwardly quiet stance, they roared inside the community. One unfortunate illustration of their power involved their veto of sorely needed elder housing. The Chinese Christian Church (CCCNE), run by the Mandarin-speaking Shih family, had clashed with the Cantonese/Toisanese-speaking CCBA. Though CCCNE had secured subsidies from the U.S. Department of Housing and Urban Development to build housing for the elderly on its land, the CCBA invoked its power under a 1963 memorandum of understanding with the Boston Redevelopment Authority (BRA) to reject the project. A service director recalled:

> [CCNE] had a couple of college people who were able to get funding. They had committed funding to build housing there, but, because of the fact that the pastor and CCBA were at loggerheads, they turned it down. They refused; they exercised their veto power only because of the fact that they didn't like Pastor Shih. They actually had the money, and they came to CCBA asking for permission to build. CCBA wouldn't give them permission to build.[18]

CCCNE lost the subsidy and the $4 million housing project, and the church soon left Chinatown for Brookline.[19] The land it had wanted to use for elder housing remains vacant today.

During the 1970s, the BRA began to document the adverse effects of growth on the environment and public health. Chinatown, for instance, was suffering from severe air pollution and had the highest tuberculosis rate in New England. The ongoing destruction of its low-income housing for new development was clearly the main factor in making the neighborhood the most overcrowded in the city and in limiting the amount of open space.[20] Fittingly, the neighborhood now hosted the highest concentration of parking lots in the city.

Despite knowing that growth was damaging the community, the BRA released T-NEMC's master plan in October 1978. The plan laid out the basis for expanding into the heart of the Chinatown residential area. It included new hospital construction on Oak, Ash, Nassau, and Harrison streets, which would threaten the QSCC's day care program and the YES program for at-risk teens. It rescinded the medical center's promise to give up land on Oak Street for elder housing and expanded student housing and office and research space into the area bounded by Tyler, Harvard, and Harrison streets. As a Massachusetts Institute of Technology–Harvard University study on Boston's future observed:

> A major issue here is the survival of Chinatown as a residential community. The neighborhood is squeezed between institutional expansion on the one hand and new commercial development on the other. . . . Chinatown's future will be a clear test of whether ethnic and special purpose neighborhoods can remain in the central city in the face of large-scale economic development.[21]

BOSTON'S COMBAT ZONE

In 1974, the BRA officially designated an area abutting Chinatown as the city's adult entertainment district. Known as the Combat Zone, it was now the only neighborhood zoned for pornography sales and strip clubs.[22] During the late 1950s and early 1960s, when redevelopment dismantled the West End and Scollay Square to make way for Government Center, it also dispersed many of that area's red-light businesses. Many of them shifted to Lower Washington Street, which had already built up an entertainment reputation, and they now began to offer strip shows and other associated commerce. Similar businesses spread to other neighborhoods as well, including fashionable Back Bay and Beacon Hill, Kenmore Square, the South End, and the Prudential Center area, prompting numerous local protests.[23] Alarmed, the BRA explored various plans to isolate the industry, and eventually it decided to confine adult entertainment to a specific zone.

The redevelopment authorities selected a section of Lower Washington Street beside Chinatown, a community with little social or political power, except for the Chin brothers' influence. Neither the city nor the neighborhood's insular and isolated leadership tried to stop them, and press and BRA appraisals of the situation rarely acknowledged the impact the decision had had on Chinatown's residents. In a letter to the *Boston Globe,* a West Roxbury reader expressed shocked at that indifference:

> I have just been shown an editorial in the Sept. 20 *Globe* in which Boston's Combat Zone was discussed. I was amazed that while the yet-to-be realized Park Plaza was mentioned, no mention was made of Chinatown, which directly abuts the Combat Zone. That you fail to consider the plight of these fine citizens who have to go through that horrible area with its drunks, filth, vomit, prostitutes and pimps every time they go the Boston Common and to the department stores is beyond my comprehension. Chinese mothers must drag their children hurriedly through the maze of near-pornographic photos plastered all over the place.[24]

The decision of Chinatown's leaders to passively support the location of the Combat Zone was, in White's terms, a failure to squeak. A few representatives at the zoning hearing even voiced their approval, citing the potential for economic growth. As a former resident said,

Chinatown's leaders bought "the bill of goods": that is, the claim that the Combat Zone would bring new business to neighborhood restaurants. Peter Chan, the little city hall manager, and Bob Lee, who owned Bob Lee's Islander Restaurant on Tyler Street and was chair of CCBA, both testified in favor of the decision. Chan did express some resignation but believed that support for the zoning would "give our government enough faith to function properly and [be in] . . . the general best interests of the city." *Sampan* reported that CACA, supported by T-NEMC, offered the only dissenting neighborhood voice at the hearing.[25] The city did not see the need to call a community meeting. As Tom Lee, a local pastor, later testified, "Most residents, most businesses probably didn't know that it happened until after the fact."[26]

In November, the city passed new zoning regulations for Lower Washington Street without modifications. Although planners proposed the development of two housing projects for Chinatown along Harrison Avenue, with the goal of offsetting some of the effects of the new zone, those suggestions never came to fruition. The city thus gave the neighborhood all the troubles associated with the city's adult entertainment without meeting any of its needs.

The Combat Zone was a neighborhood burden for decades. The area attracted sex traffic that spilled onto the doorsteps of residential Chinatown and into the Josiah Quincy Elementary School playground. Used condoms on neighborhood streets became common. Crime rates increased, and drug dealing was widespread. The Combat Zone was the scene of violent confrontations—most sensationally, the killing of a Harvard University football player in 1977. Neil Chin recalled, "From Beach Street, you could go into Lagrange Street heading west, and the prostitutes from the Combat Zone establishments would actually stop the cars by standing in front of them and really physically pulling the people out. I saw them, and I actually couldn't believe it."[27] To get to the Orange Line subway stop, immigrant women and their children had to walk swiftly past animated neon signs for pornographic bookstores, peep shows, and strip clubs featuring waving female legs and other body parts. Words and colors blared, but Chinatown appeared to have no voice.

YELLOW BUSES AND YELLOW BUSING: THE NEW ACTIVISM

In 1965, at the height of the civil rights movement, Massachusetts passed the Racial Imbalance Act.[28] It called on "all school committees [in the state] to adopt as education objectives the promotion of racial balance" and required local school systems to eliminate racial imbalance in any school that was more than 50 percent nonwhite.[29] In Boston, this triggered a struggle between Black parents and community leaders and the city's school committee, which, nearly a decade later, precipitated a court order for a busing plan to resolve educational inequities.

On a hazy, sunny afternoon in late June 1974, just after the end of the school year, U.S. district court judge W. Arthur Garrity, Jr., ordered the immediate desegregation of the city's public schools. In his ruling, he found the Boston school committee guilty of deliberately maintaining a segregated school system. The record was clear. As Mel King noted, "Judge Garrity was faced with overwhelming evidence. The School Committee had kept excellent records of its policies and plans to keep the schools segregated; and the long history of Black parent protest, court cases, and attempts to have the existence of de facto segregation publicly recognized provided a cumulative record of the resistance to voluntary desegregation."[30] Even many anti-busing activists could not and did not defend the school committee's record.[31]

For more than a decade, Boston's African American community had been striving for better educational opportunities in the public schools. In the years before the Racial Imbalance Act was passed, Black parents affiliated with the National Association for the Advancement of Colored People (NAACP), led by the activist Ruth Batson, discovered that the city was spending significantly less money on Black students than on white students. Their investigation revealed other disparities as well, such as outdated and blatantly racist curricula, the tracking of Black students into vocational classes, and the use of less experienced teaching staff in majority-Black schools. After participating in hearings and lobbying the school committee, without results, they organized what they called "Freedom Schools" for Black children and instituted a series of boycotts, rallies, and marches that attracted national attention. They also ran reform slates for school committee seats, although they rarely won those elections.[32]

Passage of the Racial Imbalance Act did not resolve the impasse with the Boston school committee, and Black community efforts and campaigns increased. The NAACP, which had established desegregation as a national priority, brought a series of lawsuits against the school committee. Yet the committee continued to resist change: the education of Black children remained decidedly inferior to the already-dismal education of white children in the Boston school system.[33] According to the historian Ronald Formisano:

> For nine years, after the passage of the Racial Imbalance Act, the Boston School Committee . . . refused to take steps to bring about any significant school integration. Through delay, counterattacks, and the most transparent obfuscation and tokenism the committee held the line against a growing black population. Meanwhile, the number of racially imbalanced schools climbed upward. As residential segregation increased the committee in no way tried to ameliorate the situation; instead, in most cases where it could choose it acted to perpetuate or even actually increase imbalance in the city's schools.[34]

Throughout this fierce battle, the city's other communities of color were ignored. At best, they were treated as pawns. For instance, in 1966, the school committee decided to classify Chinese as "white" so as to be able to report a lower number of racially imbalanced schools.[35] Committee chair Louise Day Hicks even used Chinese children as a wedge against Black children, calling them "industrious" and claiming that they wanted to avoid association with Blacks.[36]

The Racial Imbalance Act had many shortcomings: its focus on Boston, the immediacy and scale of its requirements, the class implications of allowing suburban elites to impose dramatic solutions, and the act's failure to address overall educational quality in school systems.[37] Underlying these issues was the growing contention between an increasingly assertive African American community and the Irish American and Italian American leaders who had monopolized Boston's positions of public power. White leadership refused to cede elements of control that might have enabled stakeholders to find alternatives to what became the eventual plan. At the last hour, in June 1974, the state legislature's Black caucus put forth a decentralized community-control plan to avoid the impending court order, but the overwhelmingly white Boston teachers' union blocked the compromise.[38] The city's smaller constituencies of color—the Chinese and Latino communities—were soon to be caught up in the tumult.

The court's remedy for the segregation of Boston's schools was a two-part school desegregation plan: a temporary phase 1 plan for the rapidly approaching 1974 school opening and a permanent phase 2 plan. Phase 1 focused on citywide schools, about 40 percent of the system, and involved redistricting, busing, and the formation of parent councils. It involved busing between and 17,000 and 18,000 students. Phase 2 included more sweeping changes: revising area borders, constructing new schools, and implementing a controlled transfer policy. Students could attend either a school in their community district (where the school committee determined enrollment) or a citywide school (if a seat was available).[39]

Phase 1 of the desegregation plan began with the opening of classes in September. The city's white communities were immediately ready to fight: they had mobilized a mass resistance that would shape the city's national image for years. In the months before the June court order, antibusing sentiment had been growing; a crowd of 25,000 opponents had gathered to protest at the state house in April. Their fierce opposition eventually led to school boycotts and widespread violence. When the school year opened, 25 percent of Boston's students, primarily white, were absent. Militancy in the white enclaves of South Boston, East Boston, and Charlestown was dramatic. Mayor White told Judge Garrity that enforcement of phase 1 had cost the city more than $2 million in its first eighteen days of implementation. Conditions intensified. Over the course of the school year, buses were stoned; school walkouts and scattered violence were endemic. Gunshots were fired at schools and at the *Boston Globe offices;* transit stations were trashed; a student was stabbed. State troopers and Boston police, often in riot gear, monitored the buses. The governor put five hundred National Guard troops on alert. Yet for Chinese high school students, the students in the community who were bused in phase 1, the 1974–75 school year was relatively peaceful. School buses took them to the North End and to Charlestown, and no incidents of violence were reported.[40]

Phase 2 of the desegregation plan, which incorporated Chinatown's elementary school students, was implemented in September 1975. In June, parents of students in all schools that had been deemed racially imbalanced received letters informing them that their children would be bused that fall to schools outside their neighborhoods. Chinatown parents were among those who received these letters. To this point, Chinese primary students had been studying at the old Josiah Quincy School in Chinatown and at the Abraham Lincoln School in Bay Village, bordering the neighborhood.

All of the letters, however, were written in English. Unable to read them, two Chinese parents brought their copies to Suzanne Lee, a twenty-five-year-old teacher who was just finishing her first year at the Quincy School. Lee was among a handful of Chinese American teachers who been recently hired to work among a hostile cadre of long-time Irish American and Italian American teachers.[41] After reading the letters, she told the parents that their children would apparently not be returning to Quincy in the fall. "Where are they going to go?" the parents asked. The letters did not answer that question.

Lee had long been a volunteer at the Saturday English Classes, an activist-inspired, adult-education program housed at the Quincy School. She discovered that the letters were a main topic of conversation among the program's participants, mostly female garment workers. She offered to convene a meeting so that she could explain the content of the letters to a larger group of parents. This meeting, held in early July at the Chinese Christian Church on Harvard Street, led to the formation of the Boston Chinese Parents Association (BCPA). Its membership and activities increased quickly. Parents were alarmed by the school department notices, and their fears were stoked by the ongoing murder trial of two Chinese brothers involved in a fatal brawl with a gang of white youth in Charlestown.[42] BCPA meetings grew from scores of parents to hundreds.

Eventually, Chinatown parents learned that the school department planned to bus nearly 1,000 Chinese elementary and high school children to Charlestown and the North End, areas where violence and racial tensions were high. Lai Miu (May) Yu, a garment worker living in Castle Square and one of BCPA's earliest active parents, recalled media images of mobs of white demonstrators throwing rocks at buses full of children. All three of her sons had been reassigned from local schools to attend the Harvard Kent School in Charlestown. "[The boys] were too small, small and scared," she feared. Fanny Wong, age seven at the time, remembered, "We didn't know what was happening. Suddenly, all your friends were asking, 'Did you get your letter?' We were scared about going to a new school, and we heard all these things about Charlestown—we heard they were bombing the buses—and we didn't want to go there."[43]

Though BCPA had been founded as a clearinghouse for information, its members struggled to get city officials to acknowledge their concerns about safety, communication, and representation. In their rulings and actions, neither Judge Garrity nor the Boston Public Schools had considered students other than African American and white ones. Soon after BCPA formed, Chinese parents sent letters to Garrity and the school system but received no response. They repeatedly tried and failed to get their concerns onto the school committee's agenda.

Eventually, they decided to call on the CCBA for assistance. Some believed that, as the recognized leaders in the neighborhood, CCBA members would be able to influence city decisionmakers. But BCPA's meeting with CCBA forced them to recognize the truth. As four parent representatives and Suzanne Lee met with CCBA members at the organization's dark Oxford Street office, more than a hundred other parents and supporters waited for news in a large auditorium at Tufts Medical School's Posner Hall on Harrison Avenue. The CCBA responded coldly to the parents' petition for aid: "The few men at the meeting were resistant. 'We don't have time for this,' Suzanne recalled them saying, 'And who do you think you people are that you can go against the government? You know you don't speak English, and you are a bunch of ignorant women.' The women left that meeting enraged and with a shattered image of community leaders."[44]

Subsequent interactions did not reassure them. Judge Garrity had ordered parent councils for all schools. As Chinese parents arrived for the Harvard Kent School's council elections at city hall in mid-July, they saw white parents picketing outside. Upon entering, the Chinese parents found that seats on the court-mandated parent council were reserved for Black or white parents only.[45] In August, the parents were allowed to visit the Charlestown schools that their children would attend. At the Harvard Kent School, white parents were again picketing outside. The building itself, built only two years earlier, impressed the Chinese parents, but they "were concerned about the atmosphere."[46]

BCPA members had to rely on themselves. They had been ignored and dismissed by institutions and community leadership. According to Suzanne Lee, their only advocates were about a dozen young Asian American activists (including me), who formed a support committee. Its role was to perform parent-requested work such as translating, offering input, and interacting with mainstream society. By September, it had formalized itself as the BCPA Support Committee.

The BCPA began publicly speaking out on July 30. Lai Miu Yu, who was outgoing and bold, took on the role of public spokesperson. In a press conference, the parents issued nine demands to the school system. These included a set minimum number of Chinese students, teachers, and aides in each school to which Chinese students were bused; a set minimum number of Chinese escorts on buses; the hiring of Chinese administrative staff who could communicate with the parents; and safety provisions involving bus dropoff and pickup locations and police details at schools. The BCPA requested a response by August 8, though it did not specify what actions it would take if it did not get one.

On August 6, the school committee granted the Chinese parents a hearing. At the end of the workday, May Chen, Betty Chu, and Nancy Mah, with Suzanne Lee serving as interpreter, met with school committee members in a cramped, stuffy room and began describing their concerns. Almost immediately, three committee members got up and left; only John Kerrigan and Paul Ellison remained to listen to the women. The two exhibited what the women described afterward as a "condescending and racist attitude." According to Chen, "when we sat before them, all those two did was to whisper and snicker while we were intent on answering questions. I want to know what they thought was so funny—the fact that we can't speak English, that we're Chinese?"[47]

Kerrigan and Ellison made no promises to meet any of the BCPA's demands. So on September 3, a few days before the new school year began, parents sent out a press release pointing out the inaction of "the Boston School Department, individual school administrators, Judge W. Arthur Garrity, Jr. and the Citywide Coordinating Council" and vowing unspecified "severe actions."[48] Once again, they received no response, and on September 7 members of the BCPA voted unanimously to institute a school busing boycott. They issued another press release, reiterating their grievances and declaring their intentions: "Chinese parents are united in boycotting all schools because we feel that school and court officials, by not taking concrete action on our demands, have demonstrated an overall disregard for the rights of all Chinese parents and students."[49]

The boycott was sudden in action but had been long in gestation. According to Suzanne Lee, parents apparently had been discussing it among themselves for some time. Lee got married that summer and had scheduled her weeklong honeymoon between important busing-related meetings. When she returned, the parents told her that their boycott would begin the next day. Astounded, she asked, "How can you notify everybody? This is crazy! It's the night before school starts. How can we make this happen?" They said, "We have a way."[50]

BCPA members telephoned every Chinese family with children scheduled to be bused and urged them to boycott the schools. On September 8, the women woke up at dawn and stood at local bus stops to inform parents about the action. As a result of their mobilization, the BCPA boycott was more than 90 percent effective for the 1,000 Chinese students scheduled to be bused. It even extended to Chinatown's Quincy School, which only 30 Chinese students out of a total population of 146 now attended.[51]

The boycott prompted the aloof institutions to respond. At Harvard Kent School, where she was now teaching, Lee was surprised to find a message from the U.S. Justice Department waiting for her at the front office. Since August, the Community Relations Service of the Justice Department had been supporting Federal Judge Garrity in monitoring Boston's desegregation.[52] A Justice Department Chinese American staff person asked for an immediate meeting with the parents. "Everybody's working!" Lee responded. "They're working, I'm working. We can't meet with you until the night. And whether or not they can meet with you immediately is another story." The staffer continued to demand an immediate meeting, and Lee wanted to know what the urgency was. The staffer told her, "We need the Chinese kids as a buffer." Lee understood this to mean that the Chinese students were to act as a buffer between the Black and white students.[53]

Undeterred by Justice Department pressure, the parents continued the boycott for two more days. Finally, to end the impasse, the Department of Justice and school department agreed to implement nearly all the BCPA demands, except the inclusion of Chinese teachers and aides at schools where Chinese students were assigned. The teaching staff was beyond their jurisdictions and required action from the teachers' union.

The BCPA's success attracted attention. Its members began communicating with Latino parents in El Comité de Padres, a parents' organization that faced similar issues with the Boston school system. El Comité was particularly interested in bilingual education issues. The Black caucus also reached out to BCPA to discuss people-of-color representation in school issues. John O'Bryant, an African American candidate for the school committee, asked for BCPA support. The field director of the Boston teachers' union, whose members were generally hostile to newly hired teachers of color, asked BCPA to back its ongoing strike action.

For the Chinatown community, the impact was profound. The BCPA victory was the first time that neighborhood activists had succeeded in achieving their goals. Through their demand for fair treatment, they had gained greater visibility. The neighborhood's working people had challenged institutional dictates and structures and won. Moreover, the women of BCPA had achieved a victory against the male-dominated traditional power structure in Chinatown. Abandoned by the CCBA and ignored by other established organizations, these factory workers had nonetheless been able to build on their own skills and networks. They had spent their days hunched over deafening industrial sewing machines and their evenings and weekends organizing on behalf of their children. Some of the women had no family support for their activism. One husband locked a core BCPA member out of her home when she returned from a night meeting. Others punished their wives by withholding their pay or by gambling their earnings away. The Lee Family Association admonished Suzanne Lee's father for failing to "control" his daughter's political activities.[54] Yet these "ignorant women," in CCBA's terms, demonstrated that they could win a community victory through their own intelligence and determination.

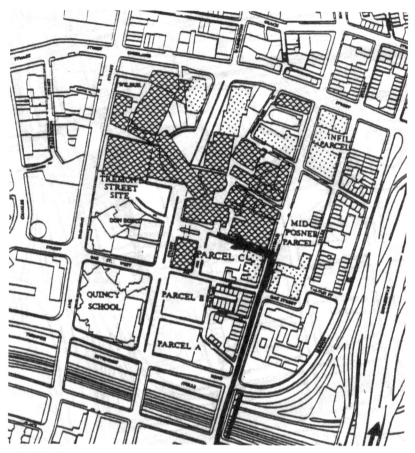

FIGURE 5. Hatched and dotted areas indicate Tufts–New England Medical Center's presence in Chinatown, 1994. From New England Medical Center Hospitals, "Draft Project Impact Report; Draft Environmental Impact Report; Parcel C Garage" (Boston, February 28, 1994).

Outside the community, the BCPA forced institutions to acknowledge the Chinatown neighborhood. After failing for much of the summer to get decisionmakers at the city, state, and federal levels to recognize them and respond to their needs, the parents forced these authorities to meet their demands for safety and representation. Not merely "others" or a "buffer" population within the Black-white busing narrative, Chinese parents forced institutions to treat them as people. As Thomas Chen has explained, "though Chinese Americans were numerically a small proportion of the city's population, BCPA mobilized a potent critique of power relations in Chinatown and the city at large. It forced urban elites to reconsider Chinatown and its residents as a political constituency, and it challenged and exposed the limits of Chinatown's traditional authority figures."[55]

Now the parents began to form relations with other city populations, which reshaped their outlooks. Chen notes, "[The campaign] altered how Chinese Bostonians viewed themselves as urban citizens . . . and helped BCPA members to develop a better understanding of racial hierarchies and their relative position in these hierarchies." BCPA members not only developed a new consciousness, but they also pushed relations across racial lines that could effectively support Chinatown's future mobilization.[56]

There were numerous aftereffects of this victory. One BCPA leader, Xin-Hua Lee, the mother of a bused seven-year-old girl, later became a leader in organizing the first rent strike in Chinatown at Tai Tung Village. Many of the activist leaders of BCPA later became founding members of the Chinese Progressive Association. As I have discussed, various actors linked to the Boston public school system—parents' organizations, school committee candidates, the teachers' union, and elected officials—began consulting with the grassroots Chinatown organization. Yet even though BCPA tried to stay involved with educational issues, most of its members turned their attention back to the daily challenges of their low-income lives of color. BCPA did not survive as an organization. Nevertheless, the parents' work set an activist tone in the community and opened a new door to future organizing in Chinatown.

TUFTS–NEW ENGLAND MEDICAL CENTER LOOMS

In chapter 2, I discussed the Free Chinatown Committee's early organizing against T-NEMC construction in the neighborhood. As the 1970s progressed, it became clear that the medical center would be Chinatown's major urban development challenge. T-NEMC pursued a very aggressive expansion strategy in these years. Because the city saw the medical complex as an important contributor to Boston's economic and public health, it facilitated this expansion. In 1973, T-NEMC constructed a new building on Washington and Kneeland streets as well as three other new facilities in the area. By 1978, it had unveiled a new master plan

FIGURE 6. Protest for elder housing at the opening of T-NEMC's human nutrition center, 1979.
Courtesy of the author.

that envisioned hundreds of millions of dollars in new construction. Imminent construction of three new large buildings loomed, each covering several hundred thousand square feet. In 1979, Jerome Grossman assumed the presidency of T-NEMC and initiated a period of growth.[57] In subsequent years, the center's expansion plan would lead to the eviction of scores of Chinese residents, mainly the elderly but also some families, as T-NEMC tripled in size.[58]

TIMELINE 1. T-NEMC Looms

1978	T-NEMC master plan presented.
	T-NEMC denies site on Parcel C for Chinatown elderly housing. Housing Task Force forms and organizes protests.
1979	Jerome Grossman assumes leadership of T-NEMC.
	Evictions of Chinese tenants on Harrison Avenue begin.
	BRA finds two sites for elderly housing in Bay Village.
1980	T-NEMC's USDA nutrition center constructed,
1981	T-NEMC buys Kneeland Street garment buildings outside of master plan.
1982	New T-NEMC master plan presented. Health science building proposed.
1983	Community coalition calls for moratorium on T-NEMC expansion.
	CCBA forms a seven-person committee with Housing Task Force.
	T-NEMC and CCBA sign agreement.

In 1978, the Chinatown community tried to build a new elder housing project. The developer Stanley Chen had secured federal funding to build 230 units of subsidized housing; the problem was that T-NEMC owned or was the designated developer for all available parcels appropriate for such construction in Chinatown.[59] The hospital complex was unwilling to relinquish its rights to a lot on Oak Street, Chen's preferred housing site. Although T-NEMC'S development consultant acknowledged to the BRA that neither of them had lived up to their obligations to the Chinatown community, the medical center would not consider any land swap or concessions.[60] For its part, the BRA claimed that it was powerless against T-NEMC, though the agency had taken much of the site from existing housing through its power of eminent domain.[61]

This stalemate so frustrated young activists in the community that they created a new coalition of service agencies and action organizations to fight for housing. Soon this coalition proved unsustainable, but one of its members, the Community Task Force on Housing and Land Development in Chinatown, continued to organize as the Chinatown Housing and Land Development Task Force (shortened to the Housing Task Force here). Its November 1978 flyer calling for a public rally conveyed the neighborhood's sense of unequal justice:

> When nobody wanted the Southeast Expressway, where was it built? Chinatown! When nobody wanted the Mass Turnpike, who got stuck with it? Chinatown! When nobody wanted the parasitic institution of Tufts–New England Medical Center, where was it dumped? Chinatown! Now when we have federal money to get some much needed housing for the elderly built in Chinatown, who stops us—Tufts![62]

In 1979, after much agitation, the BRA resolved this conflict by securing two smaller sites for elder housing in adjoining Bay Village.[63] Nonetheless, the Housing Task Force continued calling for a review of the medical center's expansion plans, organizing public demonstrations, aiding tenants to resist evictions, and carrying out land and housing work. It was able to mobilize support from the Chinese Progressive Association, Saturday English Classes, the community's health center, and student groups.[64]

The contrast between the influence and power of the neighborhood compared to the hospital's was evident in another contemporary development project. T-NEMC wanted to build a state-of-the-art human nutrition research center for the U.S. Department of Agriculture (USDA). Its construction of the fourteen-story building on the corner of Washington Street and Stuart Street (the extension of Kneeland Street across Washington) proceeded without delay. Jean Mayer, the well-known and well-connected president of Tufts University, had lobbied successfully with his numerous contacts in Congress to bring the nutrition center to Boston. At the center's groundbreaking ceremonies on December 14, 1979, T-NEMC's board of governors (which included a Saltonstall and a Cabot, both from long-established Boston families) sat beside numerous politicians. Meanwhile, outside in the snow, the Housing Task Force and other community groups had organized a demonstration. The protesters, 150 strong, marched uninvited into the building and onto the stage. An evicted elderly tenant, wearing a checked winter coat and a knit cap, told everyone in attendance about the loss of neighborhood housing and land. After the protesters exited, the ceremonies continued.[65]

T-NEMC's incursions into Chinatown continued unabated. In 1981, the medical center unexpectedly announced that it had purchased two large buildings at 15 and 35 Kneeland Street, the center of Boston's steadily shrinking garment district. This news stunned the community: T-NEMC hadn't included the buildings in its master plan, nor had it informed the BRA of its intentions. The buildings housed twenty-five garment shops that paid their employees (mostly Chinese women) meager wages but provided vital health insurance for their families. T-NEMC's purchases displaced all of the shops and six hundred to eight hundred garment jobs—between 40 and 50 percent of the garment jobs in the area. A wave of protests from community members and garment business owners prompted the city to try to moderate the losses. After three months, it found new spaces for the shops, mostly in South Boston. The loss of these neighborhood businesses dealt a tremendous economic and employment blow to Chinatown.[66]

A few months later, in early 1982, T-NEMC announced that it had developed a new master plan and wanted to pursue further expansion. The medical center proposed constructing its Health Sciences Building at Harrison Avenue and Harvard Street, where Chinese tenants had been recently evicted.[67] After the garment factory calamity, many in the community, especially the activist groups, were determined to challenge this new plan.

T-NEMC's proposal coincided with a series of negotiations between the CCBA and the medical center on a joint housing project. When those discussions failed, the association's president, Billy Chin, decided to increase pressure on T-NEMC. He adopted some of the neighborhood's new mobilization methods and formed a temporary alliance with the Housing Task Force. Together, they organized a community meeting in support of a coalition of housing activists. The coalition called for a moratorium on construction and formed a joint negotiation team to advocate on behalf of the community. The CCBA included two non-association members in this team: Lawrence Cheng and Regina Lee, both members of the Housing Task Force. In addition, the city's zoning board withheld approval of the Health Sciences Building due to opposition from Chinatown.[68]

The standoff continued for several months. Finally, in September 1983, after a series of private meetings, Billy Chin and T-NEMC representatives announced an agreement approved by the BRA. In an interview, Frank Chin, later recalled his own intervention with Kevin White as pivotal. White persuaded T-NEMC to grant CCBA the SCM Corporation building on the South End flank of the Massachusetts Turnpike extension in exchange for dropping community opposition. The agreement also granted CCBA $800,000 to develop housing on the site.[69]

However, the site fell vacant for more than a decade after the agreement was signed. Eventually, CCBA leased it to a businessman, and it is now the home of the C-Mart, one of the largest Chinese supermarkets in the neighborhood. To date, there has never been a public accounting of the related funds.[70] The Health Sciences Building, in contrast, was successfully completed. Part of it now stands on former housing sites of residential Chinatown.

LESSONS LEARNED

Even as the school busing campaign demonstrated new and potent avenues for community mobilization, Chinatown itself had changed. Redevelopment had forever altered the close-knit postwar community. While it had avoided extinction, the physical neighborhood was now split in two and hemmed in on all sides. The brick rowhouses of the old Chinatown remained only in pockets, squeezed among parking lots, institutional buildings, and large impersonal housing projects. Newer residents had replaced established families.[71] As it emerged from this first phase of postindustrial growth, Boston Chinatown was faced with a grim future. The growth coalition continued to dominate the city. Despite minor concessions, it maintained its "highly regressive social engineering," displacing the poor and people of color to benefit higher-status populations.[72] Chinatown was just one example among many.

The neighborhood found some solace in the new subsidized housing projects, Tai Tung Village and Mass Pike Towers, but residents also had to cope with the newly designated Combat Zone and the rapid expansion of T-NEMC, both of which created significant burdens and few benefits for the community. The loss of affordable housing units for families was accompanied by the loss of viable employment opportunities, particularly for Chinese women. Socially and politically, these experiences showed neighborhood activists that "world-class Boston" had little use for Chinatown.

To a large extent, traditional leaders were unable to see past their agendas to address the most pressing needs of their community. Too often, they provided cover for policies advocated by the White administration and T-NEMC as a way to support long-standing business interests. These decisions increased the fragility of Chinatown.

In response to such challenges, the Chinese Parents Association and other activist groups used new collective methods to challenge the status quo and organize for community interests. Their broad-based democratic approaches were essential to neighborhood successes during this and subsequent periods. In the 1970s, these organizations were still learning how to establish themselves—to sink their roots and build social networks. They discovered how to use confrontational methods, primarily mass organizing and civic activism, but were also learning that these approaches were not always sufficient, given the dynamic economic and political contexts of the era. Mobilization alone was often ineffective at dealing with entrenched city bureaucracies and the political and procedural skills of professional project development staffs.

Community activists supplemented their organizing with attempts to change the political environment. They supported reform candidates for mayor and began working more closely with emerging activist groups in other neighborhoods to ensure that any benefits from development also flowed to residents. Mollenkopf characterized the neighborhood movement as local efforts that "stressed ideas like citizen participation and neighborhood control over government programs, self-help and small enterprise as opposed to large public or private organizations, 'restoring and supporting natural coping mechanisms and helping networks rather than supplanting them with bureaucratic institutions,' and rehabilitating existing neighborhoods rather than allowing decline or creating new housing elsewhere." Such neighborhood activism became ubiquitous and chronic in postindustrial cities, including Boston's Chinatown.[73] The entrance of Chinatown's activists into the political arena permitted new relationship building and began to transcend the inherently local nature of their work.

CHAPTER 4

CHINATOWN JOINS THE REVOLT OF THE NEIGHBORHOODS, 1975–1983

As Chinatown's resistance to development schemes amplified, the growth coalition was forced to acknowledge the needs of it and other neighborhoods in the city. Development forces adapted, often by casting their projects as solutions to neighborhood housing, employment, and economic development. Such assurances were typically disingenuous, and the neighborhoods' resulting disillusionment pushed activists to enter electoral politics as an alternative path to progress.

The case of Lafayette Place epitomized this emerging pattern.[1] In 1975, Allied Stores Corporation, the owner of Jordan Marsh, one of the largest retailers in the city, proposed the construction of Lafayette Place, a $220 million project sited on the southern edge of the downtown retail district and at the northern border of Chinatown. The project had strong support among political and economic elites, who touted it as an initiative to revitalize the district. The city and the developer conceptualized it as a public-private partnership that would include $35 million in publicly funded improvements and $185 million in private investment.[2] Lafayette Place's construction would follow on the heels of the highly successful Quincy Market retail project next to Government Center and the creation of the pedestrian-friendly Downtown Crossing retail district.

For Mayor White and BRA's director, Robert Kenney, strengthening Boston's retail spaces was a significant piece of their urban redevelopment plans. The shopping district along Washington Street had had difficulty competing with the growing number of suburban malls and had languished during the city's postwar growth. Numerous well-known stores such as Raymond's and Chandler's had closed their doors, and dwindling attendance had long extinguished the bright marquees of "Movie Row." The city administration saw Lafayette Place as a critical part of a citywide development plan to build on the Boston's reputation as a pedestrian-friendly destination.[3]

TIMELINE 2. Lafayette Place

1975	Allied Stores proposes Lafayette Place; Sefrius becomes development partner.
1977	Sefrius downsizes project, brings in Canadian firm Mondev as an additional partner.
	City council approves project.
	City council appropriates $475K for Chinatown housing.
1979	Tregor decision puts city in financial difficulties.
	The city portion of construction begins.
	Mayor White wins reelection on "Boston jobs" policy.
1980	Citizens Advisory Committee forms to focus on Chinatown residents' employment at Lafayette Place.
	Proposition 2½ passes, limiting tax increases.
	City halts garage construction and improvements due to budget problems.
1981	City revises garage agreement with developer.
1982	Construction resumes.
1983	Chinatown reorganizes around community employment at Lafayette Place but fails.
1984	Lafayette Place opens.

Allied Stores Corporation planned to build Lafayette Place on Jordan Marsh's excess land, and the BRA agreed to support the project by building a 1,500-car parking garage under the complex at city expense. Allied Stores solicited an international developer, Sefrius Corporation, to do the construction and worked with the BRA to develop the initial plan.[4] That agency used its many planning and development powers to move the project forward, obtaining the zoning variances and tax limits necessary to accomplish the first stage of the project (the Jordan Marsh renovation) and supporting Sefrius when it secured an $8 million federal urban development action grant (UDAG).[5]

PROMISES AND SMOKE-AND-MIRRORS

Despite public investment and support, the Lafayette Place project did not go smoothly. Various players began to quarrel about the division of project costs. Sefrius had trouble finding investors; and after bringing in a collaborating partner, Montreal-based Mondev International, it substantially revised the project and reduced its commitment by $70 million. The city also delayed action on the garage.[6]

While the BRA failed to solicit comments from Chinatown in the initial 1975 proposal, its officials were quick to tell regulatory authorities and the public about the project's perceived benefits for the neighborhood. As late as December 1979, the BRA was circulating the idea of a pedestrian walkway from the garage into Chinatown, calling this a way to stimulate business. In the project's final environmental impact statement (EIS), the BRA did acknowledge possible negative impacts: rising property values, increased development, traffic congestion, and resulting health issues. But it continued to tout anticipated benefits such as 1,100 retail and hotel jobs, job training programs for construction workers, retail space within the project, and a flow of Lafayette Place patrons into Chinatown businesses.[7]

In their applications for UDAG and for chapter 121A regulatory and tax relief, the city and the developers repeated these rosy projections. They proposed giving Boston residents, "especially those . . . in the neighboring Chinese community," preference for construction jobs, a "substantial share" of the permanent jobs in the complex, and entrepreneurial opportunities in the proposed retail spaces.[8] But Chinatown residents were worried. At the UDAG hearing, testimony from the neighborhood's service providers and members of the newly formed Chinese Economic

Development Council (CEDC) emphasized the need for employment opportunities and the mitigation of negative environmental effects on the community. The development, CEDC noted, "could be a positive factor in improving Chinatown, but only if the community's concerns were addressed."[9]

Despite assurances from the BRA, the neighborhood anticipated negative effects. The community was worried about the 125 commercial tenants that would be displaced by the project—predominately garment industry shops, the main employers of working-class Chinese women. The BRA proposed relocating some of the tenants, though it did not say how many. Residents were also concerned about the environmental hazards listed in the EIS, although the BRA claimed that those adverse effects were acceptable. To mitigate them, city councilor Ray Flynn had attached an amendment to the council's approval for the project. It authorized a city-backed loan of $475,000 to CEDC for housing development. Due, in part, to this amendment, both CEDC and CCBA gave "guarded endorsements" to the project.[10]

As a way to ensure that Chinatown would see some benefits from the project, community members formed the Chinatown Citizens Advisory Committee on Lafayette Place. Committee members included Tunney Lee, a planner from the Massachusetts Institute of Technology; David Moy of the Chinese American Civic Association; and representatives from CEDC, the Chinese Progressive Association, the Vocational Education Project, and the Asian Workers Coalition. Significantly, the CCBA was not active in these efforts. Nevertheless, the committee represented a broad organizational cross-section of the community.

The Citizens Advisory Committee was concerned about employment, economic development, and mitigation issues associated with Lafayette Place. In a letter to Mayor White, it made several proposals, including bilingual training programs for construction and permanent workers, an on-site counselor, construction and permanent jobs reserved for Asians, guaranteed retail space for community businesses, and mitigation of adverse traffic effects. Committee members believed that, with proper community-based planning, some positive results were possible.[11] They were also aware that White had already made some moves toward their proposals. During his 1979 reelection campaign, he had issued an executive order requiring city projects that received chapter 121A assistance to employ a workforce of 50 percent Boston residents, 25 percent minority workers, and 10 percent women in both construction and permanent jobs. The order gave committee members faith that the city would hire Chinese workers, although they worried that these employees would not have access to bilingual support services.

As it turned out, the committee's hope that the city would respond to Chinatown's needs was misplaced. During his reelection campaign, White had shown concern about the lack of progress with Lafayette Place construction jobs while ignoring the broader effects of rising rents and land values. "If [local people] want to sell their land," he remarked, "then they give it up."[12] He offered no overt support for construction jobs for Chinatown residents or for community-based businesses in the project, and he encouraged Chinese commercial interests to expand into the Leather District and the Combat Zone, two areas that the city was having difficulty revitalizing.

In the spring of 1980, despite initial reluctance from the White administration, the Citizens Advisory Committee initiated a series of meetings with the city. To members' disappointment, the sessions produced no firm commitments regarding any of their proposals. According to David Moy, the committee had been "sort of naïve . . . , getting only good faith commitments [that] did not produce the jobs that we wanted."[13] The only concrete results were lists of construction schedules and scheduled labor needs, a far cry from the committee's requests and the mayor's executive order.

The consequences of the *Tregor* decision and the Proposition 2½ referendum (discussed in chapter 3) delayed Lafayette Place for a few years. The city resumed construction in 1982 after reaching a partnership deal with Mondev International. As work restarted, the Citizens Advisory Committee reformed as the Chinatown Employment and Training Opportunity Coalition (CETOC). Some of the coalition's participants had changed, but their advocacy remained strong; and member Ken Yee wrote hopefully about the need for "sharing the downtown prosperity with the communities."[14] Yet in subsequent meetings between CETOC personnel and the developers' representatives, project officials seemed oblivious to the neighborhood benefits outlined in the UDAG application, the EIS, and other requests for public relief and approval. They were uninterested in community issues. Project manager Marco Ottieri declined to guarantee any employment opportunities for Chinese among the projected 1,000 permanent jobs, nor would he offer discounted space for community businesses in any of Lafayette Place's 187 retail stores or 23 restaurants. He refused to open up function rooms for the use of community organizations. I was present at this particular meeting: to me, it seemed like he was dismissing poor people who were requesting alms. According to activist Lawrence Cheng, who was also present, the developer did nothing because "no one forced him to."[15] CETOC sought help from the mayor and the city council, to no avail. It had to concede. With little chance of success, the group had neither the will nor the resources to pursue the issue.

Lafayette Place opened in 1984 with numerous barriers and blank walls facing Chinatown and the Combat Zone. In the media, the retail complex was immediately derided as a "dead whale." Another developer compared it to a "Chinese wall."[16] None of the "substantial benefits" cited in the public review and public subsidy applications were evident to Chinatown residents. One or two Chinese workers had been temporarily hired during Lafayette Place's construction, but no one recalls that any Asians were permanently employed at the complex. Suzanne Lee told me that community discussions with the management of the attached Swissôtel later produced "eight or ten" housekeeping jobs.[17] The only entrepreneurial opportunity was a standard Chinese stall in the food court, which did become an inexpensive place for elderly Chinese to eat and socialize.

Soured by the results of the decade-long Lafayette Place saga, many of Chinatown's leaders had given up on the notion that development could foster community vitality. Clearly, the public-private partnerships essential to White's growth coalition policies were detrimental to the lives of the neighborhood's low-income residents. The urban development scholar Scott Cummings has written, "When private investors are drawn to profit opportunities in the central cities, revitalization and redevelopment plans typically reflect an attempt to change the use of land from one class of users to another. . . . The initiatives often compel local government to support the interests of business elites over those pursued by members of the middle and working class."[18] This is true even when such elites adopt the veneer of middle- and working-class interests. Cummings's description encapsulates the Lafayette Place/Chinatown situation. Already skeptical, neighborhood activists began actively seeking alternatives.

THE 1983 CAMPAIGN FOR MAYOR

White's last term as mayor was marred by accusations of scandal and corruption, including a federal probe regarding alleged patronage. Open hostility toward his policies on busing, education, and urban revitalization had stoked tensions between city government and the neighborhoods. During the same period, federal funding for various services, education, and public health was eroding under the Reagan administration, significantly confounding Boston's fiscal issues.

The *Boston Globe* had endorsed White's three previous three reelection candidacies, but in a July 1982 editorial it called for him to relinquish his seat: "Of the half-dozen candidates now running, any of them would be preferable to Kevin White in 1983."[19] Former state representative Mel King was the first candidate to announce his intention to challenge White, and eight more hopefuls soon joined the race. In May 1983, White announced he would not seek reelection.

Most of the mayoral candidates were familiar officeholders with roots in Boston's Irish and Italian establishment: current and former city councilors, a sheriff, the head of the Massachusetts Bay Transit Authority. Candidates from the Socialist Workers party and the U.S. Labor party also joined the race. David Finnegan, a radio talk-show host and the former head of the Boston school committee, presented himself as "the most conservative, business-oriented, downtown candidate in the field." Eventually he emerged as the frontrunner, raising the most money and inheriting the largest number of White's supporters.[20] Notably, Finnegan was the only major candidate who opposed linkage payments. (Linkage was a policy that proposed to extract fees from downtown development projects to fund housing and other community-based construction in the surrounding neighborhoods.)[21]

Neighborhood activists around the city had long chafed at White's downtown focus, and they mobilized heavily during the mayoral campaign. Massachusetts Fair Share, a citizen activist organization, was able to get two neighborhood-oriented, nonbinding referendums onto the ballot. One backed linkage payments; the other established neighborhood councils with veto powers over local development.[22] Meanwhile, two candidates emerged as champions of neighborhood interests: King and the populist city councilor Ray Flynn.

King stood out sharply against the other candidates and their agendas. The son of a union organizer, he was the only Black candidate in the race—tall, bearded, with a preference for bowties and overalls. A long-time community activist, King promoted a progressive agenda, calling for systemic change in how the city was governed and speaking out on international and social justice issues. Regarding neighborhood issues, he advocated shifting power from city hall to the neighborhoods and proposed new policies directed toward city residents. This was his

FIGURE 7. Chinatown activists campaigning for Mel King, 1983. Courtesy of Northeastern University Libraries, Archives and Special Collections.

second candidacy for mayor. During his 1979 campaign, he had run on a "Boston jobs for Boston people" platform.

The King campaign focused on neighborhood, race, gender, and other social issues. According to the historian James Green, the alliance he created reflected his "strong ties to the Latin and Asian communities of color and . . . include[d] groups like lesbians, gays, and feminists."[23] When the civil rights icon Jesse Jackson came to Boston to campaign for King, he called this alliance a "Rainbow Coalition." King's campaign soon adopted the label, and Jackson himself later used it for his presidential runs.[24]

In contrast, King's opponent Ray Flynn had built his political career on a base of socially conservative voters and his own progressive economic views. The son of a South Boston longshoreman and a cleaning woman, Flynn had been a basketball star at Providence College. Early in his political career, he had fought against busing for school desegregation, a stance he never renounced. He was a committed Catholic, strongly against abortion and homosexuality. After a stint as a state representative, he had won a seat on the Boston city council, where he advocated for rent control, public housing, and restrictions against condominium conversions.

Adopting a populist approach, Flynn began to win some activist support in city neighborhoods and from groups that focused on economic justice issues, such as the Massachusetts Tenants Organization, Massachusetts Fair Share, and 9to5, a women workers group. Flynn based his political strategy on retaining his conservative white base in high-turnout areas such as South Boston while reaching out to other white working-class communities and liberals. He campaigned on a platform of economic redistribution in favor of the neighborhoods but avoided what he saw as secondary social issues, such as race, abortion, and sexuality. Over time, as he embraced more progressive ideas, he ended his opposition to the Equal Rights Amendment for women and his support of the death penalty. His efforts to help poor and working-class communities continued to draw support from members of the activist community. Many of them were sympathetic to King but felt that racial issues would keep him from winning the election.[25]

Like Flynn, King actively campaigned in Boston's many predominantly white neighborhoods. As a result, white activists divided themselves between King and Flynn, but people of color largely unified under the banner of King's Rainbow Coalition. Most activists in Chinatown, especially those involved with the Chinese Progressive Association and the Housing Task Force, supported King, due in part to his plan to link downtown development to neighborhood benefits. He had long been a figure among the neighborhood's rising activists. As a child in the New York Streets section of the city, he had had Chinese American friends, and he later attended the old Quincy Elementary School. King was a long-time supporter of the Asian American movement. He had joined demonstrations against T-NEMC expansion and the eviction of Chinese tenants. As a candidate, he continued to advocate for greater community control over land in Chinatown, expanded English language classes, jobs for residents, and additional health and social services.[26]

While King's visibility in Chinatown gave him a key neighborhood advantage, Flynn's dismissal of race as an issue in the city marked a more substantial difference between the two candidates. Flynn characterized the city's housing, education, and employment problems as issues facing all poor people, whereas King saw them as systemic challenges for communities of color. The relevance of race was clear to Asian American activists. Many had recently taken part a national campaign highlighting racism against Asian Americans, and their anger over the death of Vincent Chin, a Chinese American beaten to death in Detroit by two white autoworkers, was still burning. In the greater Boston area, Southeast Asians—Vietnamese, Cambodian, and Laotian refugees— were frequent targets of arson, vandalism, and beatings. Several had been murdered in hate crimes. King's willingness to address these issues drew many Chinatown residents into his campaign.[27]

Asian Americans established Asians for Mel King, a formal committee within the Rainbow Coalition. Its activists, most of them Chinatown residents, worked alongside other neighborhood and constituency subgroups, including Latinos for Mel King, Lesbian and Gay Committee for Mel King, and Jamaica Plain for Mel King. Together, they formed the core of a campaign structure that was primarily grassroots-driven and not dependent on large donations or other mainstream resources. As the campaign's momentum grew, its decentralized and ad hoc nature became more formalized, but it maintained active neighborhood and identity group mobilization to ensure a strong presence in the communities.[28]

Asians for Mel King produced handmade buttons, planned neighborhood rallies, released translated campaign materials, organized marches through Chinatown, and held one of the campaign's first fundraising house parties. Representatives spoke at rallies and events, educating people across the city about the issues facing Chinatown and Asian Americans. Thanks to their work on this campaign, Chinatown activists established lasting connections with activists from other parts of Boston.

Asians for Mel King was a diverse group, but nearly every member was from the new activist sector in Chinatown and the broader Asian American community. Regina Lee, a housing advocate and the daughter of a former president of New York Chinatown's CCBA, was one of the first Asian activists to volunteer for the campaign. Others included Julian Low, a musician in the burgeoning Asian American cultural scene; Suzanne Lee, a public school teacher and education advocate (see chapter 3); Thomas Chan, also a public school teacher; and Kam Yuen Lee, a recent immigrant and part-time community organizer.

The spontaneous organizing strategies of Asians for Mel King competed directly with the well-honed methods of the established Chinatown machine. That apparatus depended on trust in the Chin brothers' recommendations. Billy Chin described politics as a personalized and transactional process: "You get the people to vote not just based on the principle of voting. . . . You base it on friendship, too. . . . I call you up to do me a favor. . . . You go out to vote, it's for me. Many of them [the Chinatown residents] do it like that."[29] For a time, the two hedged their bets, waiting to see which candidate would best support their interests. Close to the election, however, they threw their support to Flynn. As in other elections, they directed neighborhood voters with numbered slips indicating their preferred candidate's ballot position. Now, for the first time in Chinatown elections, Asians for Mel King went door to door with bilingual spiels and campaign flyers, publicizing King's platform and its relevance to the community.[30] As Regina Lee told a reporter, "emerging leadership in the community . . . says to the city government [that] the community is important and deserves to be recognized."[31]

A September poll indicated that Finnegan, King, and Flynn were in a virtual dead heat. Then, in the October preliminary election, Flynn and King finished a surprising one-two, separated by a fraction of a percent. Flynn's and King's survival testified to the depths of neighborhood discontent that had fueled their candidacies. King, in particular, made history as the first person of color to win a spot on the final election ballot in a Boston mayoral race. The columnist David Nyhan wrote in the *Boston Globe,* "The winners of the first post-White mayoralty preliminary are two candidates who weren't supposed to be there."[32]

Most political pundits favored Flynn to win the final election. Their predictions were logical. One out of four city residents claimed Irish heritage, and the city's electorate was comprised of an even more substantial proportion of Irish Americans. Boston was the nation's most Irish city, and an Irish American male had held every mayorship since the 1900s.

In Chinatown, the garment workers' union and the Chin machine were Flynn's leading advocates. The Chins used their business base effectively to support his candidacy; they also endorsed Albert "Dapper" O'Neill and Jim Kelley, conservative candidates for city council, who were furious opponents of integration, affirmative action, and busing. Billy told his employees at the China Pearl Restaurant that they could not vote for King. He and his brother also pressed owners of other restaurants and groceries to put Flynn signs in their windows and call on their workers to support the Chins' candidate.

Nevertheless, Asians for Mel King, encouraged by the preliminary results, campaigned ardently for their candidate. Going door to door, organizing sound trucks, and distributing leaflets at local Asian markets, they sought to counter the Chins' institutional advantage with higher energy and enthusiasm. They also spoke out publicly against reported anti-Black statements in the community. For their part, the Chins used their influence at city hall and got members of their operation appointed as staff at Chinatown polling places. These officials would sometimes pull levers for those whom they were assisting, particularly the elderly. Lawyers for Asians for Mel King successfully removed one such staff person for polling violations.[33]

On election day, Flynn handily defeated King, winning nearly two-thirds of the total vote, with 80 percent of the white vote and 10 percent of the Black vote. In Chinatown, the results were mixed. Flynn won Chinatown's core voting precinct but lost the two surrounding ones, both of which had large proportions of Chinatown voters.

Boston voters supported the referenda on linkage and neighborhood councils by two-to-one margins. Chinatown had a record voter turnout—a sign that its neighborhood activism had increased exponentially. For the city as a whole, the election marked a turning point: commentators saw it as an indication of widespread dissatisfaction with White's development focus. Clearly, future candidates for city office would have to negotiate neighborhood issues with some care now that local activism and populist protest had established themselves within Boston's political calculus.[34]

King's supporters were undeterred by his defeat. Their election night "Rainbow party" was a tumultuous celebration held downtown at the venerable Parker House Hotel, a place that many volunteers from communities of color had never before entered. For them, it symbolized the numerous doors that the campaign had opened. Several Chinese immigrants, watching clips of the joyous party on TV, thought King had won.

Mel King's 1983 campaign for mayor was a demonstration of local activism's potential to transcend the neighborhoods' inherent parochialism. Yet as Susan Fainstein and John Mollenkopf have pointed out, the 1980s neighborhood movements had limited success in effecting social reform. Even as they were able to mobilize large numbers of people, these movements had significant weaknesses related to local focus and the structural source of their issues. To overcome these obstacles, single-interest movements had to broaden their links and ideas and build coalitions.[35]

Nonetheless, for Chinatown's progressive electoral activists, the King campaign was a significant milestone. In their first foray, they had taken a huge risk: they had supported a Black candidate in a socially conservative community and in a city with unbroken decades of white dominance. They had organized against an entrenched local electoral machine, the local union, and a candidate from Irish South Boston, the most politically mobilized neighborhood in the city. Yet in the final Chinatown ballot, they had achieved a neighborhood stalemate.

The activists had ensured that Chinatown voters possessed the information they needed to vote in their own interests. This direct challenge to the Chin apparatus signaled a deep divide between the established political machine and emerging activist networks and set the tone for future electoral contests in Chinatown. Importantly, it also created a bridge between Asian American communities and other communities of color. King and his Rainbow Coalition actualized deeper connections among different people of color. As they worked on the campaign, activists in Asians for Mel King regularly interacted with people from many constituencies and neighborhoods. In this way, they established an Asian American presence in Boston that had previously been absent from civic discourse. After the campaign, city activists formalized the Boston Rainbow Coalition into an organization that continued to organize around critical issues. The coalition was a significant citywide force for many years, and relations among its members increased coordination and collaboration among communities of color. Eventually, May Louie, a founder of the Chinese Progressive Association and a member of Asians for Mel King, became its chair. Asian Americans also played a significant role in Jesse Jackson's national Rainbow Coalition and were involved in his 1984 and 1988 presidential campaigns.[36] Their visibility helped deepen their partnership with the African American community.

LIMITS OF THE POPULIST GROWTH COALITION, 1984–1989

Ray Flynn's comfortable victory in Boston's 1983 mayoral election did little to ease the obstacles to effective governance confronting the city, including a significant municipal deficit. Nevertheless, faced with continued community activism, he implemented many neighborhood-friendly ideas, including the linkage program for large-scale development. For downtown projects, the program's initial formula required that, for every additional square foot above 100,000, developers contribute $5 to a fund for neighborhood housing. It levied a parallel $1 charge per square foot for job training. Flynn later increased the required contributions, gave tenants greater protections against eviction, and implemented other programs to stimulate the development of affordable housing.[1]

While he continued the growth focus of previous administrations, Flynn took a more nuanced stance toward the demands of neighborhood groups. He brought in Stephen Coyle as the new head of BRA. A smart, high-powered, politically astute administrator, Coyle had grown up in nearby Waltham and understood developers. Together, he and Flynn expanded the informal collaboration among business leaders, bankers, construction unions, and developers to include citizen activists, creating a new "populist growth coalition."[2] Flynn's populist growth machine extracted explicit benefits for city neighborhoods and incorporated neighborhood activists in development decisions. The historian Pierre Clavel writes:

Coyle's task was to find a way both to serve neighborhood interests and others (such as preservationists) who opposed the projects and to indicate that at least some of the projects could go ahead. . . . Flynn and Coyle announced their decision at the end of October [1984] at a press conference supported by the release of a ninety-one-page BRA report called *Downtown Projects: Opportunities for Boston.* They couched approval of nine of the eleven projects (a tenth would follow shortly) in terms of a social contract: developers would get progress and profits, but they would also contribute to "economic justice."[3]

Previous growth coalitions had promoted all growth, advancing the idea that it would inevitably benefit the city as a whole, but that notion had often overlooked displaced city residents. Flynn's policies to redistribute some growth benefits and include neighborhood decisionmakers injected populism into his administration. The linkage policy was what allowed the growth coalition to transfer benefits from development to neighborhoods. The idea was that as development expanded, available funds for neighborhood improvement would flow. The coalition assured city business interests that linkage contributions would be small enough so as not to hinder development.

By 1990, Boston, whose population had remained majority white for a far longer period than other northeast cities had, was beginning to catch up with national demographic trends. Its total population was now 40 percent people of color. African Americans composed a quarter of the city's residents, and Asian and Latino percentages had almost doubled.[4] But Flynn's election had revealed serious cleavages between people of color and the mostly white electorate.[5] The city administration had few connections to African American communities. Mel King's influence continued through the work of the Rainbow Coalition and the Coalition for Community Control of Development. The latter, which operated out of the Rainbow Coalition's South End office, was fighting for neighborhood veto power over development. During Flynn's first term, an African American community effort—the Greater Roxbury Incorporation Project—fought to reincorporate the Black sections of the city into a separate municipality called Mandela.[6] Boston voters eventually defeated the Mandela effort at the ballot box, but the city's ongoing racial divisions tarnished its image nationally.

In an attempt to bridge barriers between city government and communities of color, the Flynn administration skewed the implementation of linkage policies. As a result, three neighborhoods received the bulk of the linkage funding: Charlestown, Roxbury, and the South End.[7] Roxbury was the center of the African American community, and directing linkage funds there had great symbolic significance for overcoming racial divisions in the city. It also helped Flynn built a relationship with the community where he was politically weakest. His administration also supported the work of that neighborhood's Dudley Street Neighborhood Initiative (DSNI). As that group's staff members noted, "the Flynn administration, it seemed, needed a Roxbury group to recognize that was not considered hostile."[8]

By all measures, the city's economic base—the source of the linkage funds—was developing rapidly. Each year the increase in downtown office space was measured in millions of square feet. New revenue from associated property taxes offset much of the damage done by Proposition 2½. By 1986, Boston had a budget surplus and no longer needed to offer incentives to stimulate development. Now developers lined up outside city hall, and Coyle and Flynn could test the boundaries of the linkage system, though they never burdened the business community enough to deter growth. Given the prosperous economic times, the business community was, for its part, overwhelmingly supportive of the policy. According to one researcher's estimate, the cost of linkage was less than 1 percent of the total cost of construction, far too modest a sum to place a burden on developers.[9]

Still, the small revenue stream through the linkage program did not begin to solve the housing needs of the neighborhoods. BRA estimated that the funds met, at best, only 6 percent of the housing demand.[10] The scarcity of affordable housing remained a critical issue, even after decades of downtown development. Three years into the Flynn administration, a BRA poll of residents found that housing remained their primary concern. Nevertheless, the current political and economic environment opened ways in which to address neighborhood interests within the city's overall growth agenda. It also supported the emergence of innovative models of community organizing and agency. Groups such as Roxbury's DSNI and various community development corporations (CDCs) around the city took advantage of these opportunities.

The DSNI neighborhood was at the junction of the Roxbury and Dorchester neighborhoods and bordered a busy mass transit bus terminal. In the 1950s, population in the area had become increasingly Black and Latino. In response, banks had drawn a "red line" around the area, refusing to open branches, make loans, or make other investments in the neighborhood.[11] Absentee landlords, arson, and the illegal commercial dumping became common. The situation was dire, with a third of Dudley's land gone to waste. Finally, in 1984, the local Mabel Louise Riley Foundation initiated a process to create a coalition of human service agencies to address these issues. Neighborhood residents began demanding and achieving control, exercising their leadership by forming DSNI in 1985.

DSNI saw the Flynn administration as an opportunity to leverage its community development strategy. Its executive director, Peter Medoff, was familiar with many of the citizen activists who worked in city hall. DSNI organized to win improved city services and, especially, to clean up the garbage-strewn neighborhood. Most dramatically, through an organizing campaign known as "Take a Stand, Own the Land," and the skillful courting of various department heads, it convinced Flynn to partially transfer the city's power of eminent domain to the community. This bold idea originated with DSNI's pro bono attorneys and the BRA's Stephen Coyle, and today DSNI remains the only U.S. community that has been granted such authority.

Eminent domain allowed DSNI to force the sale of privately held vacant parcels in the center of the community. The city also turned over numerous public parcels that had come into its hands through tax foreclosures. DSNI was thus able to assemble land on which to implement the community's mandate for "development without displacement." The organization placed all of this property into a community land trust to ensure long-term community control and permanent housing affordability. As its staff noted, however, "eminent domain would not [have] go[ne] forward, whatever the circumstances, [in areas] where there were strong institutional players to challenge it, such as in Boston's Fenway and Chinatown neighborhoods."[12]

Boston's CDCs, under the umbrella of the Massachusetts Association of Community Development Corporations, were founded as a way to create a role for local communities in development and planning; but over time many retreated from advocacy to focus on development activities. This shift aligned with the Flynn administration's push to construct more affordable housing in order to alleviate rental pressures on the city's real estate market. City hall saw opportunities in city-owned properties such as vacant land, foreclosures, and surplus buildings, but it needed partners to develop affordable housing projects. CDCs eagerly embraced this role, and the city helped them form the Boston Housing Partnership, which facilitated their collaboration. During this period, the number of CDCs in Boston expanded to more than thirty. By the end of Flynn's tenure as mayor, they were producing hundreds of housing units annually.

It was clear to neighborhood leaders that growth had created opportunities to extract benefits for community residents. Most of this growth was occurring downtown and did not directly impact the physical landscape of most Boston neighborhoods. For the majority of these areas, the greatest threat was now gentrification through a rising cost of living and shifting urban demographics. For Chinatown, however, the situation was more nuanced. Because it was located in the heart of the downtown commercial district, growth meant not just gentrification but also incremental extinction through the loss of precious neighborhood land.

THE NEIGHBORHOOD AND THE POPULIST GROWTH COALITION

Chinatown continued to change. New immigration brought more diverse Chinese groups to the neighborhood. Chinese from Vietnam established numerous stores. Mandarin-speaking Chinese from the mainland, especially Fujianese (many of them undocumented), were a growing presence. The formerly close-knit neighborhood, where everyone "had that same kind of experience . . . , saw the same outlooks, and . . . shared the same values," now featured new faces, new languages, and new ideas.[13]

Some community organizations were adjusting to Chinatown's shifting demographics, but others were unsettled by these challenges to the existing neighborhood hierarchy.[14]

TIMELINE 3. The Neighborhood and the Populist Growth Coalition

1985	First Chinatown Neighborhood Council appointed.
	First parcel-to-parcel linkage program selects Kingston-Bedford and Parcel 18.
	Long Guang Huang campaigns against police abuse.
	Community campaigns against the Combat Zone.
	South Cove Manor nursing home completed.
1986	P&L and Beverly Rose garment workers campaign.
1987	Chinatown master plan process initiated.
	BRA chooses Columbia Plaza Associates for Kingston-Bedford development.
1990	First Chinatown master plan completed.

FIGURE 8. Young activists collecting petitions in support of Long Guang Huang, 1985.
Courtesy of Northeastern University Libraries,
Archives and Special Collections.

The neighborhood still retained elements of a close-knit community. Howard Wong, who lived in Tai Tung Village in the 1980s, recalled:

> I had people watching out for me. . . . Old Golden Gate was one of the toughest places around. All the waiters were tough. You don't want to run out on a check at Golden Gate. . . . But one time me and my friend, Danny, finished a movie at midnight. We were teenagers. We [went] in. . . . We sit there, and they wouldn't serve us because they wanted us to go home. It was too late [at night]. . . .
>
> My mom yelled out the window for someone to find me at Pagoda Park. Literally, Pagoda Park is all the way down the other side [of the neighborhood]. Some kid would roll up . . . on his bike, and he said, "Your mom going nuts. She's looking for you." They knew enough to know where you were, enough to look for you, to find you.[15]

Nonetheless, Wong recognized that the neighborhood was changing and that familiar places were disappearing before his eyes.

Chinatown's political relations were also shifting. Although the Chin brothers had supported Flynn's candidacy for mayor, they had entered his campaign late, and this kept their ties with city hall fragile. They could not count on the access and influence that they had enjoyed under Kevin White's administration. Tellingly, Frank Chin resigned his post at the purchasing department; and Flynn chose Marilyn Lee of the Housing Task Force, an activist organization, as his Chinatown liaison rather than someone from the Chin cadre. Yet despite their diminished political influence, Chinatown's traditional business leadership adapted. The Chins were behind the 1985 construction of South Cove Manor, a nursing home located across the Mass Pike overpass in the South End. In 1986, the Chinese Consolidated Benevolent Association (CCBA) changed its legal status from for-profit to nonprofit, allowing it to pursue public housing and job-training funds.[16]

During this period, a surge of neighborhood mobilizations permanently changed Chinatown's perspectives on civic activism. On May 1, 1985, an undercover detective named Francis Kelly attacked a Chinese restaurant worker, Long Guang Huang, on Kneeland Street in view of residents and T-NEMC workers. Huang, age fifty-six and weighing about a hundred pounds, had arrived in the United States only six months earlier and spoke no English. The attack sent him to the emergency room. The public nature of this act, which occurred in broad daylight on a major street, outraged the entire community. Residents were further incensed to learn that Kelly had charged Huang with soliciting a prostitute, resisting arrest, and assault and battery on an officer.

The incident was a turning point in local activism. CPA issued a flyer calling on the "entire Asian community" to support justice for Huang, and the CCBA released a list of grievances directed at Police Commissioner Francis Roache. Amid swelling outrage, a coalition of community organizations called for a meeting with Roache. Suzanne Lee and David Wong, the chairs of the once polar-opposite CPA and CCBA, led the coalition. The coalition also drew up a petition with a list of demands that included dismissal of the charges against Huang, Kelly's suspension, more Asian representation in the police department, citizen review of the police, and closure of the Combat Zone. As a *Sampan* reporter wrote, such "unity [was] perhaps unprecedented" in the community.[17]

For the first time, all of Chinatown's varied groups were assertively mobilizing behind a single cause. The coalition held weekly rallies, and community members packed the courtroom during Huang's trial, filling the seats and standing seven deep in the back of the room. Mel King, along with African American community leader Chuck Turner, the Rainbow Coalition, the Four Corners Neighborhood Association, and the Greater Boston Civil Rights Coalition, spoke out in support of Huang. The campaign organized several marches, including highly disruptive actions during the height of rush hour. As a result, both Flynn and Roache visited the neighborhood multiple times during the next seven months. Flynn even came to Huang's home, bringing him groceries and publicly angering the policemen's union.

After examining the evidence, Roache called for a disciplinary hearing on Kelly's actions. The coalition forced Boston's powerful police department to open the hearing to the public, a highly unusual move. The court eventually exonerated Huang, and the police department suspended Kelly from the force.[18]

In Chinatown, the Huang campaign's broad support and success legitimized protest politics, once eschewed by the traditional leadership, as a viable tool for addressing community demands. It marked a dramatic change in the mindset of the neighborhood. The mobilization also strengthened Chinatown's links with the African American community, which had long-standing issues with policing in its own neighborhoods. The rest of Boston began to see Chinatown residents as mobilized and engaged, and the media intensely followed the Huang story. As a *Boston Globe* writer observed, "Chinatown, a community which has endured the encroachment of the seedy Combat Zone as well as commercial and residential development that has seldom benefited its citizens, had been waiting for an issue it could bring before the city as symbolic of past grievances. The treatment of Long Guang Huang became that issue, and Huang, unwittingly, became their symbol."[19]

For activists, the Huang campaign opened new mobilizing methods and revealed new targets. The Asian American Resource Workshop, which had developed some expertise in media relations through its work against anti-Asian hate crimes, publicized the Huang story.[20] Legal service lawyers and activists familiar with hate-crime issues adapted their judicial strategies and coordinated with community organizers.

After the success of the Huang campaign, activists followed up by organizing for the removal of the Combat Zone. They conducted widely publicized midnight patrols of the neighborhood, armed with flashlights, cameras, and notepads to record license-plate numbers. They invited local leaders such as Mel King to accompany them on their patrols. They coupled this effort with a call for community control of the neighborhood.

This campaign was less successful than the Huang action had been. Though activists' efforts culminated in a community rally that brought out the mayor and city council members, they received only vague and unsatisfactory promises that development projects in the Combat Zone area would eventually drive out the adult entertainment businesses.[21]

But organizers were not deterred, and in 1986 the Chinatown community took on another milestone issue, one involving Chinese garment workers. P&L Sportswear, located in East Boston, was the largest garment factory in the city. When it shut down at the end of 1985, 350 people lost their jobs, two-thirds of whom were Chinese women. Neither the company nor the International Ladies Garment Workers Union offered much support to these workers.

One evening, as some of the garment workers' children were watching the local TV news, they learned that the state was contributing $350,000 to retraining programs for displaced meatpackers in the Newmarket area of Boston. They asked their mothers why the government was ignoring the garment workers. The mothers had no answers. So in March 1986, encouraged by the success of the Huang campaign, these workers sought help from CPA. In April, another group of garment workers, who had recently lost their jobs at Beverly Rose Sportswear in the South End, joined the P&L workers.[22]

To help the garment workers convince the state to fund their retraining, CPA facilitated a democratic, participatory model of organizing in which the workers designated their own leaders and made their own decisions about group aims and actions. No community-wide coalition formed around this issue, but CPA and a sizable support committee, primarily composed of college students, were primary allies. Their assistance was indispensable in negotiating the language divide among the workers (who were mostly Chinese-speaking but did include a few Italian speakers), doing legal research and publicity, and working with mainstream institutions. Suzanne Lee was again at the center of things; and her affinity for workers, her outspokenness, and her bilingual skills were invaluable.[23]

Signaling the workers' newly felt empowerment, an early flier declared, "We garment workers feel that the government has the responsibility to provide job training for us to change to other jobs."[24] For the first time in their history, Chinese workers and activists marched in front of the state house, where they lobbied and negotiated with city and state officials. As a result of their mobilization, the state authorized funding for job retraining funding, giving Boston the responsibility for implementation.

Once they had achieved a promise from the state, the workers began debating about how best to work with the city officials who would institute the retraining program. Against the advice of CPA and their support committee, they insisted on negotiating the implementation plan en masse: "We've been garment workers for so long and received the worst treatment from anyone around us—from government officials to other non-Chinese workers—that sometimes we believe that we are nothing! Now, most of us know that we are somebody. We will make them listen to us. We know what is best for us."[25] When the city refused to meet with the mass of workers, they conducted a sit-in at city offices until Kristen McCormick, the head of the Department of Jobs and Community Services, came down to talk to them.

As negotiations continued, the workers continued to rely on their new sense of power. For instance, they rejected a lengthy two-year English-language program proposed by the city, and they insisted on helping to design their training program. After months of wrangling, CPA and the workers won concessions from various city and state agencies to provide a shorter bilingual training and reemployment program designed, with worker input, to place the workers in the food, hotel, and finance industries. In the end, the retraining program placed 90 percent of them successfully. The process of achieving and developing a retraining program had been an empowering one. A core of the former garment workers went on to form a workers' center project at CPA, sparking other worker organizing in various ethnic enclave industries.[26]

In succeeding years, Chinatown's residents used their new, more aggressive attitude to solve other community issues. The Quincy School Community Council (QSCC) prevailed in court against T-NEMC to win control of two tenements on Oak Street in residential Chinatown. The medical center had sued to stop the BRA's transfer of the buildings to QSCC for its childcare center. QSCC responded by organizing a public demonstration as well as legally challenging T-NEMC. The council was the first of the local service agencies to adopt militant mobilization methods as part of its organizing conventions. Soon thereafter, allying with groups in Dorchester, Chinatown's community activists helped stop a proposed merger of T-NEMC with Saint Margaret's Hospital of Dorchester, which would have moved Saint Margaret's to the Chinatown area.[27]

Perhaps most significantly, Chinatown's activist organizations and service agencies lobbied successfully for a neighborhood council. During the 1983 election, the nonbinding referendum to establish such councils with local development veto power had passed by a significant margin. Flynn had supported the concept, and his administration decided to roll them out in selected neighborhoods. Chinatown's traditional umbrella association, the CCBA, strenuously fought the establishment of the council. However, in another sign of the community's evolution, broad support from other organizations overwhelmed CCBA's objections.[28] While Flynn withheld veto power from the councils, the new bodies would nevertheless give neighborhoods a voice in the planning process. They would play an advisory role in matters concerning the delivery of city services, licensing, and regulation.

In June 1985, Chinatown, along with four other neighborhoods, were each allowed to establish a council. The Chinatown Neighborhood Council (CNC) was unique. In contrast to the other three, it gave actual neighborhood residents only a minority voice. Instead, it was intended to serve the larger Chinese American community, of which Chinatown was the center. Any Asian American living in Massachusetts, regardless of citizenship status, would be allowed to vote for CNC representatives. The council's structure apportioned a total of twenty-one seats among businesses, agencies, organizations, Chinatown residents, and others, with residents allotted only five seats.[29]

The neighborhood councils represented a significant change in local decision making around development. Flynn retained the prerogative to appoint the first members of each of the neighborhood councils. The CNC's statement of purpose noted that initial members "were appointed by the Mayor because they c[a]me from diverse groups or reflect different segments of the community."[30] Marilyn Lee-Tom, the city's liaison to Chinatown and South End, fought fiercely and successfully to keep the council's composition roughly representative of the broader Chinese community.

Creation of the CNC had significant implications for Chinatown. Now CCBA was no longer the neighborhood's recognized representative to the city; instead, the council had been designated to work out community issues linked to the delivery of city services. Its creation was also a concerted attempt to unite the various groups in the neighborhood. Among its members were the Chin brothers; the executive directors or representatives of service organizations, activist organizations, traditional organizations, and four tenant associations; a student; and a postal worker. Three representatives came from CCBA, two from the Chinese American Civic Association. Carol Lee from the Housing Task Force, Suzanne Lee from CPA, and David Wong from CCBA were co-moderators. The three were dedicated to bringing the different parts of the community together, and their collaboration proved to be a step forward.

DEVELOPMENT HOPE AND ACTUALITY:
CHINATOWN'S AND T-NEMC'S MASTER PLANS

Between 1984 and 1989, the city and developers spent $700 million on construction projects in or within two blocks of Chinatown.[31] While the failure of Lafayette Place had dampened efforts to revitalize the downtown retail area, stakeholders had hatched new and ambitious schemes, including the BRA's plan for what it called the Midtown Cultural District. The proposed district would consolidate a butterfly-shaped area of scattered theaters west of Washington Street, opposite Chinatown and bordering the Combat Zone. It was a complex plan that would require every development within the area to include a cultural component. Coyle invested much of his reputation in this vision, which he saw as "[his] legacy in the heart of the Hub."[32] The first project in the Midtown Cultural District would be Commonwealth Center, which would include an office tower and new hotel development along Washington Street.

Although Chinatown was in the midst of frantic development, the neighborhood itself remained politically marginalized. According to a 1998 review, it had received none of the first $47 million in linkage funds, despite the fact that it was dealing with significant development, far more than in other areas that did receive those funds.[33] In Carol Lee's opinion, Coyle thought that that Chinatown should simply let development happen and wait to receive eventual benefits. Midway through his tenure at the BRA, she, along with Marilyn Lee-Tom and Suzanne Lee, decided to try to expand his perspective. They hit on the idea of familiarizing Coyle with Chinatown. Carol Lee recalled:

> [We decided] let's make him come down and see what it's like down here, and this is why it's important to us not to have a parking garage here. So we gave him a tour of the neighborhood. It happened that there a little kid riding a bike in the parking lot, in between the cars and stuff, and he

thought it was the most horrible thing for a kid to have to live like that. Because like he comes from the suburbs where kids play in the yard or in nice quiet streets. And he was like totally appalled. And it was because of that that he decided, "Okay, institutions take a back seat to Chinatown."[34]

After that tour, observers saw a change in Coyle's attitude toward Chinatown. Now the BRA began stressing the neighborhood's concerns. In 1987, Coyle opposed a T-NEMC garage proposal, writing that, "with less than four acres of publicly owned land remaining in Chinatown, the construction of new affordable housing must be the top priority." He also decided that all remaining city and BRA land in Chinatown should be reserved for housing.[35] This priority was a clear indicator of how far he had moved in his planning for the neighborhood.

In July 1987, the BRA initiated the Chinatown master plan, the city's first in-depth study of the neighborhood. The idea had originated with the Housing Task Force, which had been unable to secure foundation funding for the research to move the project move forward. Focus groups organized by the CNC supplemented various BRA-directed studies to support the project.

The Chinatown master plan set essential goals and guidelines for community development, but its most potent components were the zoning restrictions that limited building heights in the neighborhood.[36] The goal of those restrictions was to privilege residential housing over commercial and institutional structures. Between 1980 and 1987, new housing construction in Chinatown had stalled: only thirty-nine new units were built, despite high demand. The waitlist for affordable housing in the neighborhood had grown to 2,000 people, equivalent to an additional 615 units. Applicants could expect to wait up to eight years for placement. Moreover, existing housing was in deplorable condition, while property values had more than doubled between 1983 and 1987.[37] A newspaper article about the living conditions of working families in Chinatown described twelve people sharing three bedrooms, a living room, and a kitchen. In a windowless bedroom, one set of parents slept with two children in a double bed. A cot was set up for their other two children to share. There was no other furniture, and their possessions were stacked in tall piles on the floor. Similar arrangements characterized the two other bedrooms.[38]

Meanwhile, Jerome Grossman, the CEO of T-NEMC, continued to move forward with the hospital's expansion plans in the neighborhood. In 1980, the medical center obtained air rights over Washington Street and began constructing a connector between a new pediatrics hospital on the west side of Washington Street and medical facilities on the east side of the street. In 1984, it completed the Health Sciences Building on Harrison Avenue and won approval to build the 1-C South Building.[39] To do so, Grossman engaged in a land swap. The BRA traded a parcel on the corner of Washington and Oak streets for the controversial plot of land that was to be known as Parcel C. With the South Building, T-NEMC now extended uninterrupted along the east side of Washington Street from Kneeland to Oak, nearly fulfilling all of its original 1965 plans (see fig. 5 in chapter 3).[40]

The prospects for new neighborhood housing construction nevertheless seemed to be brightening. The Chinatown master plan and the land swap cleared the way for community development abutting the Massachusetts Turnpike extension on the corner of Marginal Road and Washington Street. Within the BRA's proposal to balance populist concerns and development in the Midtown Cultural District, planners had also included an affordable housing component. Despite some opposition from preservationists such as the Boston Preservation Alliance, they have given priority to the community with the greatest need, Chinatown.[41] Through proposed linkage projects and Coyle's newfound empathy, there seemed to be a reliable stream of funds to finally stimulate housing construction and meet some of the demand in Chinatown.

STATE OF THE NEIGHBORHOOD: A TURNING POINT?

The 1987 collaboration between the BRA and the CNC to produce a community master plan gave everyone the opportunity to assess the Chinatown community after two decades of struggle. Looking at the 1987 BRA-supported surveys, the most recent decennial census data of 1980, and the community study under the aegis of Action for Boston

Community Development (discussed in chapter 2), we can see how far the community had traveled since 1970 in its self-sustainment. Now Tarry Hum of the Asian Community Development Corporation sensed a turning point. In the Chinatown master plan, she wrote:

> It is with great excitement and hope that we witness the completion and final adoption of the Chinatown Community Plan. We recognize the historical significance of the comprehensiveness of the Chinatown Community Plan. More importantly, we take pride in the community-wide planning effort and consensus on the Plan's goals and vision. We look forward to working with the City to make the vision expressed in the Plan a reality for all Asians.[42]

But how realistic was this vision in 1987? The four detailed BRA surveys—on housing, land use, business, and users of Chinatown—as well as its Chinatown neighborhood profile, compiled from census data, indicated that the population's socioeconomic status had changed little since 1970. They described the residents as primarily families, with high proportions of elderly and children, who had low levels of income, high labor-force participation, and low unemployment. "The workforce remained primarily in service and factory occupations, working in restaurants and shops and garment manufacturing businesses." Forty-two percent of the families reported their income to be less than $10,000 a year, even though family size in the neighborhood was larger than the city average.[43] In a survey of every building in the area, the BRA estimated that 5,100 persons lived in the neighborhood and that 21 percent of the housing units were overcrowded. Chinatown's population density was higher than fifty persons per acre, three times that of the city.[44]

The BRA's reports indicated regression in some areas. While in 1970 the Chinatown family median income figure was 74 percent of the citywide median, it was 66 percent of the citywide median in 1980. Furthermore, the housing survey showed that 97 percent of Chinatown units were deteriorated, a higher percentage than that in the ABCD report in 1970.[45]

Other figures indicated some modest progress. By 1980,, while most of the population remained in service or blue-collar work, a growing percentage was engaged in white-collar work (Much of this change mirrored the deindustrialization trend in the U.S. economy). There was a slight improvement in educational attainment but an increase in the proportion of residents with eight years or fewer of education. Housing was significantly less overcrowded, at 21 percent from the 1987 housing survey, but "much greater than the nation and higher than all other Boston neighborhoods."[46]

By 1987, having scratched out some progress, partially driven by a changing society, partially by residents' own extraordinary efforts, Chinatown was at a turning point. Qualitative change in the neighborhood's quality of life and accessibility remained aspirations. But with a growing unity in the community, a supportive city administration, and a buoyant economy, positive change seemed possible.

NEW LINKAGE PLANS: KINGSTON–BEDFORD

In 1985, Coyle had introduced a bold extension of the established linkage concept: his parcel-to-parcel linkage program. As rationale for the program, the BRA's 1986 report noted that poverty in Boston had increased despite the $7 billion invested in downtown commercial development since 1977:

> The vast majority of new jobs created since 1976 have gone to better off, better educated suburban residents. A recent survey conducted by the Boston Redevelopment Authority shows that 78 percent of the employees in Boston's large downtown office buildings are suburban commuters. While downtown development has substantially increased the municipal tax base, the growing disparity between downtown and neighborhood investment, the influx of new middle income households seeking to live near their jobs and thereby creating displacement pressure on long term residents, and the lack of business opportunities for minorities downtown and in the neighborhoods, have raised questions about how to manage downtown development to improve the quality of life of neighborhood residents.[47]

Under the new parcel-to-parcel program, investors would be allowed to develop a high-demand, publicly owned downtown parcel only if they also developed a low-demand, publicly owned neighborhood parcel in an outlying neighborhood. The city would solicit proposals for the development of both parcels. It would also use its leverage to promote other neighborhood benefits, including a role for community investors, donations for job-training funds, and social services. The community investors would participate in the developments as minority-ownership partners.

That same year, the parcel-to-parcel linkage program identified its first sites: the city-owned Kingston-Bedford project on the northern edge of Chinatown coupled with the state-owned Parcel 18 on Ruggles Street, located in the southwest corridor cutting through Roxbury.[48] Public support from the city and the state would cover 28 percent of the project's cost. Both BRA reports and media coverage focused on Roxbury, the center of Boston's African American community, as the primary neighborhood of concern. In the preliminary environmental impact statement (EIS), the BRA discussed Roxbury at length and mentioned Chinatown only briefly. In some places, as in the section on the need to build up the neighborhood economy, it did not discuss Chinatown at all. That omission was curious because previous BRA reports had cited census figures showing that Chinatown had a lower median family income than Roxbury did.[49] This disparity in focus was an indication that factors other than need were at play in directing linkage implementation.[50]

The BRA saw the estimated $400 million Kingston-Bedford/Parcel 18 projects as a way to build neighborhood support for the city's populist growth agenda. The agency intended to expand how growth could benefit developers and business interests as well as residents. It was particularly interested in building support in the Black community through direct investment and the promise of new benefits. The Mandela secession campaign had pressured Flynn during his first term and had further strained his relations with African Americans. Because he wanted to highlight his ability to spur development in that community, Chinatown received far less focus. Nonetheless, it was crucial to the first parcel-to-parcel linkage project, as it would be directly impacted by the proposed development. The BRA was seeking the "highest possible density development" on the Kingston-Bedford site, and Chinatown faced severe consequences.[51] This was clear, even to observers outside the community. As the *Boston Globe* editorialized, Flynn "surely doesn't want to treat Chinatown's needs lightly, merely because its residents, many of them foreign-born, lack a voice and political clout."[52]

Still, many in Chinatown were optimistic. The project was the first significant one to specifically direct funds toward Chinatown, and supporters felt that the neighborhood would finally obtain the stream of linkage funds it needed to rebuild.[53] Coyle told community leaders that Kingston-Bedford and spinoff projects were likely to generate more than $22 million in housing, job training, and economic development funds. Given the intense engagement of all parties in the growth coalition and the neighborhood in this redirection of wealth, the future seemed bright—especially for members of the chosen minority investment team, who, the BRA specified, would have a 30 percent share of the two projects.

The neighborhood's participation in the Kingston-Bedford project primarily followed the BRA's proscribed procedures. Because no community entities were large enough to take part in a project of this magnitude, the BRA allowed them to organize into potential minority development partners that could qualify to become part of the larger development team. The BRA and the two neighborhoods would review the qualifications of the proposed minority development teams. The teams that passed that review would then submit community development proposals, one of which would be selected. According to the *Boston Globe,* both the city and community observers felt that the resulting partnerships could effect "a significant reordering of the economic leadership within the minority communities."[54]

Five African American/Chinese American investor teams applied for the Kingston-Bedford/Parcel 18 projects. Not surprisingly, one of the top qualifying teams included the Chinatown businessmen who had campaigned for Flynn in 1983: Frank and Billy Chin; Davis Woo, the president of CCBA; and David Wong, a co-moderator for CNC. The African American members of this team were also prominent businessmen—among them, John Cruz, the proprietor of the city's largest Black-owned construction company, and Ron Homer, the president of Boston's largest Black-owned bank. With public support from both Flynn and the *Boston Globe,* they formed their partnership under the name Columbia Plaza Associates. Their main competitor was the Boston Development Collaborative, which included four CDCs and individual investors, some of whom were new immigrants and professional Chinese.[55]

The BRA's community review procedure allowed Chinatown and Roxbury entities to study the qualifications and ideas of the candidate teams and conduct the environmental review process. The BRA designated the CNC to represent Chinatown in the community review process. The Parcel 18+ Task Force, formed specifically for this project, represented Roxbury. Although the neighborhoods could make recommendations, the BRA established the framework for project evaluation and reserved the right to make the final selection.

As I have mentioned, the BRA required developers to provide specific benefits within Kingston-Bedford/Parcel 18 for housing, job-training programs, minority businesses, employment opportunities, and potential community space. According to agency estimates, linkage funds numbered in the millions. For housing alone, the BRA anticipated $7 million in linkage funds, which would be divided equally between Chinatown and Roxbury. Still, it continued to focus mainly on the Black community, talking expansively of anchoring the neighborhood economy in Roxbury through this effort.[56]

The Kingston-Bedford portion of the linked parcels involved two structures designed for mixed use: an office tower, retail space, a parking garage, and a hotel. Various proposals estimated that the structures' gross square footage could be as much as 900,000, with heights as high as thirty-four stories. The parking garage would provide six hundred to eight hundred new spaces. By any measure, this would be a large project, but at the time it was unprecedented. During this period, the existing buildings across the street, which included Ming's Market, then the largest in Chinatown, were six to eight stories high.

The negative impacts of this enormous development were projected to be even more severe than those of Lafayette Place. In assessing the various proposals, the EIS noted, "All build alternatives will have a moderate to significant adverse impact on traffic." Other problems included degradation of air quality; an increase in noise; crowd, pedestrian, and parking congestion; and wind and shadow effects. The report also noted that property values adjacent to the site were likely to increase by at least 30 percent, yet Chinatown would not have compensating opportunities for employment or business.[57] Lawrence Cheng, who had been instrumental in creating the Chinatown master plan, was skeptical about neighborhood benefits: "Traffic will be terrible. Maybe you can get some construction jobs; I doubt that. If you are lucky, you can maybe train a group of residents to become maintenance people. . . . I don't see any possibility of any retail moving into the ground floor of these developments."[58] Jerry Chu, a resident, pointed out that the basic problem with linkage is that you're saying, "If you give me money, I let you do this." This results in too many projects that are too large.[59]

The CNC tried to interest Chinatown residents in reviewing the construction proposal. Yet even though it held frequent meetings, it failed to engage the community entirely. The council outlined the project to the community in two bilingual meetings; but according to Suzanne Lee, most attendees found the developers' highly technical descriptions incomprehensible. Moreover, the council had reasons for not trying to broaden residential engagement in the process. Some members felt that the CNC itself was reasonably representative of the community and thus well positioned to act as its voice. Others, such as Carol Lee, felt that the council was spreading itself too thin, due to the high volume of development, so it could not organize effectively within the community.[60] In addition, internal tensions were high because individual CNC members had interests in one or another of the potential minority partner groups, most notably Columbia Plaza Associates. After arguing over the issue of conflict of interest, the council decided to allow affected members to participate in discussions about those partner groups but not vote on their selection.

Eventually, three minority partner applicants emerged as finalists: Boston Development Collaborative, Columbia Plaza Associates, and Interlink Associates. Each group had the opportunity to describe the benefits it was offering and to include community input in their proposals. All lobbied the council heavily, often with free meals and payments for business-related expenses. In the final round, the CNC recommended Boston Development Collaborative, and Roxbury's Parcel 18+ Task

Force recommended Columbia Plaza Associates. The council preferred the Boston Development Collaborative because it believe it was more sincere about community input and more specific about its benefits. But feelings were heated; and after the CNC announced its recommendation at a BRA hearing, Frank Chin began berating Suzanne Lee and had to be restrained by another Columbia Plaza partner, Paul Chan. As it turned out, Chin's anger was unnecessary: the BRA eventually chose Columbia Plaza Associates.[61]

In February 1988, Columbia Plaza Associates chose a majority partner, Metropolitan Structures of Chicago, and completed its proposal. Metropolitan Structures and Columbia Plaza's final design exceeded the most intensive development alternative initially described by the BRA. Their plan for the Kingston-Bedford site included 990,000 square feet of new development, with the tallest building at thirty-five stories. Their proposed benefits package included $6.7 million in new housing funds, $1.3 million in job-training funds, and financing for a community development fund with a minimum of $10 million.[62] The plan called for the Chinatown and Roxbury communities to divide the funds.

ECONOMIC COLLAPSE AND ITS NET EFFECTS ON THE NEIGHBORHOOD

The projected benefits from the new parcel-to-parcel initiative proved to be illusory. By late 1988, Boston's market for office space, and Chinatown's hopes, were collapsing. The "Massachusetts miracle" was over. As financing for Kingston-Bedford evaporated, Ron Homer, a Columbia Plaza investor, publicly called for the elimination of the linkage payments associated with it.

Kingston-Bedford was just one of many significant projects in or near Chinatown that developers canceled or delayed because of the recession. Neither Commonwealth Center nor the Midtown Cultural District ever reached the implementation stage.[63] Columbia Plaza Associates continued to have difficulties. The Parcel 18 site found few interested tenants. It took vigorous city and state support to identify a state agency to occupy the building in 1994. Paul Chan estimates that investors lost $25 million.[64]

Eventually, construction did begin on Kingston-Bedford (now called One Lincoln Place). In 1992, Columbia Plaza donated $1 million before the project was completed.[65] Half of those funds went to Roxbury; the other half supported the creation of housing in Chinatown. The Asian Community Development Corporation's (ACDC) Oak Terrace housing and the Chinese Economic Development Council's Mei Wah Village projects divided Chinatown's share equally.

Kingston-Bedford's limited linkage benefit contributed only marginally toward addressing Chinatown's housing problem. Nonetheless, it allowed ACDC to realize its first housing project. It had initially hoped to build more apartments but settled for the eighty-eight primarily multibedroom units in Oak Terrace. Even then, the total cost of the project, completed in 1994, was $13.5 million, and only half of the units went to low- and middle-income residents. CEDC's plan for elder housing in the community was even more constrained. Its funding for construction did not become available until 1996, and it scaled down its plans significantly, building only forty-two units on a corner of its parcel.[66] Together, these two developments bridged Chinatown's other large housing projects, from Tai Tung to the east to Mass Pike Towers to the west. While the $250,000 that ACDC and CEDC each received from Columbia Plaza Associates did help to cover costs, it was supplementary at best.

These construction projects illustrated the gulf between the scale of affordable housing development and the level of need. When Oak Terrace applications became available, a thousand people waited for hours outside the ACDC offices.[67] As the lines demonstrated, the community was struggling make up for the units lost to T-NEMC encroachment. Nevertheless, the housing activists behind ACDC, many of whom had started in the Housing Task Force, had succeeded in realizing the first significant expansion of affordable housing in Chinatown in two decades.

But the Kingston-Bedford process had shattered the ability of Chinatown's various groups to collaborate. This rupture in community cohesion was evident during the CNC's first election. The traditional leadership publicized a surprise slate of candidates to replace many of the council's agency and activist representatives, who, in turn, responded with their own slate of candidates. Some felt the election itself was being manipulated. Observers accused candidates and campaigners of filling out ballots for voters, complained that people were voting without proper identification, and lamented about loss of control over ballot distribution. Many felt that voters often had no idea of who the candidates were.

The election touched off two weeks of controversy, which the city declined to address. Two elected members of CNC's board as well as its executive director resigned in protest. Suzanne Lee and others felt that the actions of Chinatown's traditional leaders were an apparent retaliation for the council's rejection of Columbia Plaza Associates.

In the end, the election displaced most of the progressives from the council. Of its twenty-one original members, thirteen ran for reelection. The defeated incumbents included Suzanne Lee; Warren Eng, a founder of CACA; the chair of QSCC; and an activist tenant from Castle Square. Other prominent progressives who were defeated included representatives of the Housing Task Force and the Workshop and the director of the QSCC. The new council members included local business owners and city workers, who had little idea of the issues involved.[68] The reconfigured CNC was now firmly in the hands of business owners and the traditional leadership and became less engaged as a critical arbiter of development, community needs, and conflicts of interest. Fragile neighborhood relations had shattered, and this divide among the sectors would hobble the community for years to come.

POPULIST GROWTH'S CONSEQUENCES

During the Flynn-Coyle years, Boston's neighborhoods felt they had an excellent chance to thrive. Robust growth provided a substantial base for linkage benefits, and the Flynn administration was dedicated to transferring some of the wealth generated by downtown growth: to promote "business growth *and* neighborhood renewal."[69] This growth agenda was a narrower one than the scholars Fainstein and Mollenkopf had envisioned as necessary for transformation. While sectors of the neighborhood movement did grasp some strands of political power in the Flynn administration, they failed to build connections to other movements, which could have created a qualitatively stronger force. Flynn reached out to CDCs and neighborhood groups that were, according to his staff, part of the "pragmatic left."[70] Most were not from communities of color or from the other constituencies in King's Rainbow Coalition.

In this environment, the city did build some affordable housing and advanced some protections for renters. Neighborhood groups had a more significant role in the process. Yet Boston's essential growth dynamic remained the same. None of these advances could address the city's continuing gentrification, the displacement of low- and middle-income residents, and the marginal role of neighborhood groups in development.

During Flynn's tenure, Chinatown built a modest number of housing units and made a down payment on future units. These limited gains were critical to sustaining the community. But the populist growth coalition never provided the stream of funds that would allow Chinatown to address housing supply in any significant way. Linkage yielded only a few hundred thousand dollars for a neighborhood in which a single significant housing project required tens of millions of dollars. Of the five hundred units in Chinatown that Coyle promised would be built in six years, only 130 were built in eleven years, primarily with non-linkage funding. It became clear to many that supporting a neighborhood development strategy based on growth and the promise of linkage funds would never meet community needs. The major community achievement during these years was the creation of the Chinatown master plan in 1990, which defined the neighborhood's vision for future development and fixed its physical boundaries. While the plan produced no new housing, it was a blueprint around which the community could mobilize.

This new political and economic environment coincided with the maturity of community organizing that bonded many organizations with community members. Since Lafayette Place, neighborhood organizing had evolved in many ways. Local campaigns associated with Mel King, Long Guang Huang, the garment workers, the Oak Street buildings, and Saint Margaret's Hospital had established Chinatown as an active neighborhood player in the city. They also demonstrated the development of social networks that, despite continuing divisiveness with the business leaders, supported both the agencies and the activist organizations. New relationships among these organizations and their clients or members were based on shared ideals, obligations, and trust. Together, they overcame many of the divisions triggered by Chinatown's increasing diversity.

A number of community members began to see mass organizing as a useful tool, and their methods were becoming increasingly militant. They did not use such tactics with development issues during this period, but employing it against police brutality and in support of workers' rights had demonstrated its effectiveness. Mobilization also began to be tied to other forms of community agency, such as citywide networking and use of regulatory policies. Yet the neighborhood's limited success in claiming a full share of public benefit from economic development proved that it needed to become a much greater civic force. Chinatown had to build on its maturing state of mobilization to win concrete progress in sustaining the neighborhood. Without it, the neighborhood would slowly recede.

"TO BE OR NOT TO BE" FOR THE PARCEL C GARAGE, 1990–1993

An economic collapse created the setting for the most momentous development struggle in Chinatown's history. The recession began in 1989, and by December the office vacancy rate in Boston had climbed to 12 percent. The Bank of New England, the second largest in the region, went bankrupt as a result of bad real estate loans; and the region's largest bank, the Bank of Boston, wrote off $300 million in losses for the last quarter of the year. The federal government set up the Resolution Trust Corporation to liquidate the assets of insolvent savings and loan associations, eventually closing 750 of them. By 1990, Boston's downtown office rents, which had recently commanded rates second only to New York's, were being offered at discounts of 25 percent. By the end of that year, office property values had plummeted by an average of 25 percent, and there were a record number of vacancies. Between 1990 and 1992, more than a hundred banks failed in New England.[1]

The weakening economy undermined the Flynn administration's leverage to extract concessions from developers. Once supportive, they now openly questioned linkage payments, calling them a barrier to growth. By 1991, Coyle was telling a reporter that the BRA's role had changed from "managing the boom to trying to encourage new investment."[2] The slowdown in office construction triggered a budget crisis at the agency. As the administrative center of city planning and development, it had depended on income from the sale of city-owned parcels. When developers no longer demanded this land, that revenue stream dried up. The agency began running severe deficits, and its ability to initiate new projects weakened.

The city tabled its grand development plans. The Midtown Cultural District, which the BRA had worked so hard to develop and around which it had made so many commitments to win Chinatown's support, disappeared from discussions. The Commonwealth Center hotel, office tower, and retail project was canceled in 1991. Pedestrians had open vistas of parking lots and empty storefronts, vestiges of large-scale developers' land acquisition and demolition.

To escape this dispiriting climate, Coyle left his city post in 1992 to work for the AFL-CIO Housing Investment Trust in Washington, D.C. A year later Flynn also exited city government, accepting an ambassador-ship to the Vatican. In his wake went his so-called "Sandinistas"—Alex Bledsoe, Peter Dreier, Don Gillis, and Neil Sullivan—citizen activists who had provided much-needed leadership for progressive urban policies.[3]

After Flynn's departure, city council president Tom Menino became Boston's interim mayor, ending almost a century of Irish American con-trol over the office. A native Bostonian with Italian roots, Menino was a slow, determined, self-described "average guy." Political commentators derided him as "Mayor Pothole" for his focus on tangible constitu-ent services. Some called him "Mumbles," a reference to his mangled speaking style and meandering syntax.[4] Menino lived in Readville, a neighborhood on the far outskirts of the city. He had formerly worked in the declining Westinghouse-Sturtevant factory, which made large industrial fans; and as a city councilor he had represented District 5, a mostly Irish American area with a minority of Italian Americans and an even smaller concentration of African Americans.

Menino was a working-class scion without much advanced educa-tion, but he had nursed a lifelong interest in politics, and his political ambitions would eventually surprise many of his detractors. His hero was Harry Truman, the only president without a college degree. He har-bored a vindictive streak toward those who opposed him. Nonetheless, he won the mayor's seat in the next election and went on to become the longest-serving mayor in Boston history.[5]

Menino shared Flynn's and Coyle's focus on neighborhoods, but his approach to development was more orthodox. He considered it inherently beneficial. Though the linkage policies remained in place during his early administration, he discussed no ambitious parcel-to-parcel linkage packages and took no new policy approaches to redistributing benefits to the neighborhoods.[6] Nor did the BRA undertake new initiatives. After Coyle left, Flynn had replaced him with Paul Barrett, a tough, aggressive, former athlete from Flynn's own South Boston neighborhood. Though Barrett had little background in planning and development, he made multiple attempts to address the urban economic crisis and the BRA's budget problems. Since the start of the recession, half of the agency staff had been let go, but he now moved quickly to slow the downsizing. He tried to follow Coyle's recession strategy of pursuing growth industries in the city—health care, biotechnology, and education. Acknowledging development's current realpolitik, he declared:

> The need for offices and hotels has plateaued in Boston. . . . Seven of the city's top employers are institutions like MGH [Massachusetts General Hospital], Northeastern [University], BU [Boston University]. That's where the local economy is going, whether I like it or anyone in the city likes it. And that brings all the issues around development— issues of traffic, people's abilities to stay in a neighborhood, the ability to build affordable housing—closer to people's homes.[7]

Barrett suggested a new motto to guide Boston's future: "We have to grow the city and make institutions grow." Under his tenure, that machine became less populist. It returned to embracing its traditional constituents—developers, bankers, and the construction industry—and turned to conventional incentive strategies to attract capital. There were fewer obvious political opportunities for neighborhoods.[8]

NEW LEADERS, EVOLVING ORGANIZATIONS, EVOLVING NEIGHBORHOOD

According to the 1990 census, the Asian American population had almost doubled in Boston in over the course of the past decade. Yet the population of Chinatown had barely budged from its 1980s figure of 5,000. At the same time, the Chinatown Coalition's community assessment report had noted an increase in ethnic, cultural, linguistic, and political diversity: "Asians living in Chinatown and Boston [were] of Vietnamese, Vietnamese-Chinese, Burmese-Chinese, Laotian and Cambodian ancestry."[9] In response to this increased diversity, social service agencies were adapting to serve a broader racial and ethnic population, one that was Asian rather than Chinese. The Chinese American Civic Association, one of the neighborhood's two largest multiservice agencies, renamed itself the Asian American Civic Association (AACA). Boston Chinese Youth Essential Services became Boston Asian Youth Essential Services (YES).

As they expanded into communities in and around Boston, Asian populations were also becoming more dispersed. The South Cove Community Health Center established a satellite clinic in Quincy, just south of Boston, which now had a large Asian American population. The Golden Age Center established branches in Quincy and in the Boston neighborhood of Brighton, which had an established Chinese population. While Chinatown itself was not growing, its energetic leaders—Caroline Chang, Stephanie Fan, Regina Lee, Ann Wong, David Moy, Richard Chin, Beverly Wing, Ann Moy, and others—continued to build on existing organizations and establish new ones: service agencies, nonprofit developers, and grassroots activist groups. This generation of organizers—some U.S.-born, others recent immigrants—felt a broad sense of responsibility for their constituents. Compared with the traditional leadership, they took a more equitable view of their rights as American citizens, had greater familiarity with local institutions, and used various means of negotiation to achieve their ends.

The largest of the service agencies—the South Cove Health Center, the Quincy School Community Council (QSCC), and the Asian American Civic Association (AACA)—were now multimillion-dollar operations. Together, they helped form the Chinatown Coalition (TCC), a new umbrella entity intended to encourage interagency collaboration. The Asian Community Development Corporation (ACDC) had completed its first project, Oak Terrace, on Washington Street, facing the Josiah Quincy Elementary School. The Chinese Economic Development Council (CEDC) had acquired properties closer to the business area (the 31 Beach Street building and the Oxford Place apartments) but lost another (the China Trade Center on Washington and Boylston streets) to creditors.[10]

The activist groups also established and engaged in new smaller-scale efforts. Both the Asian American Resource Workshop, under my direction, and the Chinese Progressive Association (CPA), under Ann Wong's, now had more than five hundred members and were expanding their range of activities to include services and youth leadership programs. During the Flynn years, these groups developed more effective mobilization methods and mounted numerous campaigns that incorporated cultural symbols, community-centered policies, and media strategies. While individual organizations and their leaders still initiated neighborhood mobilizations, the broader community of residents had become more actively engaged. Moreover, organizing methods had become increasingly militant. These activist groups began to evolve to better address the realities of Boston's changing political and economic situation.[11]

The traditional umbrella group, the Chinese Consolidated Benevolent Association (CCBA), both flourished and struggled. It was now the neighborhood's largest developer and landowner but had also been damaged by debilitating internal disputes. Its holdings included the Tai Tung Village housing project and the former SCM building site. It had developed affordable housing complexes such as Tremont Village apartments in adjacent Bay Village and Waterford Place in the South End. Yet new leaders and businesses within the organization were increasingly aggrieved at the Chin faction's long dominance and their expectation that others should follow their directives.[12]

Churches began to play a more community active role during this period—among them, Saint James Catholic Church and the Boston Chinese Evangelical Church, which called itself the "largest Asian church in New England."[13] The Harry Dow Legal Fund was founded to support legal activism, particularly for the disadvantaged. Athletic and social groups as well as committees focused on specialized issues such as beautification or anti-drug programs also formed.

Some organizations adopted the CCBA's traditional strategies, accommodating themselves to established city institutions and working within mainstream economic development channels. They established relations with the mayor's administration and supported its initiatives in the neighborhood. The Chinatown Neighborhood Council (CNC), a creation of the city administration, had once represented community interests (see chapter 5). Now, however, it had become the most prominent among these accommodationist entities. Others included the AACA, the Golden Age Center, and the Chinatown YMCA. Their executive directors would often appear at ribbon cuttings and publicized corporate donation events supporting new developments or city initiatives.

Some groups maintained a degree of independence from the city administrations. For instance, to distance itself from Boston's community school network, the QSCC eventually changed its name to Boston Chinatown Neighborhood Center (BCNC). However, the activist groups continued to challenge what they saw as an unjust and unequal status quo, pushing for changes in decision making, legislation, and regulations.[14]

Greater cooperation was evident among the various groups, and the community began to appreciate the importance, and difficulty, of using collaboration to achieve results. Their success in combining efforts during the Long Guang Huang campaign and the broad representation of the first CNC had not succeeded in maintaining a substantial, consistent neighborhood accord. The divergent interests of business leaders, service providers, and activist organizations had made coming together around a common agenda difficult, as the council's first election had shown (see chapter 5). Cooperation was possible only at particular junctures, when the community or the authorities undeniably demanded it. Zenobia Lai, a legal services lawyer, observed, "I think there are a lot of organizations in Chinatown that give people the impression that Chinatown is really organized, but, I think, the truth is, it is really not."[15] Paul Chan, a community developer who worked with CCBA, agreed that though

Chinatown was more organized than other neighborhoods, it was not highly organized.[16]

The activist groups were working, but conditions in Chinatown were difficult to change. Data from the 1990 census and city statistics listed the neighborhood's median income at 70 percent of the citywide level and showed a poverty rate of 28 percent—50 percent higher than the city rate. Employment in once-stable industries had changed, but the population remained mainly working class. Chinese women who had once been garment workers were now employed in hotels, back offices, and light manufacturing. An increasing percentage of residents were elderly; they now formed one-fifth of the neighborhood's population. But they would prove to be reliable participants in community mobilization.

THE NEIGHBORHOOD COUNCIL AND T-NEMC

After the business leaders' victory in the 1988 CNC election, Bill Moy began the first of a remarkable succession of terms as a council moderator, a post he held for three decades. Self-confident and intimidating, Moy could dominate a room. The council's meetings, once inclusive affairs, were now held without public knowledge or input and conducted entirely in English. Anonymous council members complained that a small number of people made all of the decisions.[17] Apparent conflicts of interest existed among CNC members, but there was little complaint. When the BRA ended its financial support of the council, T-NEMC began funding the salary of the executive director and hired one of the co-moderators. In his position as a moderator, Moy functioned as T-NEMC's liaison to Chinatown and later also as liaison for the Central Artery/Third Harbor Tunnel project.

One of the first major decisions that the new council faced concerned the 1988 dispute between T-NEMC and QSCC over two Oak Street rowhouses that the latter used as a community center. T-NEMC sued to prevent the BRA from turning over the buildings to QSCC. Despite the urging of QSCC, the Chinatown Housing and Land Task Force, and the

BRA, the CNC refused to take a side in the dispute. Marilyn Lee-Tom of the Housing Task Force pointed out the irony in "hearing the city defending the community's right to use its own land" rather than getting such support from the CNC, the community's nominal representative.[18] Years later Moy summarized his stance in the statement "T-NEMC has been a good friend to the community."[19]

Except for the expanding medical complex, little construction occurred in or around the neighborhood during the early 1990s. But even as other industries languished, the health industry was thriving. As early as the 1960s, health-related organizations and businesses were the largest employer in the commonwealth. The BRA predicted that the health industry's employment and earnings growth between 1990 and

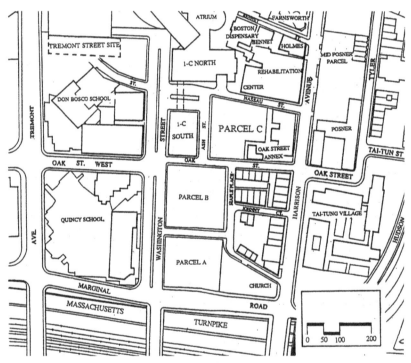

FIGURE 9. Parcel C in context. From New England Medical Center Hospitals, "Draft Project Impact Report; Draft Environmental Impact Report; Parcel C Garage" (Boston, February 28, 1994).

1995 would continue to outpace the rest of the state economy, as it had for over a decade.[20]

As Boston planners began to trumpet the industry's role in driving the urban economy, T-NEMC presented yet another master plan for expansion. Most of this 1990 plan laid out ideas for more intensive use of the land it already owned. Upward growth included construction of the 1-C project, including a North Building containing a new emergency area and a South Building housing a new maternity wing and a community hospital. New construction and renovation would expand the number of hospital beds, and further research facilities were under consideration on Washington Street.[21] T-NEMC's growth encircled the area bordered by Harrison, Oak, Ash, and Nassau streets, now designated as Parcel C. The new North and South buildings and their rehabilitation facilities would look down at the remaining rowhouse buildings and a parking lot. T-NEMC's renewed designs for this site would affect Chinatown for years.

PARCEL C DEVELOPMENT

The Parcel C site had a long and controversial history. Under the 1965 urban renewal plan, the BRA had used eminent domain to take ownership of the score of rowhouses on Oak Street. It had demolished these buildings, which had housed dozens of Chinese families, to prepare the site for T-NEMC expansion. T-NEMC had made some unsuccessful attempts to build on the site, but the community had continually opposed the projects. In the late 1970s, a Chinese American developer's futile effort to build elder housing on the site became the catalyst for creating the Housing Task Force. In 1986, T-NEMC had proposed building a garage on the site, but the first CNC rejected the plan. T-NEMC's appeals to the BRA failed to win city approval. Tufts University and Saint Margaret's Hospital had also tried unsuccessfully to move facilities there. As I have mentioned, in 1988 T-NEMC filed and lost a lawsuit intended to prevent the BRA from transferring control of two buildings to QSCC. These were the last two standing brick rowhouses on Oak Street abutting the Parcel C boundaries.

TIMELINE 4. Parcel C

1965	BRA takes area by eminent domain for T-NEMC, demolishes housing.
1978	Despite protests, T-NEMC does not relinquish its right to site to allow for an elder-housing project.
1986	T-NEMC proposes garage on Parcel C; first CNC rejects project.
1987	BRA rejects garage.
	Tufts University and Saint Margaret's Hospital propose a move to Parcel C; Chinatown community rejects move, which fails.
1988	T-NEMC sues to prevent BRA from transferring two remaining buildings to QSCC.
1989	Court upholds transfer of two buildings to QSCC.
1990	BRA arranges a swap of land with T-NEMC for Parcel C, designates it for Chinatown.
	BRA plans community center for six Chinatown organizations.
1992	BRA designates fifty-five spaces on site for ACDC project parking; BRA and T-NEMC propose garage on Parcel C.
1993	CNC supports garage.
	Parcel C coalition forms.

In 1990, after years of dispute between the neighborhood and the medical center, the BRA arranged a land swap for the parcel. This swap allowed T-NEMC to build the 1-C South Building on Washington Street, adjacent to the parcel, which increased the medical center's number of beds and expanded other health services. The city designated the Parcel R3/R3A area, which was adjacent to Massachusetts Turnpike extension and included Parcel C, for community use and marked it as lying inside a proposed Historic Chinatown District.[22]

Chinatown's most glaring problem was the critical shortage of housing in the neighborhood, but it had many other needs as well. So the city initiated a process to decide on community development plans for Parcel R3/R3A. The city called for a minimum of 220 housing units on R3/R3A. Washington Street, Marginal Road (along the Mass Pike), Maple Place, and Oak Street bordered the area. The parcel encompassed the original Pine Street Inn, a homeless shelter, and an old commercial building.

One of the BRA's difficulties was deciding between competing Chinatown nonprofit developers. Lawrence Cheng, Tunney Lee, and other activists had formed Asian Community Development Corporation (ACDC) to provide an alternative to the Chinese Economic Development Council (CEDC). These activists were not alone in having serious concerns about CEDC, which had chosen to retain its chair, George Pan, even after his conviction for defrauding the U.S. government.[23] Although all of its program directors had walked out after that decision, CEDC nevertheless wielded influence as Chinatown's only community development corporation. ACDC hoped to change that dynamic.

The BRA decided to deal with the competitive situation between ACDC and CEDC by dividing the development rights for R3/R3A into Parcels A, B, and C. According to Lawrence Cheng, the agency tried to give something to everyone in order to win neighborhood support for the proposed Midtown Cultural District plan. So in 1988, CEDC received Parcel A, and ACDC received Parcel B. Parcel C was to be used to build a community center and a parking lot for the two housing projects. The center would be a separate initiative because neither of the CDCs considered the project feasible.[24]

To develop the badly needed community center on the Parcel C site, the BRA worked with seven agencies—AACA, the Workshop, the Chinatown Boys' and Girls' Club, CPA, QSCC, the health center, and South Cove YMCA—most of which needed facilities for their operations.[25] In 1990, six of them formally incorporated as the Chinatown Community Center (CCC). Although QSCC did not sign the incorporation papers, it participated in the initial discussions and remained an active and interested party.[26] Because the local CDCs were not interested in developing the parcel, the BRA proposed finding linkage funds to build a 90,000-square-foot community center and organized a national competition to design it.

As the economy fell into recession, planning for the community center was put on hold. But when ACDC's plans for its Oak Terrace housing project slowly reached fruition, it asked the BRA and CCC to set aside fifty-five parking spaces in Parcel C to meet federal financing requirements. The BRA and CCC agreed. Now, with no active development, much of Parcel C became a 24,000-square-foot surface parking area bordered by three small streets. Still standing were three small, mid-nineteenth-century Greek revival brick rowhouses, the remnants of a style that had once proliferated on the site. Last used as T-NEMC offices, these buildings were now vacant. Although the BRA owned most of the land, the QSCC retained a small corner, used as a playground for the Acorn Day Care Center housed in QSCC's Oak Street buildings.[27]

Parcel C was in the Chinatown residential area. Across the street was a line of brick rowhouses, cousins of the three isolated buildings on the parcel. In 1993, families occupied these rowhouses, including the Mahannas, one of the few remaining Syrian families who had populated the neighborhood before the Chinese had moved in. Mary Mahanna, who was employed in the Quincy School lunchroom, and her son Paul moved easily through the area and often worked with the neighbors. Other residents were the working-class Moy family, including Marie, an active and gregarious native-born Chinese American who clerked at T-NEMC, and her immigrant husband, who worked in the restaurants. Next to these rowhouses, construction was proceeding on Oak Terrace, ACDC's Parcel B housing project.

Because of Oak Street's location, children and families from Chinatown's largest housing project, Tai Tung Village, traveled through the narrow block to get to Quincy School, the central operations of QSCC, and the health center. QSCC operated out of the school, primarily after school hours. The health center and QSCC facilities were thus located in the same building, across Washington Street from Oak Terrace. Quincy Towers, a highrise filled with small apartments for the elderly and the Golden Age Center, occupied the corner plot and looked down over the Quincy School facilities.

As the economy continued its decline, the BRA decided to dispose of Parcel C.[28] It approached T-NEMC in the fall of 1992 and proposed allowing the medical center to build its long-desired garage on the site. In an attempt to allay community objections, the development package would include some Chinatown benefits among those offered to the various stakeholders. The packages were relatively simple. The BRA would receive $3.8 million from T-NEMC to stabilize the agency's fiscal situation. (Two years later the BRA would announce that it was running an $8 million deficit on its $12 million annual budget.) T-NEMC would be able to construct a 455-space parking facility on the site, relieving the parking congestion associated with the growing medical center, Tufts University Medical School, the USDA Human Nutrition Research Center, and the Tufts University Veterinary School. Chinatown would gain a community center, albeit smaller than the one original planned (10,000 square feet located under the garage); the fifty-five existing parking spaces for Oak Terrace (valued by T-NEMC at $1.8 million); or a cash settlement of $1.2 million.[29]

For Chinatown, the negative impacts of this Parcel C plan would be both environmental and social. The neighborhood would lose what some felt was the last remaining piece of land available for community development. Residents attached a great deal of symbolism to the parcel, and they thought they had kept it when they had agreed to previous T-NEMC expansion on Washington Street. They saw this new plan as yet another broken city promise. Instead of a community center, there would be a busy garage in the midst of their residential area, a place where traffic safety and environmental issues were already problematic. Along with noise, wind, shadows, and other adverse effects, the owners of the Oak Street brownstones expected the garage construction to destabilize their homes, as construction of the 1-C buildings had done.[30]

Although the medical center's EIS report listed no appreciable adverse effects from this development, Chinatown had a litany of concerns. Community members pointed out that T-NEMC plans placed the garage against QSCC's Oak Street buildings, which housed the Acorn Day Care Center and a playground, and also bordered a vital link between Tai Tung Village and the service facilities on Washington Street. The garage could potentially affect the elderly residents of Quincy Towers, families in Oak Terrace and on Oak Street, and children in the Quincy School, all of which were adjacent to or less than a block away from the proposed garage.[31] The garage thus touched many of the social networks in the densely populated neighborhood. Abutting residents as well as representatives of CPA, QSCC, and the Workshop were among those who spoke out most loudly against the plan. Lydia Lowe of CPA asked, "Why are our community's needs always last on the priority list?" In a letter to the *Boston Herald*, a resident characterized the proposal as "selfish, irresponsible, and racist."[32]

T-NEMC and the BRA brought the plan first to the neighborhood council and then communicated with CCC members. (By this point, the Chinatown Boys' and Girls' Club had dissolved, so it was no longer among them.) While the majority rejected the proposal, both AACA and the YMCA were supportive. They, along with the council, proposed that

CCC negotiate with T-NEMC. The other members agreed to ask for a meeting and to present a counterproposal for added community benefits. However, the more activist groups also wanted a full community review process to discuss any new agreements with T-NEMC. In their view, the community should decide whether the tradeoffs were beneficial.

In March 1993, T-NEMC finally agreed to meet with CCC. Larry Smith, the medical center's vice president and general counsel, spoke with members in the AACA's facilities in the basement of the old Quincy School. Also present were AACA and YMCA representatives, Lydia Lowe, David Moy, and the Workshop's representative (me). Smith stunned us by beginning the meeting with the statement that T-NEMC would make no changes in terms: all issues were beyond discussion. I responded by telling him that the garage was unacceptable and vowed that the next meeting would be in the streets if T-NEMC tried to build it. The meeting ended without any change in position.

The CNC, clearly determined to see the garage proposal go through, began to publicly criticize the CCC members who opposed the garage. The council claimed that the CCC only wanted more money and had entered the process too late. But when the council met to make its decision on the Parcel C development, one hundred residents and community representatives crowded into what was usually a small session and spoke uniformly against the proposal.

The gathering was tense and emotional; both residents and a council member shed tears. One resident recounted a painful experience with T-NEMC that had resulted in the death of her husband during medical treatment. But eventually the council, comprised mainly of members living outside the neighborhood, voted twelve to two in favor of the proposal. Attendees were enraged. Lydia Lowe, who was usually low-key, vowed, "We plan to fight this all the way." Judi Chan, a young teenage resident, said, "I feel betrayed by [the council]. . . . New England Medical Center is taking the land here little by little. This is Chinatown. We want to keep our neighborhoods like they are."[33]

Three of the five remaining organizations in CCC (the Workshop, CPA, and the health center), along with QSCC, subsequently called a community meeting of residents. At this gathering, residents of Oak Street, including Marie Moy and Mary Mahanna, spoke strongly against the garage, and Lowe of CPA pledged her support. All promised to continue their opposition to the garage construction. Thus began an intense, popular campaign against the Parcel C garage.[34]

FIGURE 10. Wen-ti Tsen and David Fichter, *Unity/Community: Chinatown Community Mural*, 1986, acrylic, 40 ft. x 30 ft., Boston. The Chinatown history mural was painted on the side of 34 Oak Street before the building was torn down and replaced by the Metropolitan housing development. Courtesy of Wen-ti Tsen.

LEADING AGAINST THE GROWTH MACHINE, 1993–1998

A core of committed activists, led by the primary activist groups in Chinatown—the Chinese Progressive Association (CPA) and the Asian American Resource Workshop—anchored the campaign against the Parcel C garage. They organized in early June 1993 as the Coalition to Protect Parcel C for Chinatown, also known as the Parcel C Coalition. CPA had developed significant roots among immigrant workers through years spent championing their issues. The Workshop, a place for younger, English-speaking Asian Americans, was active in media issues, opposing hate crimes, and introducing Asian American studies curriculum into local high schools and colleges. The Quincy School Community Council (QSCC), the most extensive service agency in Chinatown, also joined the campaign. While its executive director, David Moy, did not involve his staff, he participated energetically. QSCC's many roles among the community's immigrants added a broader legitimacy to the coalition. A core of young, activist lawyers—Zenobia Lai and Chi Chi Wu of Greater Boston Legal Services (GBLS), Andrew Leong from the University of Massachusetts, and Elaine Tung, a pro bono corporate lawyer—also fiercely took up the issue. They brought with them some law students, who would become very active in the campaign.[1] Marie Moy, who served on the

QSCC board, and other resident abutters became active. Henry Yee, the energetic president of the Tai Tung Tenants Association, was passionate about the rights of Chinatown residents, and he was among the Parcel C Coalition's most active core members. Another activist, Howard Wong, born in Chinatown, wrote, "Parcel C is just a small plot of land, but it can represent a lot. It represents to me in some way the future. . . . But the future I see now seems bleak. In the past, when I walked out of the Tai Tung Village courtyard, I used to see the old houses facing me on Harrison Avenue. But now all I really see is the looming shadow of NEMC's new buildings. It towers over them—it towers over us."[2]

TIMELINE 5. Parcel C Campaign

June 1993	Parcel C coalition forms, organizes first street protests against T-NEMC garage.
	BRA board approves garage.
July 93	Coalition calls for a community referendum.
	BRA offers an alternative site for a community center.
August 1993	Coalition rejects any offer involving a garage.
	Coalition presses mayoral candidates on garage.
	Coalition works with other neighborhoods opposing BRA.
	State environmental agency hears Chinatown objections to the garage.
September 1993	State announces T-NEMC garage environmental review required.
	Chinatown votes against garage in referendum.
December 1993	CNC election retains garage supporters.
April 1994	Coalition presents a new plan for Parcel C.
May 1994	State rejects T-NEMC garage environmental review.
July 1994	Coalition offers same lease terms as NEMC for Parcel C land.
August 1994	Family Fun Day rally at Parcel C, community Parcel C plan presented.
October 1994	Coalition communicates a plan for civil rights lawsuit.
	City Hall transfers Parcel C to CCBA.
1995	Tufts announces expansion plans.
1996	Ramp DD campaign takes place.

The Parcel C Coalition attracted a dozen other organizations, including the Chinese Consolidated Benevolent Association (CCBA), several of its affiliated family associations, the Tai Tung Tenants Association, activist organizations, a few businesses, and social service agencies.[3] It adopted a town-hall method of organizing but also formed several committees. Despite this broad support, Zenobia Lai observed that "a lot of people . . . didn't support the Parcel C struggle." They thought "we [were] a bunch of crazy nuts and that we [wouldn't] win because we [were] going against the City. We [were] going against the New England Medical Center. They ha[d] more resources. They ha[d] more money. They [were] perceived to be more powerful than us, which was a bunch of grassroots organizers."[4]

The coalition's membership reflected the deep, intertwined loyalties and agendas in Chinatown. Organizations that didn't participate were as significant as those that did. The Chinatown Coalition (TCC) did not play a role because its members included T-NEMC as well as Chinatown organizations that both supported and opposed the garage. One TCC member later expressed regret that the group did not attempt to resolve differences that arose around Parcel C.[5] The Asian Community Development Corporation (ACDC) also had conflicting interests related to the Parcel C proposal. While it privately expressed sympathy, it felt unable to take a public position. An ACDC member, reflecting on past battles, expressed a sentiment that many people held: "Don't ever try to fight against big money. We fought against big money, against Thompson, against New England Medical Center, and look where it got us. They got whatever they wanted. So, don't think that we can fight big money, we can't."[6] The city, moreover, reminded ACDC that financing arrangements for Oak Terrace depended on Boston's goodwill. Except for QSCC and the South Cove Health Center, the service agencies found it difficult to advocate for the community because of institutional entanglements.

Despite widespread opposition to the garage proposal, there was also vocal support for it, most loudly from the Chinatown Neighborhood Council (CNC). The council's co-moderator Bill Moy, its executive director Davis Woo, and the Asian American Civic Association's (AACA) director Chau-Ming Lee testified in favor of the garage at the BRA hearing. According to Woo, "if the garage proposal is rejected, we will have turned our backs on the substantial money that would come to Chinatown." In his view, it was an arrangement "that reflects the reality of today." The CNC's other co-moderator, Bobby Guen, a dentist raised in Chinatown, echoed that argument. Stating "There's no money out there," he suggested this was the best deal available. Bill Moy charged that the Parcel C Coalition was manipulating residents and students. While a small minority of the CNC called for self-reflection, most were determined to, as one council member put it, "stand our ground" and support the garage.[7] Thus, the stage was set for a defining test of wills, replete with competing visions for Chinatown: residents against Boston's powerful mayor, the BRA, and one of the city's most important industries.

THE CAMPAIGN

Aroused by T-NEMC's and the CNC's deafness to their concerns, opponents of the Parcel C garage began to campaign furiously as soon as the coalition was formed. During the eighteen-month campaign, the Asian American Resource Workshop and the CPA dedicated their entire staffs (each contributing a half-dozen people) to the work. The workshop took responsibility for media and administrative support. CPA concentrated on community organizing. The law students associated with the legal service lawyers began to investigate various legal options to stop the construction. The Parcel C Coalition actively drew on Chinatown's history as a victimized community to mobilize residents, directly defying the city and its plans.[8]

Lydia Lowe was responsible for coordinating CPA's campaign against the garage. She was a transplanted Californian who had come east to attend college in the 1980s. Lowe had been an enthusiastic and capable student organizer and had contributed to building a network of Asian American student organizations on the East Coast. She had joined CPA staff in 1987 after volunteering on the support committee for the P&L garment workers. In 1991, after becoming its executive director, she had spent a summer in Hong Kong to learn the Cantonese dialect so she could organize in Chinatown.

On the opposite side of the issue was Richard Chin, who represented the Chinatown YMCA on the CNC and was a supporter of the garage. Born in Chinatown and now living in the South End, Chin was the son of a laundryman and a garment worker. He had spent time at the Y in his youth and, after graduating from college, worked in a succession of community service organizations before assuming the directorship there. While Chin was aware of the systemic racism in Chinatown's history, he believed residents needed to work within the constraints of existing structures to improve the conditions of the community.

Lowe and Chin held two very different conceptions of Chinatown. Lowe saw it as a critical refuge for working people and the center of the region's Chinese community. She strongly felt that it would lose those roles if Chinese residents were no longer able to live in the area.[9] Chin believed that Chinatown needed to accommodate development to save whatever community it had left—to give up something to gain something else.[10] These opposing perspectives played out between the factions in the Parcel C garage campaign.

The Parcel C Coalition began by employing organizing methods that previous neighborhood campaigns had developed: petitions to the mayor and the BRA, community meetings, and public demonstrations. The issue resonated in the neighborhood: the coalition collected 2,500 petition signatures, and three hundred people attended the first demonstration. The Workshop developed an intense and relentless media campaign with frequent press-release blitzes. Terri Oshiro, its program director, remembers writing and putting out releases daily during the height of the campaign. The coalition intended to keep the issue in the public eye. Over the course of eighteen months, it generated seventy-five articles, letters to the editor, and editorial pieces in the Chinese- and English-language press.[11]

The community packed a three-hour BRA hearing to debate approval of the project. Nonetheless, despite residents' "impassioned plea," the agency's board voted unanimously to approve the garage. David Moy, who attended the meeting, editorialized in the *Sampan* that the BRA board had "ignored a petition with over 2500 signatures, the testimonies of community residents and organizations, and the knowledge of a community demonstration which drew over 300 or more community people." He concluded that the board "had already made up its mind to support the NEMC proposal even prior to the hearing."[12] The pressure also forced the CNC to spend its subsequent meeting explaining its vote and responding to criticisms.

Because the garage needed state environmental approval, the Parcel C Coalition began to organize around the regulatory process. In late August 1993, it lobbied the Massachusetts Department of Environmental Protection (MDEP) to require the fullest environmental impact review (EIR). T-NEMC argued that a full review was unnecessary, but the coalition's legal support team coordinated a vigorous action. Fifty people attended the hearing and presented twenty oral testimonies and written comments. The neighborhood had prepared by conducting its own traffic studies. Local youth, advised by Doug Brugge, a community health specialist, had stood on street corners for hours counting cars. Their traffic numbers were two to three times higher than those submitted in T-NEMC's preliminary EIR. The Parcel C Coalition legal team also provided testimony from abutters and the health center staff.

These efforts persuaded MDEP to rule in the neighborhood's favor: in September, the agency required T-NEMC to conduct a new and complete EIR.[13] For T-NEMC, MDEP's rejection was a crucial setback. It took the medical center another six months to resubmit a draft EIR. That delay gave Chinatown an invaluable chance to mobilize.

Meanwhile, in July 1993, Menino had stepped in as interim mayor (replacing Flynn), and the election campaign for the next mayoral term began almost immediately after he took office. The Parcel C Coalition took advantage, prodding candidates to take a stand on the garage issue. This approach effectively elevated Chinatown's grievances within Boston's politics. Most of the six candidates for mayor leaned toward opposing the garage, but Menino, the eventual victor, was noncommittal. He said that he would meet with both sides before deciding.[14] Unfortunately, he failed to live up to that promise.

Given T-NEMC's and the city's unwillingness to budge on the garage issue, the Parcel C Coalition introduced novel methods for mobilizing the neighborhood. For instance, it proposed a neighborhood referendum to allow residents to vote directly on the plan. It wanted to put the concept of democracy to the test. When the city refused, the coalition itself funded and organized the referendum. Even though the vote would lack formal recognition, the coalition felt that it was important to allow the community to express its voice as both the city and the CNC had denied it any representation. The American Friends Service Committee agreed to serve as a neutral third party to oversee the voting.[15]

As an attempt at a compromise, the BRA offered Chinatown a city-owned parcel on Tyler Street, part of which was the site of the Chinatown Y, as the location of a new community center. The coalition considered and unanimously rejected the offer. For these activists, the Parcel C garage was no longer open to negotiation. Organizations were bound by their commitment to Chinatown's residents. Suzanne Lee, the coalition's co-chair, declared that "expecting people in that area to put up with a garage" was a threat to their health and safety.[16]

Moving forward with the community referendum, volunteers passed out leaflets door to door and on street corners. They sent sound trucks rolling through the streets to inform residents about the referendum. They produced fact sheets and posters encouraging people to vote. The result was significant voter turnout, with people waiting by the dozens outside voting sites. In the end, the community rejected the garage proposal by a decisive vote of 1,692 to 42.[17]

The referendum's success strengthened organizational calls to elevate the community's voice in local decision making, but the city declared the referendum irrelevant. Lowe told the *Boston Herald*, "This is a basic issue of democracy. The people in this community should be allowed to decide." The BRA's Paul Barrett retorted, "We're not going to run this city and this agency by referendum."[18] David Moy wryly noted that the nonbinding referendum's "results [were] every bit as binding as the past promises of the BRA and New England Medical [were] true."[19] It was clear that the relationship between Chinatown and the BRA had changed since the more cooperative boom years of the 1980s. In the face of conflicting organizational voices, the vote gave the garage opponents a legitimacy that would shape the community response to Parcel C.

POST-REFERENDUM MOBILIZATION

The Parcel C Coalition tested additional avenues of protest. In December 1993, it tried to elect a more responsive neighborhood council. After a fierce campaign with competing slates, the CNC held the election in a few polling sites under a driving rain. Restaurant vans and their owners delivered scores of workers to the polls. The incumbent slate of candidates prevailed, preserving the council's status quo.[20]

With the help of Chia-Ming Sze, a prominent local architect, the Parcel C Coalition put forward alternative plans for the site. The plan packet, prepared with architectural renderings and cost estimates, called for developing a community center using the existing buildings and creating open space that could be realized with modest funding. This proposal directly challenged the BRA's and the CNC's initial justification for the parcel sale—that the economic environment had so deteriorated that resources to develop a center were unavailable.[21]

The coalition's legal committee researched the possibility of replacing T-NEMC on the prevailing lease for Parcel C. The coalition asked the BRA to extend to the Chinatown community the same terms for Parcel C that it was currently giving to T-NEMC: $1 a year. At a July 1994 news conference, the coalition offered a stack of ninety-nine dollar bills to the agency for a neighborhood lease of the site for ninety-nine years. The BRA declined to respond.[22]

Facing the city's indifference, the coalition considered occupying Parcel C for a weekend, turning it into a tent city as Black activists led by Mel King had done on a South End parking lot in 1968. While some Chinatown activists were excited about the idea, others were concerned about asking community members to put themselves in harm's way. For those who were not U.S. citizens, an arrest could endanger naturalization prospects or lead to deportation. The coalition opted instead for a Family Fun Day to dramatize the possibilities of Parcel C as a recreational space for Chinatown's residential community.

In August, volunteers arranged games, activities, and performances for youth, adults, and the elderly on the Oak Street lot. Across the Oak

Street buildings they strung banners that read "No Garage on Oak Street" and "Community Center on Parcel C" in English and Chinese. Performers staged a mock dedication ceremony for the imagined community center and recreation area, complete with a ribbon cutting and firecrackers. As coalition member Terri Oshiro said, "We wanted the community to see what a recreational and community center would be used for if we win the struggle. We want the city to know if they won't help us, the community will take ownership of the issue."[23]

The campaign also developed new sources of support. The Conservation Law Foundation, Boston University's School of Public Health, and the Environmental Diversity Forum helped guide the neighborhood's environmental regulatory strategy. With the Conservation Law Foundation, the coalition explored the possibility of filing a legal suit against the city for violating an EPA-ordered parking construction freeze in the downtown area that had been in effect for several years. The Sierra Club and the American Lung Association lent their names in support. Health Care for All helped publicize and lobby around the responsibilities of health care institutions and organized independent protest activities.[24] The coalition also secured Boston Foundation support to help organize the campaign.

Most importantly, Chinatown developed relations with other neighborhoods that had become involved in redevelopment controversies with the BRA. There had been neighborhood battles in Allston-Brighton, which was facing expansion of the Boston College football stadium. West Roxbury was fighting a proposed Home Depot facility, and a central city cross-neighborhood alliance was working against a proposed asphalt plant in Roxbury. Because Chinatown's campaign was the most sustained, intense, and active of these clashes, it mobilized a broader movement among Boston neighborhoods that demanded greater accountability in the city development process. This citywide network building put substantial pressure on the BRA to reform its practices and policies.[25] The visibility of the Parcel C campaign was critical in changing perceptions of the Chinatown neighborhood from passive and unknown to active and engaged. It also transformed a neighborhood-specific campaign into a citywide call for change.

ENVIRONMENTAL REVIEW VICTORY AND DIVERSE TACTICS

Meanwhile, the Parcel C Coalition's legal committee stayed involved in the state's environmental review process. On the last day of February 1994, T-NEMC submitted the draft EIR that the state had demanded. In response, coalition lawyers produced a lengthy list of the draft's omissions and deficiencies. Their comments, which were supported by those of other experts, moved MDEP to reject T-NEMC's draft EIR in April. MDEP required T-NEMC to file a supplementary EIR to remedy those problems and also supported a coalition request that the EIR be translated into Chinese.[26]

In the interim, the Parcel C Coalition worked to establish lines of communication with city hall. The architect Chia-Ming Sze offered to intervene with Mayor Menino to try to set up a dialogue on community concerns. But like other communication attempts, this, too, failed.[27] Despite Menino's campaign promise to meet with both sides of the garage issue, his administration did not acknowledge the coalition. Their increasing alienation was a consequence of several factors, including the CNC's dominance, the activists' break with the Chin group (Menino's close allies), and the mayor's tendency to hold grudges against those who disagreed with him. As a local columnist later observed, "personal petulance rules the day in Menino's Boston."[28]

Though the city and T-NEMC were unaware of it, the community coalition was becoming weary. The campaign had lasted for more than a year, diverting energy and resources from the already challenging work of sustaining small community organizations. Despite the activists' intensity and inventiveness, the city and the BRA remained intransigent. Increasingly impatient, coalition members made plans for a demonstration at City Hall Plaza, announcing them in *Sampan.* Zenobia Lai of GBLS spearheaded an effort among coalition lawyers to prepare associated civil rights charges against the city for discriminatory urban policies against the neighborhood. The legal team based its complaint on perceived civil rights violations under Title 8 and equal protection statutes. On October 21, 1994, the coalition communicated its intentions to the Menino administration.[29]

Three days before the planned rally at city hall, Mayor Menino made a surprising announcement: T-NEMC had withdrawn its proposal for the garage. The administration designated the parcel for neighborhood housing and turned the land over to the CCBA. Despite the victory, many in the community were still upset with how the city had managed the issue. Lydia Lowe recalled, "We had been sending a letter or making a phone call every week to the mayor's office. A few months in, that was what we decided—'Let's just send in a letter every week,' and there was never a single response to all those letters. And at the end, even when they decided not to build a garage, they wouldn't even notify us. So we were angry at the city."[30]

Larry Smith, T-NEMC's interim chief operating officer, who had dismissed the community's opposition a year earlier, blamed the Parcel C Coalition's "skillfully orchestrated media campaign and a series of high profile events" for the withdrawal of the garage proposal.[31] T-NEMC's retreat never acknowledged the neighborhood's expressed opposition and legitimate concerns, nor did the elites engage in any serious dialogue about them. The coalition concluded the campaign by organizing a victory march and later a community banquet.

THE FIRST EFFECTS OF THE PARCEL C CAMPAIGN

Following the campaign, the Parcel C Coalition transformed itself into the Campaign to Protect Chinatown (CPC) to deal with land issues in the neighborhood. It was now comprised of a smaller core of activists who engaged in urban environmental and neighborhood research and resident organizing.[32] Yet a gulf remained between Chinatown's residents and the community's social structure. In 1994, T-NEMC developed a twenty-year plan for development that challenged the boundaries drawn by the Chinatown master plan. It included expansion into the east side of Tyler Street and new research facilities on the remainder of the east side of Harrison Avenue down to Tai Tung Village. The plan also proposed building a shell for the South Cove YMCA, which for twenty years had conducted programs in a pressurized fabric structure. The BRA and the CNC approved.

The new plan, revealed just as the Parcel C controversy was being resolved, did not provoke the same response as the garage had. Many of the Parcel C campaign's leaders were exhausted and reluctant to engage themselves so soon in yet another battle. They also recognized the needs of the Chinatown Y. Nonetheless, the medical center expansion plan was potentially divisive.[33] Neil Chin, who lived close to Oak Street, pointed out to the CNC that it was a violation of the Chinatown master plan. Elena Choy, who lived on Harvard Street with her mother, had been unaware of the plan before the council approved it and expressed anger at how the decision had been made.[34] Henry Yee of the Tai Tung Tenants Association unsuccessfully approached organizations to try to stop the plan. Clearly, there were few mechanisms in place to ensure accountability to resident voices within organizational structures. To date, T-NEMC has realized only the Harrison Street construction described in its plan. The east side of Tyler, where the Y bubble once stood, remains vacant and is used as a parking area.

After three years, CCBA failed to advance the development of the Parcel C site. With BRA support, other community leaders initiated an open dialogue about the parcel. In February 1998, ACDC and CPC collaborated to create a community process for decision making around the site.[35] Eventually, Parcel C became the proposed Metropolitan development, and ACDC and Edward Fish Associates became the developers.

ACDC and Fish Associates designed the Metropolitan to be a twenty-three-story mixed-use project, 46 percent of which would be affordable residential units. The remainder were market-rate and luxury units. The scale and composition became a source of tension between the developers and the activists who had fought for Parcel C. ACDC had adopted a "new urbanist" vision of Chinatown that embraced a multi-class, mixed-use community in contrast to Chinatown's traditional role as a haven for working people.[36] The Metropolitan far exceeded the Chinatown master plan's height regulations, and most occupants would be higher-income residents. ACDC, moreover, was a junior partner to the private developers, whom it needed to fund and complete projects. The project nevertheless increased the units available for working people. It was completed in 2004, and both ACDC and CPA were to claim organizational space within the development.[37]

In 1996, the community applied the mobilization lessons from Parcel C in a successful campaign against a proposed Interstate 93 exit ramp called ramp DD, part of a large-scale project to move the city's central artery underground. The state's Department of Transportation had designed the ramp to exit onto Marginal Road, which bordered the Quincy School.[38] A coalition called the Chinatown Central Artery/ Tunnel Task Force formed to fight the ramp, modeling its tactics on those of the Parcel C Coalition. Unlike the Parcel C controversy, the community was unanimous in its opposition to ramp DD. The coalition organized marches, lobbying, a media strategy, negotiations, and public protests, including a parade of two hundred community members to the state house. Residents vowed to lie down in front of the bulldozers. With the help of the city, planners rerouted the ramp.[39]

THE COMMUNITY FINDS A VOICE IN THE CITY

Chinatown grew in intangible ways through the Parcel C organizing process. The mobilization was vital in developing social capital, capabilities, leadership, and relationships in the community. Historically, it was the neighborhood's broadest mobilization in response to its many land issues. In Zenobia Lai's eyes, it established the progressive organizations as "key players in community politics" and incorporated residents into civic activism in an unprecedented manner, "every step of the way."[40] The Chinatown community realized its strengths in building widespread and sustained mobilization using a wide variety of methods, and its efforts established new relationships among different community groups.

Chinatown's new identity demonstrated that the neighborhood, despite its divisions, had evolved into a community that could claim and assert its perceived rights. It had centers of leadership other than the traditional associations of the pre–World War II community and the postwar ward bosses. It was a neighborhood that could reflect on and articulate a distinct vision for its future. Those who would have been most affected by the garage—the residents—were now at the center of decision making.

The Parcel C campaign renegotiated Chinatown's relationships with the rest of the city. The community drew a line regarding T-NEMC expansion: it would end at Nassau and Oak streets. As Tom O'Malley, Barrett's successor at the BRA, said, "The community and their response to the garage sent a very decisive message, even if it was not only contentious but divisive at the time, that it had to be a holistic community process. . . . The institutions are no longer going to expand in that direction. The housing is going to be permanently affordable."[41] T-NEMC learned a lesson and became more cautious in how it worked with the community. Since then, it has not directly confronted Chinatown around a development project. It has also paid more attention to its relations to the neighborhood and has hired local Chinese Americans as community liaisons.

The campaign also altered Chinatown's relationship with city authorities. Lydia Lowe observed that the referendum made politicians take notice of groups beyond the Chin allies and start to work with them. It signaled to the city that public bodies had to communicate more broadly and engage a more diverse set of stakeholders beyond the CNC. The city began to engage in more public processes around development; it translated documents and provided interpreters at hearings. This was a sea change—a recognition that residents had a legitimate voice.[42]

Chinatown's relations with other mobilized neighborhoods changed as well. Now perceived as one of the most active communities, it became a meaningful participant in citywide neighborhood issues. Other neighborhoods began to call on Chinatown to join cross-neighborhood initiatives.

But there were negative effects as well. Among the harmful results of the Parcel C campaign was the opening of old wounds. The campaign had exposed the attitudes and weaknesses of the CNC and provoked very public divisions in neighborhood attitudes toward growth. These divisions would allow the growth coalition to nominally comply with a policy of neighborhood oversight while violating it in practice. Development forces could always point to a partner in the community that favored a proposed project.

Another effect of the Parcel C and ramp DD mobilizations was the strain the campaign imposed on the neighborhood's organizing resources. The active organizations were all small groups, most with a staff that numbered in single digits. They had to reallocate resources away from their established campaigns and programs to organize around development issues. Their investment provided the day-to-day coordination structure for the campaign, and much of the energy came from community volunteers outside the neighborhood. Law students, activists, and other bodies supplemented the young, elderly, and abutting residents. While residents came to invest themselves in neighborhood development, organizations continued to play the leading role in mobilization efforts. This tension between the residents and organizations was evident in the responses to T-NEMC's new plan, with residents wanting to fight and organizations feeling that they lacked the capacity.

The scholar Manuel Castells has defined urban movements as a fight for residents' use values rather than the city's exchange values, the maintenance of autonomous local culture, and the search for increasing power in local government. Chinatown's mobilization had transcended protest and deepened in all three of these aspects. It had also begun to overcome the limitations that Castells saw in many urban movements by coupling its issues with those of other groups in the city.[43] The neighborhood's Parcel C and ramp DD actions demonstrated that it was capable of conducting very sophisticated campaigns. The community refined its use of existing mobilization methods, making the Parcel C issue the dominant development story in the city for eighteen months. It was, as Suzanne Lee observed, "the accumulation of many years of organizing work."[44]

The strengths of Chinatown's evolving organizing efforts were most effective in counteracting the harmful effects of growth but not generating positive growth. It could preserve some of the housing units and community spaces but did not often contribute to creating additional housing. Community development entities such as ACDC, on the other hand, were making incremental additions to sustaining Chinatown's working-class heart while simultaneously diluting it. Projects such as the Metropolitan provided some affordable housing but also brought newer and wealthier people into the neighborhood.

Chinatown thus remained divided. Within the neighborhood, many residents began to question growth and to look at the details of growth plans. A number of them, particularly those who had opposed the Parcel C garage, concluded that alternatives to growth strategies were necessary. Others, who saw no such options, pined for the return of optimal growth conditions, a supportive policy, and a dynamic development environment. In difficult times they felt the neighborhood must sacrifice more to support development projects. Another sector in the community occupied the middle ground and sought to combine support for growth with planning for the neighborhood.

Chinatown, while learning to value collaboration, had not yet found an arrangement for sustaining working unity within the community. Sharp divisions still divided those who had fought the garage, those who had stayed neutral on the issue, and those who had supported it. Whether the neighborhood could resolve these issues and elevate its work in a transformative direction to meet its needs within a growth machine environment is a question that would have to unfold.

CHAPTER 8

BUILDING NEW ALLIANCES, 1999–2007

A half-century of urban-renewal development had transformed Boston. Downtown was now an array of tall office buildings and residential towers. German, Canadian, and Saudi investors had bought shares in many of these buildings, and there were plans for eight new hotels. Emblematic of these changes was Millennium Place, downtown's largest mixed-use development since the 1980s. It included the Ritz-Carlton Hotel, a new movie complex, apartments, and condominiums as well as fitness clubs and shops for upscale clientele.[1]

TIMELINE 6. Chinatown's New Alliances

1999	ABN and CRA founded
2001	Liberty Place campaign organized.
2002	Chinatown settles with Liberty Place developer; city recognizes CRA.
	Civic Engagement Initiative funded.
2003	Gaiety Theatre campaign organized.
	AALDEF and CPA charge voter coercion.
	New Majority Coalition organized.
	Campaign for Parcel 24 organized.
2004	Metropolitan project on Parcel C completed.
2005	U.S. Department of Justice finds city deficient on voting-rights issues; two-year oversight ordered.
2006	Yoon and Team Unity slate elected to city council.

As development continued energetically downtown, it also spread throughout much of the city. A spine of hotels, office buildings, and residences ran through the upscale Back Bay. Large-scale development had changed the thousand-acre Seaport District in South Boston—the city's last sparsely settled area, once a bastion of old warehouses and wharves. Institutions such as the *Boston Globe,* Massachusetts Institute of Technology, banks, development companies, and government agencies had promoted this "last frontier," which now held three times more commercial space than had been available during the real estate boom of the Flynn years. They opened a federal courthouse, a convention facility, and an "innovation district" and began to plan for microunits to house the young tech workers flooding into downtown and the Seaport.[2]

But the growing popularity of city living led to unwelcome developments in other neighborhoods and created a housing crisis throughout Boston. Vacancy rates hovered between 1 and 2 percent. In 1999, the University of Massachusetts Boston hosted a panel on gentrification in the city, and one participant revealed that one hundred Boston families received eviction notices every day. Housing activists were struggling with the speed at which developers were paying off mortgages on federally subsidized housing projects built during the 1960s. These settlements allowed them to charge market-rate prices for apartments such as Brighton's Village Manor, where monthly rents had skyrocketed from $337 to $1,166. Homelessness in Massachusetts doubled between 1995 and 1999. Rents in Boston nearly doubled between 1995 and 2000: costs now exceeded those in New York and Los Angeles, trailing only Honolulu and San Francisco. Housing prices were out of reach of families earning a median income.[3]

Chinatown, Jamaica Plain, Mission Hill, the Fenway, and sections of Roxbury faced the most change in these years. The *Improper Bostonian,* a city magazine, featured a cover article titled "The New Face of Chinatown: Lured by the Cheap Rents and An Electric 24/7 Energy Found Nowhere Else in Town, Hip Bostonians Are Flocking to Chinatown to Live."[4] Previously overlooked neighborhoods such as Allston, once mostly composed of inexpensive student housing, now included an "eco-district" in which developers charged twice the area's average rents.

The growing city was also becoming more diverse. Its population of Asians, Latinos, and, to a lesser extent, African Americans was increasing faster than the white population was. By 2000, the census category "non-Hispanic whites" was, for the first time, a minority in Boston. They now formed less than half of the total population, and their numbers had dropped by more than 10 percent since the 1990 census.[5] In the meantime, the Asian American population had grown sharply, rising from 5 to 8 percent, and Latinos had risen from 11 to 14 percent. The African American population was growing more slowly, but it still formed about a quarter of the city's population. Nevertheless, compared to the white population, Boston's nonwhite residents had lower percentages of citizenship and were more divided in their political views. Because whites continued to go to the polls, they largely determined election results.

Consequently, there were signs of renewed neighborhood activism. In 1999, the Alliance of Boston Neighborhoods (ABN) formed to advocate for changes in the development process. It attracted representatives from twenty-nine neighborhood associations, stretching from Charlestown in the north to Dorchester in the south. Advocates began resurrecting proposals for rent control. Tenants' groups, supported by Mayor Menino, proposed a home rule petition in 2002, which required the approval of city council and the state legislature. Yet despite fierce organizing and support from the councilors of color, the city council voted down the petition that year and again in 2004.[6]

After a record ten-year expansion, the nation's economy began contracting in early 2001. Still, the subsequent recovery was earlier and more robust in information-economy cities such as Boston than it was in the rest of the country; and developers were ready to suggest new projects.[7] Boston's economy had been relatively insulated during the downturn. Financial services such as Fidelity Investments and Putnam Investments had exploded in the city during the 1990s boom. Boston had also become more technology- and knowledge-based, and it was now a center for management consulting, software, research universities, and biotech. In 1992, Genzyme opened an imposing $110 million manufacturing facility in Allston, overlooking the Massachusetts Turnpike. Biogen was thriving across the river in Cambridge. Health and education industries also continued to play powerful, growing roles in the local economy and kept expanding throughout the metropolitan area.

THE NEIGHBORHOOD

The new millennium proved to be a particularly intense period for Chinatown. The urban environment and forces within the neighborhood provoked numerous turning points, and new alignments developed within the community and between local organizations and groups outside the neighborhood. In 2000, Chinatown issued a second master plan—published as "Masterplan 2000"—that reaffirmed the 1990 plan's goals and summarized the progress that Chinatown had made since then. Most notable for the neighborhood's 5,100 residents were the shrinkage of the Combat Zone and the construction of 145 new housing units. However, that number was well short of the 1990 master plan's goal of 500, and the shortage was a particular problem given the doubling of Boston's Chinese population in the ensuing ten years. The "Masterplan" also noted the improved working relationship between T-NEMC and Chinatown and an increase in the number and types of businesses in the community.

Nevertheless, the 2000 plan outlined many failures. Chinatown remained relatively isolated, with few physical connections to adjoining communities. The plan also identified insufficient affordable housing and a reduction in employment opportunities, which kept new immigrants restricted to restaurants and hospitality. Fifty percent of Chinatown's geographic area was occupied by T-NEMC or paved over for parking lots. In short, while there were some positive changes, the community had not solved the core challenges of ensuring a sustainable and growing residential neighborhood.[8]

Amid these ongoing issues, the community's leadership was transitioning. Though the Chin brothers had reached retirement age, they remained active and showed little progress in grooming successors. Bill Moy continued to head the Chinatown Neighborhood Council (CNC). Suzanne Lee became the principal of the Josiah Quincy Elementary School. Lydia Lowe was now a mother with two daughters, but she maintained her steady leadership of the Chinese Progressive Association (CPA). Younger leaders emerged during this period. Elaine Ng, the daughter of Donald Ng, who had represented Asian Americans in the Third World Jobs Clearinghouse in the 1970s, became the new director of the Boston Chinatown Neighborhood Center (BCNC) in 2006. A tough, smart director, she led her organization in the mode of her predecessor, David Moy. Jeremy Liu took charge of the Asian Community Development Corporation (ACDC) and infused arts and other activities into its new urbanist vision of the neighborhood. The Asian American Resource Workshop went through a period of decline but continued to attract young English-speaking and non-Chinese American activists. There, too, a new leadership generation was emerging.

Activism had a new center. CPA was able to drive a capital campaign that allowed it to lobby for and buy commercial office space in the Metropolitan complex on Parcel C. This permanent home helped stabilize the group and solidified its role as the center of local neighborhood activism. CPA's base created a new reality for grassroots groups such as the Workshop and the Chinatown Resident Association (CRA), which had often moved offices due to the shifting currents of the neighborhood real estate market. The Workshop and API Movement, a new political collective, both began informally operating out of the premises, and the Boston Chinatown Neighborhood Center (BCNC) was next door. These facilities, all part of the Metropolitan complex, became the new physical heart of organizing in Chinatown. Grassroots mobilizing now shifted from active, multi-organizational alliances to CPA-led initiatives.

Younger immigrant leaders emerged within the Chinese Consolidated Benevolent Association (CCBA). Their goal was to identify new strategies to build on the organization's traditional dominance within the community. Significantly, these emerging leaders, such as Wilson Lee and Robert Leung, sustained the organization's internal tensions between Chin loyalists and their foes.[9] One manifestation of this was CCBA's absence from the Chinese New Year parade, in which it had played a significant role for more than a century. People allied with the Chins took charge of the event and excluded the CCBA.[10]

Another front in this conflict involved long-standing issues about space for community organizations. A public, multiyear dispute arose between Kwong Kow Chinese School and CCBA. The Kwong Kow School rented the CCBA's premises, and Billy Chin sat on the school's board. The school and CCBA became caught up in the disagreements over rent and the governance of the school that resulted in several court appearances. The conflict precipitated a demonstration organized by 1,500 of Kwong Kow's alumni, students, and supporters. The show of force was the largest in the neighborhood since the anti-Japanese protests before World War II. In 2000, the tension forced the school to vacate what had been its home for the past sixteen years in thirty-six hours. AACA had also left because of similar conflicts with CCBA.[11] It took several years before both the Kwong Kow and AACA could build a new permanent home across the street.

The South Cove Y also finally found a new permanent home, in new facilities on the west flank of Chinatown. The developer Corcoran Jennison obtained control of a closed Catholic complex, the Don Bosco Technical High School, from the BRA. It proposed new construction, but the BRA retained one building, which it leased to the YMCA. The South Cove Y, renamed the Wang YMCA, expanded its domain to serve a growing downtown population rather than solely the Chinatown neighborhood. Richard Chin now served under another layer of administration.[12]

As community leaders were grappling with internal tensions, Chinatown continued to deal with development pressures that threatened its social and cultural fabric. One such project was Kensington Place, a thirty-one-story luxury housing development proposed for the side of Washington Street that faced Chinatown. It was one of five major development projects in the Chinatown/downtown area that would increase high-end housing in the neighborhood to nearly half of all units. The Kensington proposal, located in the Midtown Cultural District, was constrained by zoning regulations that limited the height of buildings with a footprint of an acre or less to no more than 155 feet. However, the city, determined to support the developers, had given the project a special variance that allowed them include city sidewalks, streets, and other adjoining private property within the building's footprint so that it would not have to abide by the height restriction. The city also promised to take two private adjoining parcels by eminent domain to create the acre site.[13]

To fight the project, Chinatown activists expanded their work with the ABN and the city's preservation groups. Preservationists and African American artists were particularly concerned about the Gaiety Theatre, which currently occupied the proposed site. The theater had achieved prominence during the Jazz Age for hosting African American burlesque shows, and they did not want it to be razed. ACDC, hoping to develop the site into a project that included housing, also joined the campaign. The campaign organized demonstrations and gained some media attention, including a film made by students at Emerson College.[14] However, before the activists could achieve their goal of getting a hearing, the Kensington project developers knocked down the Gaiety. Steve Bailey, a *Boston Globe* business columnist, expressed his outrage in a December 2003 column: "The BRA is out of control, Kensington Place providing only the most recent example. It is an organization willing to game the system to get what the mayor wants. It holds endless community meetings but never wavers from its appointed mission. Its 'master plans' are good until the next developer wants in the door. The money, the power, are always on the side of building bigger, not smaller. The opposition, with neither money nor power, can't fight City Hall."[15]

Alongside these existing concerns, a new series of development issues arose. One was a proposal to build another mixed-use tower, initially known as Liberty Plaza, on the corner of Beach and Washington streets. In late 2004, the Massachusetts Turnpike Authority also began to consider developing a ten-acre site located where the Interstate 93 and the Mass Pike highway ramps went underground on Kneeland Street, between Lincoln and Hudson streets. The concept was a new neighborhood called Gateway Center, designed to welcome motorists into the city, and its land area would be one-fifth the size of the formally recognized Chinatown District. Then, in 2007, the BRA approved the controversial Dainty Dot development project in northern Chinatown at the corner of Essex and Kingston streets. The Dainty Dot Hosiery building was a large, historic garment-factory building built in the 1880s. The developer proposed erecting a twenty-seven-story residential structure containing market-rate condominiums on the site. The proposal both violated the Chinatown master plan and required the demolition of a historic building.[16] As with previous projects, many people protested the construction of a building that was four times larger than the zoning regulations allowed.

Already, in 2003, a coalition of Chinatown organizations, including ACDC, the Chinese Economic Development Council (CEDC), and CPA, had been working to counterbalance these trends. They began with a campaign for Parcel 24, located across from the remaining side of Hudson Street, which they intended to use as a site for Chinatown housing. Forty years ago, the land had been taken when the state was building the central artery and the turnpike extension. But after the turnpike authority relocated some structures during its Big Dig project, the parcel became available for development, and Chinatown activists staged a "speak out" to reclaim it. "The community deserves some kind of reparations for what happened to the neighborhood in the past," said Lydia Lowe. "We'll take that in the form of returning Parcel 24."[17] The campaign was different from other recent battles in that it targeted a semipublic entity rather than a private institution or developer. Typically, Bill Moy of the CNC spoke out against the campaign, but other stakeholders were supportive. The coalition organized public protests and enlisted legislators' support. Even the BRA cooperated with Chinatown against the turnpike authority; and, in 2005, the turnpike officials agreed to offer a discounted ground lease to a development partnership that included ACDC.[18]

As a result of Big Dig tunnel construction, activists were also able to garner new open space in the neighborhood. Chinatown Park, on the eastern edge of commercial Chinatown, featured displays, benches, and a play structure. It also had a small bamboo grove that shielded the neighborhood from the thirty-five-story Kingston-Bedford building, now known as the State Street Financial Center.[19]

FINDING THE ROAD FORWARD: MORE THAN CHINATOWN

Unable to find a sustainable solution to the development pressures on Chinatown, activists searched for another road forward. They began by focusing specifically on the needs of neighborhood residents. Recalling how the Menino administration had stonewalled members of the community during the Parcel C controversy, CPA and the Campaign to Protect Chinatown (CPC) began to recognize the importance of organizing residents to advocate directly for Chinatown's future. Thus, in 1999, they formed the Chinatown Resident Association (CRA). Their place-based focus on neighborhood residents was a shift away from seeing Chinatown primarily as the center of greater Boston's Chinese community. The new coalition began to focus more on Chinatown as a place where people lived and faced specific neighborhood issues. As longtime neighborhood activist Neil Chin noted during an organizing meeting with residents, "when was the last time that anyone came to ask you for your opinion about what should happen in Chinatown?"[20]

A few local housing complexes did have tenants' associations, but there had been no neighborhood-wide forum to elevate resident voices. Now the newly formed CRA would give residents leverage to challenge the nonresident-dominated CNC. An increasing proportion of Chinatown residents were elderly, and they began to play a crucial role in neighborhood organizing. For Mah Wah, a former waiter living in one of the South Cove elder-housing projects, this was an opportunity to respond to the racism and inequities that he and his peers had experienced for their entire lives.[21] Groups of elderly residents began to attend hearings and meetings, despite the fact that these gatherings were inconsistently translated. Despite problems with comprehension, they were determined to show solidarity about issues that mattered to them.[22]

The Liberty Plaza project, renamed Liberty Place, was an initial focus for CRA. Kevin Fitzgerald, the owner of numerous parking lots in the area around Chinatown, saw it as a way to profit from the growing popularity of urban living. In 2002, he proposed a twenty-six-story apartment tower with more than 400 apartments and 468 parking spaces. Located the corner of Beach and Washington streets, the site was within the designated borders of the Chinatown master plan that restricted buildings to eight stories or less.[23]

Several organizations, including the Workshop, CPA, CPC, and CRA, began mobilizing against the development. Alternatives for Community and Environment (ACE), an environmental justice organization in Roxbury, supported them. As in other recent campaigns, activists packed hearings to demand a voice, organized numerous rallies, and sent letters and petitions. But Fitzgerald had learned from past confrontations: he parceled out benefits to various neighborhood groups to gain support and helped finance new residential units for the Golden Age Center.

In a replay of the lines drawn during the Parcel C controversy, the CNC, business leaders, and a couple of the benefiting agencies supported the project. This was no surprise: activists now expected these entities to support developers. As the *Boston Globe* noted, "in recent years, the council has supported every major project built or proposed in the area; it approved Liberty Place unanimously, arguing that its higher-end housing will attract former residents back to Chinatown. The council has earned the label, among residents, of a rubber stamp for development in a community dominated by immigrants earning low wages."[24] The BRA and the mayor also actively supported the development.

The campaign met one institutional obstacle after another. After months of protest, the developer agreed to only a small reduction in the building's size and an increase in its proportion of affordable units, from 5 percent to 10 percent. Organizers responded by accelerating their tactics. "Respect the Master Plan," became their slogan, often printed on placards held up at hearings and community meetings. Representing the CPC, Greater Boston Legal Services (GBLS), argued, "Now that middle class America finds urban living desirable, Chinatown is once again asked to make room for them, so that they can walk to theaters or their upscale offices in downtown. Fifty years of accommodating the needs of middle class America is enough. . . . Chinatown demands that its master plan be respected."[25]

A central question was whether the Chinatown master plan, which represented years of work by both the city and the neighborhood, had any power to guide future development. Residents called on the city to honor their joint plan. Activists organized elaborate street performances, which depicted wealthy developers in top hats and tails, supported by city agents, evicting residents. To illustrate the effect of the proposed tower on increased traffic, the coalition organized a "car jam," circling two hundred honking cars around the Liberty Place block for an entire day. Mayor Menino was chauffeured close to the protest to observe the commotion but left without comment.

Using a tactic drawn from the Parcel C campaign, Chinatown residents and community activists demanded a referendum. After the expected BRA refusal, they launched their own amid a heated battle. The referendum asked voters to weigh in on three issues: approving the proposed Liberty Place project, rezoning the adult entertainment district,

FIGURE 11. Karen Chen and Jian Hua Tang at the election polls, November 2016. Courtesy of Northeastern University Libraries, Archives and Special Collections.

and recognizing an incorporated resident association to review and offer recommendations on development proposals that affected Chinatown. The American Friends Service Committee and the League of Women Voters agreed to monitor the vote. Although BRA representatives and Liberty Place principals claimed that most Chinatown residents supported Liberty Place (and undertook a well-funded counter-campaign against the organizers), voters opposed the project by a three-to-one ratio. By even larger margins, they approved rezoning the Combat Zone and establishing a resident review procedure for development proposals.

"We have won this battle, but the revolution is not over," said Henry Yee, CRA's president and a long-time resident of Tai Tung Village. "The residents have voted against the project, and now we need to take our message to the Zoning Board of Appeals." As expected, neither the mayor nor the board honored the residents' wishes. The developer, however, increased the affordable units to 15 percent of the total and changed ten moderate-income units into subsidized Section 8 units that most Chinatown residents could afford to rent.[26]

After nearly a year of battling the developer and the city, the Chinatown activists recognized that their options were dwindling. In December 2002, they agreed to a settlement. In that agreement, the city of Boston accepted that the CRA or a representative neighborhood council would have an authority equivalent to the CNC's. The Liberty Place developer granted $575,000 and the city $75,000 to a specially designated fund to develop thirty units of permanently affordable, low-income, single-room-occupancy housing in Chinatown. The city also agreed to help secure a site and financing and to make good-faith efforts to ensure that the project would be developed within two years. CPA would have veto power over the terms of the project and its developer. The city also agreed to discuss the future implementation of the Chinatown master plan.

The establishment of a city-recognized Chinatown resident council was a major political victory, though it came at a considerable price: dropping opposition to Liberty Place. In the past, the primarily non-resident CNC had served as the city's community advisory body on development issues in the neighborhood. But as CRA co-chair Marie Moy argued, "Chinatown residents are the most affected by development. It is only right that residents should have a voice in neighborhood affairs." In an editorial, the *Boston Globe* noted:

> Bill Moy, the familiar Chinatown leader and co-moderator of the Chinatown Neighborhood Council, remained outside the heated tent, literally and figuratively, on Monday when Mayor Menino praised the settlement. . . . Regardless of bruised feelings, there is a new political force in Chinatown. It recognizes that the traditional Chinatown could cease to exist if residential and commercial development spreads unchecked.[27]

A local philanthropic initiative opened another new road for neighborhood activists. Progressive nonprofits such as the Hyams and Miller foundations embraced the idea that political power was an element in reviving poor neighborhoods. In 2002, they began funding voter participation initiatives in Roxbury, Dorchester, Allston, Jamaica Plain, and Chinatown. CPA was their Chinatown recipient. While CPA had become increasingly active in electoral affairs, foundation support helped them focus their efforts. By later that year, Chinatown's electoral turnout had increased by 70 percent, the largest percentage gain in the city. Lowe noted in the local newspaper that this was the third consecutive year of historically high turnout, though, like other neighborhoods of color, Chinatown still lagged behind the overall city average.[28]

CPA conducted door-to-door canvassing in Chinatown. While remaining nonpartisan, it offered bilingual workshops and materials about the electoral process, the structure of government, and candidate histories and stances on issues. CPA both expanded the electorate and improved residents' ability to cast informed votes. The approach, which CPA had been building over time, was another challenge to the Chin apparatus—a sign that increasingly contested elections would pit an education and empowerment strategy against a patronage-based one.

One tactic that annoyed the Chin apparatus was CPA's continuous monitoring of elections to assure that "translators" did not pull the levers for the residents. A confrontation over this issue boiled over in 2003, when election observers, including some from the New York–based

Asian American Legal Defense and Education Fund, identified voter coercion of immigrant voters. Chinese-speaking voters reported that election workers had pressured them to vote for specific candidates and had filled out ballots for them. Similar issues were arising in other minority and immigrant neighborhoods in Boston. A subsequent state investigation found numerous and repeated violations of election law. Based on an examination of these complaints and others, a 2005 lawsuit by the U.S. Department of Justice charged that the city had denied the rights of Chinese, Vietnamese, and Latino voters with limited English skills. A truculent city administration eventually agreed to a settlement that included federal oversight over Boston elections until 2007.[29]

Community activism was also building on the citywide ties that Chinatown activists had established during the Mel King campaign and the Parcel C and Long Guang Huang mobilizations. One of their first cross-neighborhood ventures was the New Majority Coalition, an attempt to resurrect the Rainbow Coalition concept while taking advantage of changing demographics to highlight inequities in the city. In 2003, prompted by African American city councilor Chuck Turner, several race- and ethnic-based research institutes at the University of Massachusetts Boston initiated a process to establish the new community coalition. The vision for New Majority was to use it to create meaningful strategies that reflected the new demographic realities of a majority-minority Boston.[30] Member organizations included CPA, the Dudley Street Neighborhood Initiative (DSNI), the Association of Community Organizations for Reform Now, as well as tenant, Muslim, Latino, and voting rights groups. The coalition quickly went to work to elect candidates of color, including Felix Arroyo, Sr., to the city council and Andrea Cabral to the Suffolk County sheriff's office.

As the New Majority Coalition moved out of the university and into the communities, it faced numerous leadership and organizational challenges. By 2006, the community groups had assumed command and developed an agenda that covered affordable housing, funding for youth jobs, a civilian review board of police practices, law reform, and more diverse staff in the Boston public schools. CPA, which was organizationally more stable than the other groups were, stepped forward to provide some leadership. But the coalition remained fragile. It struggled along for some years, participating in a few election cycles before expiring. Despite its failure to find a sustainable model, it did create a new template for citywide work through electoral mobilization and multiracial alliances.[31]

CPA then became involved in other citywide partnerships, including the Alliance of Boston Neighborhoods, whose mission was to "serve as the voice of neighborhood interests" and "coordinate . . . in matters dealing with neighborhood concerns." ABN took direct aim at the BRA. Led by Shirley Kressel, a Back Bay landscape architect, the alliance connected numerous civic groups in neighborhoods where the BRA had promoted development. One goal was to change the BRA's charter: to separate its planning role from its development function, as was the case in most cities. ABN argued that the city should disband the BRA and publicly called for this change.[32] While it never realized this goal, it did raise awareness by providing a visible, critical view of the BRA and its role in the city.

During the 2005 city elections, Sam Yoon, a Korean American who was working at ACDC, ran for an at-large city council seat—the first Asian American to ever compete for city office. At that time, there were three councilors of color—African Americans Chuck Turner and Charles Yancey, who represented their predominantly Black and Latino districts, and Felix Arroyo, Sr., a Latino who held an at-large seat. To elevate the interests of people of color and promote a progressive presence on the thirteen-member council, the three formed a slate, Team Unity, and embraced Yoon. All three incumbents were confident of reelection, and they used Team Unity to make a bold statement about people of color's dissatisfaction with the status quo and the powerful Menino administration. Each member of the team, including Yoon, won election. Though it ultimately failed to shift the council's balance of power, Team Unity was another step in reinforcing greater community involvement in electoral politics, reflecting Boston's growing Asian American population, and demonstrating that the city's electorate was open to Asian American candidates.[33]

As the nation fell into a deep recession in 2008, activists gathered together the elements of a new mobilization approach, one that combined organizing, electoral mobilization, and citywide alliances to address community needs and social injustice in Boston. The Liberty Place campaign had demonstrated that public commitments, as enshrined in documents such as the Chinatown master plan, were situational; the neighborhood had to deploy other forms of power to ensure their realization. Activists, primarily led by CPA, began using mobilization more selectively, carefully weighing chances of success and potential neighborhood benefits against the damaging effects on the community. By mobilizing Chinatown voters, CPA had some success in changing the balance of power. While finding allies in the community was challenging, the coalition had many interests and viewpoints in common with other groups whose neighborhoods were threatened by gentrification. These citywide alliances also influenced broader civic discourse and the positions of decision makers.

BUBBLE, TROUBLE, AND TESTING A NEW VISION, 2008–2014

When the housing bubble burst in 2008, the resulting recession disrupted the economy nationally and locally. Massachusetts suffered a sharp rise in unemployment, which rose to nearly 9 percent. In Boston, development projects came to a halt. For instance, new construction on the site of the former Filene's department store stalled for lack of investors, leaving a vast empty pit in the middle of the city that embarrassed the Menino administration. In the northeastern corner of Chinatown, the Dainty Dot project, now called the Radian, failed to move forward for several years because of a lack of financing. Hospitals and educational institutions temporarily shelved their expansion plans.[1]

Employment in the city plummeted. Shortly after the 2008 presidential election, Fidelity laid off 1,300 people; and Putnam Investments, MFS Investment Management, and Bank of America soon followed suit. Eventually, there were more than 11,000 layoffs in the state's finance and insurance industries. Other businesses, including law firms, technology companies, publishing houses, construction, and retail stores, also laid off employees or closed altogether.[2]

Lower-income workers and residents faced the greatest challenges. In addition to dealing with layoffs, many immigrant workers were not getting paid because their employers were withholding their wages. In 2008, the Chinese Progressive Association (CPA) reported that a number of Chinese restaurants, Asian groceries, and Chinatown bus companies owed their workers up to four months of back pay.[3] Homeowners who had been victims of predatory lending, particularly in neighborhoods of color such as Roxbury, Dorchester, Mattapan, and East Boston, struggled to pay their mortgages as incomes declined or vanished. Homes and condominiums became more difficult to purchase as banks became hesitant to offer mortgages. Because Chinatown residents were primarily renters, they were less affected by the housing market, but protests and blockades became increasingly prevalent in Boston's other communities of color.[4]

Despite these challenges, Boston continued to benefit from a diverse economic base across the health, education, biotechnology, finance, insurance, science, and technology sectors. Thus, it was, on the whole, less vulnerable than other U.S. cities were. With the help of new federal stimulus tools, the local economy was officially out of recession by 2009.[5] At the same time, fewer people were drawn to the notion of owning a large suburban home and commuting into the city. They preferred living in a dense urban environment close to the city's jobs and cultural life. Many embraced a new rental lifestyle, and developers began move forward again, announcing plans to convert condominium projects into luxury rentals to take advantage of this resurgent market.[6]

Once again, Chinatown's central downtown location made it the focus of new projects, most of them market-rate rental complexes. The twenty-six-story Radian changed a large proportion of its planned condominiums into rental units. The Kensington opened on Washington Street. The *Boston Herald* building, located in the old New York Streets area in the South End, went up for sale. National Development purchased it and proposed the enormous Ink Block project. It would include Siena Boston (featuring luxury private-access maisonettes), three structures of market-rate rental apartments, and a 50,000-square-foot Whole Foods Market. Two other buildings, one containing the AC Hotel, would complete the project. Across the street at 345 Harrison Street, a massive block-wide project of 602 apartments and commercial space was in the works. The BRA had ten projects in the pipeline for the Chinatown area alone.[7] The recession had slowed development plans in the neighborhood—but only briefly.

TIMELINE 7. A New Vision for Chinatown

2005	Immigrant Workers Centers Collaborative is formed.
2007	Right to the City Coalition is formed.
2010	State legislature makes bilingual ballots permanent.
	Third Chinatown master plan is issued.
2011	Suzanne Lee runs for city council, is defeated; CPA creates the CPPA political action committee.
2013	Right to the City Vote is established.
	Mayor Marty Walsh is elected.
2014	Community land trust is created.
	Community reports that affordable housing is stable, new housing overwhelmingly high-income.

A NEW RESPONSE TO DEVELOPMENT

In 2010, the community revised the Chinatown master plan for a third time. The new plan reflected the changing community and changing boundaries, which now extended eastward down Kneeland Street toward the old railyard area and southward into the South End. This expanded footprint encompassed pending development projects in the Ink Block area and the Gateway District, also called South Bay. The third master plan noted that Chinatown had fewer families now that 70 percent of the housing in the neighborhood was upscale studio and one-bedroom apartments. At the same time, its population had increased by nearly a thousand people, the bulk of them higher-income and non-Chinese.[8]

Chinatown's historic rowhouses were beginning to attract land speculators. In 2014, simple three- and four-family brick houses sold for between $700,000 and $900,000. In 2015, similar rowhouses sold for $1.26 million. Looking to profit from the houses' central downtown location, developers were converting them into single-family homes or Airbnb rentals. Other developers renovated the structures to the limits of their lot sizes and building heights. The apartments became housing for students and professionals.[9]

Despite a multiyear delay caused by the recession, the Asian Community Development Corporation (ACDC) was able to move forward on One Greenway, its Parcel 24 project on the demolished flank of Hudson Street. The project included a twenty-story, 363-unit, mixed-income housing structure. While it offered significantly more affordable units than other new developments did, the majority were still market-rate. The Parcel 24 plan also included fifty-one affordable condominiums in a separate building. Angie Liou, ACDC's executive director, reflected on the difficulties of working with New Boston (its for-profit partner) and supporting affordable housing:

> For them, if the market dips, they have to go change the program. That's what happened with Parcel 24. Part of the reason that program took so long was . . . the downturn, [when] New Boston decided that they needed to go back and change the program, and that provides a level of complication to the project. We had to agree on things together. I think, as an organization, I would say that it's no small feat that we got to do [the Metropolitan] and Parcel 24.[10]

From the Radian project, the BRA's new inclusionary development housing requirements funded sixty-seven units of affordable housing on Oxford Street—known as Oxford–Ping On. Oxford-Ping On included a significant percentage of low-income units.[11] Yet despite these housing victories, Chinatown activists were unable to garner guaranteed employment opportunities in the new luxury hotels and apartment complexes. New development continued to bring few economic benefits to neighborhood residents.

Chinatown also continued to press for a community library. Its previous library had closed in 1956, a victim of urban renewal. For some sixty years, Chinatown had remained one of the few Boston neighborhoods without a branch library. Beginning in 2001, the Chinese Progressive Association's (CPA) community youth program kicked off what became a long campaign for a new library, under the aegis of the multigenerational Friends of the Chinatown Library. A few years later, progressive artists and architects created the Chinatown Storefront Library as a voluntary three-month demonstration. Staffed by volunteers, the project revealed the demand for and viability of a Chinatown branch. Nonetheless, the Boston public library system would not commit to creating a permanent one. The demonstration project, funded entirely by the community, was housed in the Archstone complex (formerly Liberty Place) and then resurfaced as a reading room at the Oak Terrace housing project. Eventually, however, it was unable to sustain itself. Chinatown youth continued to demonstrate, CPA questioned political candidates about the library, and Friends of the Chinatown Library began lobbying city officials. Boston's leaders could not ignore the issue.[12]

Chinatown's fractured political affairs continued in the post-recession climate. New groups such as API Movement forthrightly criticized the status quo and questioned the efficacy of electoral strategies. Now led by Carolyn Chou and Nam Le, the Asian American Resource Workshop also stepped up its activism, though it shifted much of its focus to Dorchester's Vietnamese community.[13] Both groups, however, worked closely with CPA.

Disputes continued in the Chinese Consolidated Benevolent Association (CCBA), with the Chin group instigating lawsuits against the current leadership. The newest point of contention arose around the old SCM site that T-NEMC had ceded to CCBA thirty years earlier in the settlement allowing further medical center expansion. CCBA had never developed the community housing it had promised on the site, instead using the flow of funds from commercial rentals to support its organization. Paul Chan, Bill Moy, and, ironically, Billy Chin, who had negotiated and failed to implement the original plan, were among those now petitioning the state attorney general to allow the CCBA to develop a housing plan. The attorney general's office sent a letter to CCBA in 2013, calling for greater transparency and restricting the use of the rent monies to affordable housing. The issue would continue to fester in disputes among CCBA subgroups.[14]

Yet efforts to foster greater cooperation among groups persisted, despite ongoing community tension. The Chinatown Coalition (TCC) continued to effectively communicate and coordinate the work of service agencies. Many of its diverse member organizations were involved in creating the 2010 master plan, another sign of the potential importance of community input in local planning issues.

The Ink Block's evolution reflected Chinatown activists' new approach to development. Its original proposal had called for a sixty-eight-foot-tall, mixed-used building. The site was located just over the turnpike barrier that separated the southern side of the neighborhood from the South End. The building would overlook one occupied by Quinzani's Bakery and a Chinese bean sprout business.[15] Quinzani's provided bread to many restaurants, including Chinese ones in the suburbs, and it had a Chinese manager.

The developer organized consultations with representatives from the surrounding community. Bill Moy and his pro-growth allies were prominent among them, but activists did engage in some limited organizing against the project. CPA negotiated with Whole Foods for employment opportunities, eventually winning 20 percent of the jobs for residents of Chinatown and the South End. In the end, Asian Americans formed more than one-quarter of the new employees hired.[16]

Chinatown's activists were now much more selective about which developments to target. They focused on the most egregious ones, such as Millennium Towers/Millennium Place, a skyscraper project whose developers had evaded much of their linkage payments. Activists had learned through harsh experience that most developments were inevitable. By now they had moved closer to ACDC's attitude that, "when possible, why not work with [developers] and leverage them to make them pay for as much affordable housing as possible?"[17]

To lessen impacts on the community, activists became increasingly engaged in advocacy for policy changes, such as adjusting definitions of affordability and changing zoning regulations. One area of progress was in organizing tenants to advocate for lower rent increases and to preserve affordable units in the face of expiring subsidy programs. Through painstaking work, they successfully made hundreds of existing units more affordable for low-income households across the neighborhood.[18] In some cases, as in Castle Square Apartments, tenants won ownership shares when the ownership of housing projects reorganized.[19]

Chinatown's evolution as an activist community reflected an emerging approach that was locally oriented but expansive, democratic, collaborative, and race-aware. At the core of this mobilization were citywide alliances, particularly with other communities of color. The demands were for equitable opportunities to ensure greater local decision making and achieve practical results for community residents. While communities of color were most vulnerable, housing for poor and middle-income Bostonians was an issue common to most of city neighborhoods.

Chinatown successfully transformed itself into a local political player, mobilizing voters and activists into citywide neighborhood networks that fought for immigrant rights and local governance. The community continued to increase its election turnout and its number of registered voters. By 2009, CPA was conducting hundreds of voter workshops and reaching thousands of households annually. It became one of the city's largest grassroots community organizations working in the political arena, and it achieved some success.[20] In 2011, much of its effort was directed toward Suzanne Lee's candidacy for city council. She was the first Chinatown-based candidate to run for city office, but the Chin group backed the incumbent, South Boston's Bill Linehan, and thus large signs supporting him popped up in the windows of neighborhood stores. Still, by running a spirited and vigorous campaign, Lee nearly upset Linehan, losing by fewer than one hundred votes.[21]

Later that year, CPA announced the formation of an affiliated political action committee to further its political strategy. Unlike the nonprofit CPA, the Chinese Progressive Political Action (CPPA) could endorse candidates and raise campaign funds. CPPA would play an essential role in the next mayoral election and support Lee's second run for city council.

Part of CPA's political focus found its expression in a successful campaign to mandate bilingual ballots in Chinatown and in Dorchester's Vietnamese community. This lengthy mobilization was rooted in a 2003 election dispute, when numerous Chinese voters charged that their votes had been improperly influenced or tampered with at the polls (see chapter 8).[22] To institutionalize bilingual ballots, activists relied on heavy community lobbying and numerous hearings, which the Chinese, particularly the elderly, attended in droves. In two subsequent elections, Boston provided a fully translated Chinese bilingual ballot that included transliterated candidate names, although the secretary of state remained opposed to making them permanent. But continued lobbying from Chinatown and Dorchester residents successfully convinced the city to issue a home-rule petition for permanent bilingual ballots. The state legislature finally approved the bilingual ballots in 2010.[23]

Through a decades-long redistricting campaign, CPA continued its effort to open up the electoral system for greater participation and emerge from the domination of the much larger South Boston neighborhood. Every ten years, federal, state, and municipal election districts are reconfigured based on the U.S. census, a process usually controlled by insiders and incumbents. The 2012 redistricting efforts were intimately related to the Linehan-Lee contest of 2011. Linehan took advantage of his position as chair of the city council redistricting committee to try to remove areas of the South End and Chinatown (where he had lost to Lee) from the district. In the end, community demand to keep the South End and Chinatown intact prevailed, though the two neighborhoods remained junior partners to South Boston.[24]

In 2012, CPA reflected on its long investment in electoral organizing and noted the progress it had made. Political candidates could no longer take Chinatown voters for granted; they needed to bid for their votes through bilingual literature and by addressing community concerns. CPA was determined to bring the community's political influence "to the next level," but it knew it couldn't achieve its goals alone. This decision became the basis for its growing leadership role in citywide alliances.

FIGURE 12. An Immigrant Workers Center Collaborative gathering, 2012. Courtesy of the Chinese Progressive Association.

Lisette Le, a Vietnamese American graduate of Tufts University, became the coordinator of CPA's citywide relations. Under her aegis, citywide work become an integral part of CPA's strategy to stabilize Chinatown.[25]

Building on earlier efforts such as the New Majority Coalition and the Alliance of Boston Neighborhoods, CPA helped launch Whose Boston, a citywide coalition that emphasized equity concerns linked to development, the BRA, and land use. CPA and its director, Lydia Lowe, were catalysts, building on the organization's long political and community history, experience, and relatively high capacity when compared to that of other grassroots neighborhood groups. Eventually, however, the Right to the City Coalition (RTTC) replaced Whose Boston as a central citywide alliance. RTTC Boston was part of a national Right to the City Coalition, which worked against gentrification "to halt the displacement of low-income people, people of color, marginalized LGBTQ communities, and youths of color from their historic urban neighborhoods."[26] Part of a global upsurge in urban activism, the national RTTC had been inspired by Henri Lefebvre's 1967 essay of that name, whose ideas had recently been reignited by theorists such as David Harvey.[27] This background gave it a broader vision and more ambitious goals for structural change than preceding neighborhood movements had possessed. As a result, RTTC was able to expand neighborhood movements into urban social movement frameworks.[28]

Formed in 2007, RTTC Boston distinguished itself from previous citywide formations because it was rooted in community-based organizations that were actively organizing at the grassroots level. Its anchor groups were CPA; Alternatives for Community and Environment, an environmental justice organization in Roxbury; City Life/Vida Urbana, a group that organized physical resistance to evictions; and the Boston Workers Alliance in Roxbury. While RTTC as a whole continued to focus on issues of displacement and stabilization, these internal groups continued to engage in organizing and develop significant constituencies.

Compared to previous coalitions, RTTC Boston was a much more effective public voice for low-income communities and communities of color. It began to sponsor some large events targeting banks and other financial institutions that were responsible for foreclosures. It organized campaigns against income inequality, home foreclosures, luxury housing development, public transit fare increases, and development tax breaks. In 2013, its successes in promoting housing for low- and moderate-income residents and fighting evictions prompted it to form Right to the City Vote, which became a vehicle for organizing around elections. With Lisette Le as its staff organizer, RTTC Vote brought more groups into efforts to mobilize voters and to focus on new legislative goals to protect residents from evictions.[29] Its first campaign platform centered on community control of land and land disposition, protection for renters, opposition against land speculation, and more job opportunities.

Meanwhile, CPA remained at the center of another citywide coalition, the Immigrant Workers Center Collaborative. Formed in 2005, the alliance eventually included nine member organizations. The collaborative was a reaction to the failure of established trade unions to organize the growing immigrant worker population. It contributed to successful campaigns for legislation that would improve wages and working conditions and prevent the abuse of immigrant workers: the state's Temporary Workers Right to Know law in 2012 and the city's executive order against improper withholding of pay in 2014.[30]

Devolution—that is, greater community control over policies affecting the neighborhood—also emerged as a new community approach. Building on the most recent Chinatown master plan and the Chinatown Neighborhood Council's and Chinatown Resident Association's advisory powers, CPA began to explore the use of a community land trust to preserve affordable housing, which the Dudley Street Neighborhood Initiative (DSNI) had successfully used to support its goal of "development without displacement."[31] A community land trust owns the land underneath neighborhood houses and other buildings. Homeowners on trust land enter into agreements with the trust for long-term, low-cost ground leases. Affordability restrictions in the lease ensure that the homes remain permanently affordable. Land trusts thus provide stability in low- and moderate-income communities.

To this point, activists had rarely turned to land trusts to areas such as Boston Chinatown, which had little available land and intense competition for development. That changed in 2014, when Chinatown's new community land trust began to press the city to turn over the few remaining city-owned parcels to the trust. Facilitated by CPA, the land trust worked with developers to develop proposals for specific sites.

FIGURE 13. Bill-signing ceremony for permanent bilingual ballots in Chinatown and other immigrant areas, 2014. Courtesy of the Chinese Progressive Association.

It moved cautiously, coordinating with nonprofit developers such as ACDC.[32] Nonetheless, the land trust concept has been slow to take hold in Chinatown, given the money involved in neighborhood land and housing. In 2015, one of the trust's board members even sold her row-house to a developer and subsequently moved out of the area. On a more promising note, DSNI has since founded the Greater Boston Community Land Trust Network to bring together emerging neighborhood efforts throughout the city and press the administration to provide proactive support to community land trusts. Chinatown's was finally able acquire its first properties in 2019, though at a high cost.

A NEW MAYOR AND A CHANGING CHINATOWN

In 2013, after a series of health crises, Tom Menino, Boston's longest-serving mayor, decided not to run for a sixth term. The scramble for his seat revealed a pent-up desire for new leadership in the city. Twelve candidates ultimately ran for mayor, including three incumbent city councilors, a state representative, a pirate radio-station operator, and a district attorney. CPA allies were also among the candidates: Felix Arroyo, Jr., a former union organizer and incumbent city councilor, and John Barros, the executive director of DSNI, running for his first political office.[33] Aside from the size of the field, the race was novel for other reasons. Nonwhites had been a majority of the city's population since 2000, and now many residents felt that it was time for a change: of the twelve mayoral candidates, six were people of color.[34]

The election was a significant test of CPA's belief that political power was the avenue to preserving Chinatown. With a more open political environment and citywide ties, could its CPPA arm successfully promote a candidate who would be more responsive to community needs and implement better policies? Though neither Arroyo nor Barros had a particularly reformist platform, both had grassroots backgrounds and sympathy for the neighborhood issues. Members were torn about which one to support. Similar tensions were evident in other citywide coalitions, but eventually CPPA and RTTC Vote campaigned for Barros.[35]

The large field of candidates and a relative scarcity of resources were serious barriers for all the candidates of color.[36] To the disappointment of many residents of color and urban progressives, Barros, Arroyo, and the others failed to move beyond the preliminary election, which instead sent two Irish American men—former union official and state representative Marty Walsh and city councilor John Connolly—to the general election. The three leading candidates of color, including Arroyo and Barros, decided to support Walsh. They positioned race and economic equity as primary campaign issues, and most political analysts considered this base of support the decisive element in Walsh's victory.[37]

After taking office, Walsh took significant steps toward diversifying his administration. He appointed Arroyo to run the city's Department of Health and Human Services, Barros to run the newly created Department of Economic Development, Trinh Nguyen to run the Department of Jobs and Community Service, and Alejandra St. Guillen to head the Office of New Bostonians. Now, for the first time, CPA had extensive ties within the city administration. Its executive director, Lydia Lowe, was appointed to the city's Housing Task Force, and other CPA members sat on various youth and education task forces. In addition, the first Asian American woman, Michelle Wu, from the South End, was elected to the city council. She would provide another significant avenue through which to convey community concerns.[38]

It remains to be seen if CPA's strategy of direct political engagement will succeed in sustaining Chinatown as a viable working-class and immigrant neighborhood. Chinatown may have reached a tipping point, given the economic realities currently reshaping Boston's downtown. During the first weeks of the Walsh administration, evictions in ten different neighborhood buildings were in process. A single-room-occupancy building, across Harrison Avenue from the original building in which Chinatown had begun, remained vacant for two years after a fire revealed numerous code violations. CPA has been unable to move the owner or the city to reclaim the building for affordable housing; instead, developers have proposed a new hotel on the site. With development trending toward luxury and high-income housing, CPA must keep drawing heavily on its hard-won ties to bring new affordable housing to the neighborhood. Nevertheless, the community is better positioned to make its presence felt.[39]

DISTORTED DEVELOPMENT

As the November 2013 election approached and Menino's reign in Boston neared its end, developers rushed to the BRA to get their projects approved. The reason for their urgency became apparent after Walsh's election. In 2014, a front-page story in the *Boston Globe* pointed out the imbalance in the city's current housing stock, noting that developers themselves were unsure if there were sufficient numbers of wealthy people to fill these luxury units.[40] A subsequent series of articles revealed how distorted the development approval process had become between January 2009 and June 2013. During those years, the nominally independent BRA was unaccountable to anyone except Menino; no outside agency had any right of review. Mayoral aides regularly sat in on BRA staff meetings, and twenty-five of the agency's forty-four highest-paid staff members donated to the mayor's political campaigns. Its board functioned as a rubber stamp for any development projects recommended by the staff; board members approved all 2,348 recommendations put before them (all but five unanimously), often without discussion. The obstacles that Chinatown had faced were part of a broader citywide problem—an unresponsive and opaque board that had allowed only token and nominal community input before implementing predetermined plans.

It was clear that the BRA had failed to address affordable housing, arguably the city's biggest problem. The agency's board had taken just three minutes to approve a $500 million project that included a $6 million discount on affordable housing fees. Other developers also received numerous discounts on such fees. At a time when both residents and elites were universally acknowledging the scarcity of affordable housing in the city, the *Globe* reported that the BRA had dispensed $18 million for affordable housing when it should have collected $75 million. Some of those housing funds didn't even go toward housing but paid for a public street improvement and a health center.[41] Linkage payments were recorded on paper and often ignored. For instance, Millennium Partners, a New York–based $4 billion limited partnership, was allowed to forego $15 million in linkage payments in its Boston construction projects. The single staff person charged with administering the collections acknowledged failing to keep up with developers.

Carrying out a central campaign promise, Walsh ordered a limited audit of the BRA. The auditing firm KPMG highlighted the disorganization in the agency, reporting that the BRA could not provide full documentation related to policies for document management, compliance requirements, inclusionary development policy payments, agency responsibilities, leases, and properties with deed restrictions. For decades, the uniquely powerful entity had assembled and disposed of city properties for private development while reshaping the city. However, it had created no systematic or even rudimentary method of monitoring developers' compliance with obligations linked to affordable housing and public benefits.[42]

Walsh's commitment to reform the BRA may lead to change, but the current development boom in Boston has forced his administration to move forward with reforms cautiously. It is uncertain if he will make systemic changes to the BRA's functions and its operational transparency. To date, the most significant change has been to rebrand the agency as the Boston Planning and Development Authority.

CHINATOWN NOW

In a presentation in the fall of 2014, the Chinatown Master Plan Implementation Committee, chaired by Lowe, told the community that 98 percent of Chinatown's 2,170 existing low- and moderate-income units were relatively stable, thanks to nonprofit owners or the renewal of affordability agreements. Yet the committee acknowledged that, since 2000, 2,664 units of new housing had been developed or approved in the neighborhood, and less than 20 percent of them were considered affordable. In addition, 91 percent of a 1,614 units constructed at the edges of Chinatown were luxury housing.

Chinatown had become indelibly different. The mixed-income neighborhood that ACDC had championed had been realized, but the benefits to the working-class immigrant population were unclear. Nevertheless, for the moment, the community's survival appeared to be assured because the neighborhood now possessed a critical mass of stable, affordable housing. Most people now lived in mid-rise apartment buildings rather than rowhouses. Though the Chinatown neighborhood had formal boundaries, the actual land on which the working-class population was living had diminished, interspersed among institutional buildings, luxury housing, businesses, and agency and organizational structures. CPA's strategy was to expand Chinatown's housing base for working-class people and sustain the residents who would live in there. That strategy remains unfulfilled, except marginally, as the neighborhood is overwhelmed by other populations and purposes.

CHAPTER 10

CHINATOWNS AND ETHNIC SURVIVAL IN A GLOBALIZED WORLD

The movement toward a globalized economy has spurred greater transnational migration. As with earlier periods of high immigration to the United States, new ethnic enclaves are forming in America's cities, including Boston. Central American neighborhoods in East Boston, the Haitian community in Mattapan, and the Vietnamese center in Fields Corner reflect the growing diversity of the city. These neighborhoods increasingly compete with the forces and actors of development, whose investors and consumers are often from outside the city and sometimes the country. This tension reinvites the query that the Joint Center for Urban Studies at the Massachusetts Institute of Technology and Harvard University articulated decades ago regarding Boston Chinatown: is there a place for "ethnic and special purpose neighborhoods in the central city in the face of large-scale economic development?"[1]

Many studies have documented what some call a "great inversion." Cities, once dominated by the working class and the urban poor after middle-class and affluent residents fled to the suburbs, have increasingly refashioned themselves as the domain of a wealthy, predominately white population.[2] This dynamic challenges the notion that a multiclass, multiracial community befits a city population.[3] Some contemporary voices demand integration into an imagined mainstream norm. Yet ethnic neighborhoods play a critical, sheltering role for immigrant and refugee populations in an unfamiliar and sometimes unsympathetic land. Such communities provide social relationships, familiar ways of seeing the world, social supports, and structures so that residents may survive and grow. They offer alternative ways of negotiating the U.S. landscape and daily life. By exposing cities to diverse perspectives and cultures, moreover, they support a more vital civic life and a more profound understanding among people. The life of such cities is more interesting, inspiring, and robust.

Diversity or perhaps the spectacle of diversity is so desirable that some cities have fabricated ethnic enclaves. This enthusiasm is most evident in the case of Chinatowns and the re-creations of historic Latino districts. Planners and developers have undertaken inventive efforts to preserve traditional Mexican American areas such as Olvera Street in Los Angeles, Market Square in San Antonio, and various Little Italys across the country, long after their imagined residents have dispersed. First seen in Las Vegas, commercial Chinatowns have since been installed or proposed in Raleigh-Durham, Atlanta, Orlando, and Austin. These "Chinatowns" reflect our modern consumer society and often center around malls, groceries, and restaurants. They incorporate stereotypical cultural elements such as koi ponds and waterfalls that rarely appear in traditional Chinatowns.[4] Such attempts to manufacture community lack a vital component: residents and their dynamic culture and creative expressions of life.

Artificial creations designed to attract economic development fail to understand the functions of these communities within the broader society. Chinatowns historically represented a marginal community's long effort to define its role within U.S. society. As such, its features cannot be prescribed and are not static. Working Chinese Americans' dynamic interactions with national institutions and the larger, primarily white population, as well as with their own cultural inheritances and practices, shaped their ethnic economy, social structures, and social practices. Their communities evolved through negotiation, conflict, culture, and an ability to leverage scarce resources for residents. As historic Chinatowns have deepened their local roots, grown in agency, and forged new relationships, they have developed more expansive visions of engagement that contrast with their early insular, defensive postures. Attempting to fossilize dated perceptions of such communities in commercial ventures diminishes these real-life dynamics.

Spectacular and commercial features such as the festivals and restaurants associated with low-income ethnic enclaves are not the most threatened elements of these communities. What is at risk is their role as living, nurturing neighborhoods with active residents and community groups. For enclaves, the main issue is how to sustain their current constituent population. Because of their social origins, traditional Chinatowns are often close to city centers and become the coal-mine canaries of urban gentrification.

America's historic Chinatowns can show other low-income ethnic enclaves a potential pathway toward sustaining durable communities. Their collective experiences form a broad sample of struggle and endurance. Not all of them have been successful. Their particular adaptations in response to the pressures shared by other communities suggest the level of agency that low-income ethnic enclaves may be able gain over their futures as well as the need for alternative paths.

Boston's was one of many Chinatowns in the eastern United States. Others emerged in Chicago, Hartford, Providence, Baltimore, Columbus, Jersey City, Detroit, Pittsburgh, New Orleans, Washington, D.C., and New York City. Early on, these Chinatowns followed similar trajectories, typically establishing themselves in low-income, immigrant, and depressed areas close to transportation hubs and the downtown. Municipal development plans often forced these fragile settlements to relocate. In Washington, D.C., construction of the Federal Triangle led the Chinese to move south of Mount Vernon Square. Detroit Chinatown was originally sited near the intersection of Michigan and Third avenues. To make room for the John Lodge Freeway, the community moved north to Cass Avenue and Peterboro Street, where the enclave went into decline, losing its last commercial establishment in 2000. In the early 1900s, Chicago moved its Chinatown from South Clark Street in the city's famous Loop to the South Side in Armour Square. The Chinese first settled in Cleveland around Public Square but divided into two distinct enclaves. Urban development, including construction of a parcel post building in the largest enclave on Ontario Street, led their migration to the smaller enclave on 55th and Euclid and then to the creation of new Chinatown on Rockwell Avenue. Baltimore's small Chinatown on narrow Marion Street moved to make way for the department stores in the city center. The community was able to migrate four blocks north to Park Avenue and Mulberry Street. In contrast, the location of Boston Chinatown has been unusually stable, despite decades of intense development pressures.

DISPERSAL AND ENDURING PATHS

Traditional East Coast Chinatowns have followed four trajectories: dispersal, displacement, rapid growth, or mobilization. Most urban Chinatowns disappeared during urban development. In 1940, Rose Hum Lee recorded twenty-eight U.S. cities with established Chinatowns, half of them in the East.[5] Of those she listed, only four or five have survived. The smaller the population settlement, the more likely its disappearance, and little documentation of these communities has survived. Urban development has dispersed or hollowed out Chinatowns in the Midwest, including those in Cleveland and St. Louis, and along the northeastern seaboard, in Hartford, Baltimore, and Washington, D.C. Often forced to move multiple times, these enclaves eventually succumbed to city development projects, changing demographics, and immigration policies.

A few found paths to survival. For instance, Chicago Chinatown, dominated by the Moy clan, endured by transplanting itself to avoid discriminatory rents and antagonism from the white population. In 1912, the siting of a new federal building in the Loop forced the On Leong tong to move its members and associated businesses to a new Chinatown. On Leong's conflict with a smaller association, the Hip Sing tong, was an additional motivation. The On Leong–led move ended at a relatively isolated industrial area near the south branch of the Chicago River at Cermak and Wentworth. Once the location of a slaughterhouse, a steel mill, a brewery, and a glue factory, the area was now in decline and far from the downtown. As a result, the community was partially insulated against gentrification and had space to develop residences and businesses.[6] In the 1980s and early 1990s, a private Chinese American development corporation secured the geographic anchor for the community's lasting viability: thirty-two acres of the Santa Fe Railroad yards that bordered Chinatown to the north. Like other Chinatowns today, Chicago's suffers from a lack of affordable housing, but 8,000 Chinese continue to live in the neighborhood.[7] This was a case in which fortune, foresight, and planning allowed the community to confront changing circumstances and preserve itself. That self-preservation did, however, require critical infrastructure to coordinate a transfer of the majority of the population to a distant location. Unlike many eastern urban Chinatowns, which are hemmed in by development, early twentieth-century Chicago offered some space for the enclave to move en masse.

Of the eastern U.S. Chinatowns that have endured, New York's is unique as an ethnic community, built up by a great flow of Chinese immigration before widespread gentrification spread into the neighborhood. Though the area began attracting many types of people by the end of the twentieth century, the Chinese enclave had grown so large that it was almost immovable. New York Chinatown began in the late nineteenth century in a ten-block area in the southern Lower East Side, a traditional landing area for immigrants. The Chinese occupied a space next to the Bowery and Five Points neighborhood, notorious for vagrants, criminal elements, and gangs such as the nativist Bowery Boys and Irish American groups. Canal Street, the Bowery, Park Row, and Baxter Street delineated the original triangle of New York Chinatown. Like Boston's, it still sits on its original settlement site.

Unlike other Chinatowns, most of which numbered their residents in the hundreds until immigration reform in the 1960s, New York Chinatown had thousands of residents by 1890. According to the 1900 census, more than 6,000 Chinese Americans lived in New York City, though the historian Jan Lin believes this was an undercount.[8] The Lee family, followed by Chins and Wongs, dominated the population. Traditional businesses—groceries, restaurants, and laundries—developed, but the community was large enough to support more diverse activities such as traditional Chinese herbal pharmacies, bakers, printers, novelty shops, tailors, and interpreters.[9]

As immigration and transnational capital flowed from Asia in the 1960s and 1970s, New York Chinatown expanded east and south into other parts of the Lower East Side and northward into Little Italy and parts of the East Village. Today the city's Chinatown dwarfs all others. The neighborhood has more than 2,200 businesses; and with an estimated 116,700 residents, its population is more than twenty times greater than Boston's.[10]

Because of the community's proximity to Wall Street, the terrorist attacks on September 11, 2001, severely crippled Chinatown. Emergency regulations imposed after the attacks limited traffic into the area, isolating it and hindering deliveries to restaurants, garment shops, and other businesses. Parking lots closed, and telephone service became erratic. More recently, the neighborhood is dealing with the gentrification that is overtaking much of Manhattan. Until now, Chinatown has been able to avoid the incursions of urban renewal programs, but new development pressures are reaching into its core, driving out street vendors and pushing up rents in residential towers.[11] Still, thanks to early rapid growth, New York Chinatown has created a community that is sizable enough to withstand significant threats. The neighborhood retains an undeniable presence and continues to support its large population. It has also benefited from an extensive organizational infrastructure, including activist and service organizations that have fought to maintain the community. Chinatown remains a significant destination in New York City, and its web of organizations and accrued political power will help sustain it into the future.

PHILADELPHIA AND BOSTON CHINATOWN

Chinatowns in Boston and Philadelphia share similar survival stories, and both clearly reveal the role of neighborhood agency in community viability.[12] In each case, the alternative to relocation and expansion was community organizing and mobilization. They were smaller communities than New York's and thus easy targets for redevelopment, but they were large enough for younger generations to develop activist campaigns and structures to mobilize against displacement.

Philadelphia's Chinatown began in the nineteenth century on the 900 block of Race Street, east of the city's wharves and the original city settlement. The neighborhood was known the Tenderloin District, an area of burlesque theaters and rooming houses. One early resident said, "You could smell beer joints all over."[13] When the Chinese settled there, the neighborhood was also home to a number of manufacturers, including a foundry, a chair factory, and a safe factory. During the last three decades of the nineteenth century, the Chinese population grew from fewer than 20 people to more than 1,000 residents. The neighborhood's population fell during the Depression and then slowly rose again but did not reach 1,000 Chinese again until 1990.

Philadelphia made various attempts to contain or eradicate the growing Chinatown area. According to the researcher Kathryn Wilson, the police first raided the community in 1882. After landowners and non-Chinese residents petitioned the mayor to rid the neighborhood of Chinese restaurants and gambling, the city instituted a health inspection drive in 1887. Beginning in 1890, police repeatedly raided Chinatown, a practice that went for two decades. In the early twentieth century, as the city upgraded roads for automobiles, local newspapers were proclaiming the death of the enclave.[14] Yet the community hung on.

Beginning in the 1960s, a series of urban renewal projects—a convention center, Gallery Mall, Independence Mall, and smaller developments—swallowed portions of Chinatown. Already, by 1966, years of demolition and displacement had diminished the community. But two events in particular ignited a neighborhood response, especially among young Asian Americans, who formed what was initially known as the Save Chinatown Movement. They mobilized first against the Vine Street Expressway, part of Interstate 676, which was designed to connect Center City Philadelphia with New Jersey.[15] Then the proposed destruction of the Holy Redeemer Church, which housed the neighborhood's only elementary school, catalyzed young activists such as Cecilia Moy Yep, who persuaded the traditional associations to support the neighborhood's first town meeting at the Free Library.

Yellow Seeds and Philadelphia Chinatown Development Corporation (PCDC) were among the early organizations that challenged redevelopment plans. What was unique to this city's Chinatown was the relative unity among its different sectors. Mary Yee, a young organizer at the time, recalled that it helped that everyone knew each other. PCDC, originally a committee within the Chinese Benevolent Association (CBA), mobilized the working generation of the American-born, such as Yep, but publicly deferred to the traditional leadership. The organization strictly confined itself to the community development arena and allowed CBA to represent the neighborhood before the city, even as CBA admitted that it lacked the skills to negotiate the issues. At the same time, the leftist college-age activists involved in Yellow Seeds decided to work with PCDC as "the loyal opposition" in a combined campaign to defend Chinatown. Yellow Seeds staff brought their ties with working people and their language skills to the primarily English-speaking PCDC founders; they even sat on the board of PCDC, and one served as co-chair.[16]

Differences were evident among the groups. Yellow Seeds and community youth preferred direct action and often challenged authority figures. They would confront the Catholic church's conservative Cardinal Krol to push him to oppose the taking of Holy Redeemer Church. Their tactics included climbing onto rubble to frustrate construction operations, "confronting bulldozers to stop demolition, picketing in front of Cardinal Krol's residence or exposing community sell-outs in print," through their community newspaper.[17] In contrast, PCDC preferred to lobby and organize a community presence at city and state hearings. Nevertheless, their united front succeeded in forcing a reduced expressway plan, saving Holy Redeemer, and winning mitigation measures, including a pedestrian pathway decorated with Chinatown motifs that crossed over the expressway. In 1975, this working alliance supported a Chinatown-sustaining urban renewal plan and then mobilized the community to win city support for it.[18] After its passage, PCDC focused on developing housing projects and advocating around land issues affecting Philadelphia Chinatown. Since then, it has completed five major housing projects, including senior housing, rowhouses and apartments, and commercial space.

The CBA, preoccupied with its traditional mediating functions and limited by language barriers, left the field to PCDC, and that organization came to dominate community planning. Yellow Seeds dissolved in the late 1970s.[19] In 1985, Asian Americans United (AAU), founded in part by former Yellow Seeds members, took up some of the older organization's roles. However, it was more focused on youth, education, and anti-Asian violence.[20] Differing approaches to community development continued, and this divergence among organizations became evident in the next big development struggle.

In the late 1990s, Philadelphia tried to build a new baseball stadium complex for the Phillies on the northern border of Chinatown. The facility would have removed the growing community's only avenue for expansion. By this time, Chinatown had become a resource for other Asian American populations in the city, and they all opposed the proposal. The organizing, however, occurred within two different structures, thus exposing rifts in the community. One coalition, the Philadelphia Chinatown Coalition to Oppose the Stadium (PCCOS), led by CBA, included businesses and many Chinese-speaking residents. It preferred to organize community actions. The other coalition, Stadium Out of Chinatown Coalition, led by PCDC, mobilized younger, primarily English-speaking residents and supporters and focused on lobbying city hall. AAU joined both coalitions and saw the need to form a unified front.

Everyone united around a PCCOS's call for a march and rally under the banner of Stadium Out of Chinatown. Nearly 1,000 people attended to oppose the project, and Chinatown businesses closed their doors in protest. The CBA, Holy Redeemer Church and School, Pennsylvania Indochina's Senior Citizens Association, Taiwan United Association, and AAU all helped to bring out supporters. Mobilization for city hearings, lawsuits, petitions, alliance building, and letter-writing campaigns followed the successful protest. Like the Parcel C struggle in Boston Chinatown, the stadium campaign reflected the maturation of the neighborhood's organizing experience with significant media consciousness and heavy political lobbying. These efforts succeeded, and the city eventually decided to site the stadium elsewhere.

Philadelphia Chinatown is hemmed in on three sides by large publicly funded projects—the Independence Mall urban renewal area to the east, Gallery Mall to the south, and Pennsylvania Convention Center to the west. Gentrification has insinuated itself into the neighborhood in new developments. The pedestrian pathway over the Vine Street Expressway to the north is Chinatown's only opening, so it has had to target property across the expressway to grow. That neighborhood was previously a light manufacturing area. While the Chinatown community has come to know the area as Chinatown North, developers and businesses, who compete for the land, have variously called it the Loft District and Callowhill. PCDC was instrumental in getting the area rezoned for housing and has developed some mixed-income projects, including elder housing. Community groups have established offices there, and a charter school and a church have opened.[21]

Philadelphia's Historic Chinatown and Chinatown North are now home to about 2,500 Chinese and 6,000 total residents and serve the 87,000 Asians in the city. Unofficially, municipal and community organizations estimate that 4,000 Chinese live in the neighborhoods today. The area's core is stable, and it is more compact and contiguous than Boston Chinatown is. Of the four hundred plus commercial entities, the most common are restaurants, followed by retail stores and cosmetic services. Almost all are small local businesses.[22]

Boston Chinatown, like Philadelphia's, has relied primarily on its own agency for survival. But each neighborhood's experiences may have lessons for the other on organizing to survive. Philadelphia Chinatown probably benefited from the working alliance that developed among CBA, PCDC, and Yellow Seeds. That united voice helped them realize a city plan to sustain the community. Such unity may have grown, however, from several differences between the city enclaves. In the 1970s, Philadelphia Chinatown was smaller and less complex than Boston Chinatown was. Its population measured in the hundreds, while Boston's was four or five times larger. In addition, as Kathryn Wilson writes, "there is no evidence that [Philadelphia] wished Chinatown gone in the 1960s."[23] Boston city administrations, however, initially supported urban renewal plans to eliminate its Chinese enclave (or at least its residential component) to accommodate T-NEMC. Philadelphia's redevelopment authority, moreover, lacked the power that BRA had to implement its vision.[24] Philadelphia Chinatown may have also benefited from the timing of the city's transportation plans. For instance, the Environmental Protection Act gave the community tools to oppose the expressway. Mary Yee, who grew up in Boston Chinatown and later relocated to Philadelphia, did not recall that such tools were available when the

Central Artery and Mass Pike Extension were dividing the community. Finally, widespread public protests in Philadelphia, particularly around earlier urban renewal projects, had contributed to the passage of protective laws and to more inclusive processes for large-scale redevelopment.

Philadelphia Chinatown's evolution consolidated control of community development in the hands of PCDC. Thus, compared to Boston Chinatown, decision making is less inclusive, less debated, and less influenced by resident voices and organizing. Existing differences revealed themselves during the stadium fight, but PCDC continues to carry out most of the community planning. While its dominance may fit into the prevailing neoliberal urban planning models (in which the city outsources neighborhood development issues to a reliable partner), it may not be the healthiest, representative, or most inclusive approach to community engagement.

The Boston and Philadelphia Chinese enclaves endure, but their residents' organizing and mobilization strategies have not eliminated threats. The Asian American Legal Defense and Education Fund's 2014 review of land use in Boston, New York, and Philadelphia Chinatowns concluded, "From 2000 to 2010, the share of the Asian population in all three Chinatowns decreased. The absolute number of Asians in New York's Chinatown also decreased during this period." Further, "the median housing value and rent values in all three Chinatowns show the rising value of land in these neighborhoods."[25] While their survival remains uncertain, Boston and Philadelphia Chinatowns' efforts to mobilize residents to protect the neighborhood can be instructive for other low-income ethnic neighborhoods that are trying to determine their destinies. The community infrastructure and the network of organizations that larger Chinatowns supported have been critical. With that base, they demonstrate that residents and community supporters can have an effect if they find appropriate methods of activism, organizing tools, and allies with common interests.

CONCLUSION

MAKING THE ROAD BY WALKING

On a sunny day in early October 2014, Mayor Marty Walsh attended the public unveiling of the last policy report from his numerous transition task forces. The event was held at the Parcel 24 project site, and the focus was his housing plan. In "Housing a Changing City: Boston 2030," Walsh set a goal for 53,000 new units, with an emphasis on affordable, low-income housing. His plan was ambitious, far exceeding the 30,000-unit goal that the Menino administration had set and failed to implement. Still, more than 40 percent of the units in Walsh's plan would be luxury or market-rate units.[1]

Despite continuing inequities, decades of activism in Chinatown and other Boston neighborhoods have created a greater sensitivity to the needs and demands of working- and middle-class residents. Yet while the ratio of market-rate to affordable housing may be a workable tradeoff in most neighborhoods, Chinatown's proximity to the epicenter of Boston development continues to threaten its survival. Numerous reports have highlighted the urgency of shelter in Boston. In September 2014, the *Boston Globe* cited the city's low rate of housing production, noting that luxury units were "expected to make up the vast majority of new apartments . . . in the next three years." A few months later, a front-page article in the *Sunday Globe* opened with this statement: "There have been three great ages of development in modern Boston. The first began . . . in the late 19th century. . . . The second came in the 1960s and '70s. . . . The third is now."[2] Homelessness in Boston was increasing, and the homeless population in Massachusetts was growing faster than any other state's. A 2013 study by the Federal Reserve Bank of Cleveland indicated that Boston was "undergoing the most rapid gentrification of any city in the country," with 25 percent of its neighborhoods enduring massive change. In subsequent years, neither the housing crisis nor community disparities abated. The Brookings Institute found that Boston now had the highest income inequality among the fifty largest cities in the country. Tenants' groups continued to protest rising rents, and officeholders searched for solutions, including restrictions on short-term rental companies such as Airbnb, higher fees on developers, and pleas and incentives for more middle-income housing.[3]

Over the course of its 135-year history, Boston Chinatown has been constantly entangled with the city's physical, social, and cultural landscape. Initially ignored as an undesirable, unhealthy landing area for immigrants, a neighborhood dominated by rowhouses, industry, and transportation hubs, Chinatown was recast in the city's postindustrial age as a compelling target for development—first, for highways and T-NEMC; later for commercial development; more recently, for luxury residences. As the area has evolved, Chinatown's commercial core has become a distinctive neighborhood and a minor tourist attraction, adding to Boston's new image as a global, knowledge-based, multicultural city.

As a residential neighborhood, however, Chinatown has struggled over the decades to transform its subaltern status and find a voice in city decision making. Its post–World War II transition crystallized those efforts, as the area gradually gained more mainstream institutions, increased voter mobilization, and made direct attempts to organize the community. Redevelopment projects triggered protest politics. After local initiatives advanced the community's agenda, the city began to recognize Chinatown's needs, though it has still not significantly addressed them.

For recent immigrants, Chinatown continues to provide important social and organizational networks, daily comforts, and routines that help them survive urban challenges in an unfamiliar environment. For long-time residents, the neighborhood holds shared meanings and aspirations. For Asian Americans throughout the city, it remains a significant space for political, social, and cultural mobilization.

But for Boston politicians and other elites, the city's future appears to depend on serving the needs of the global wealthy—housing them in the new Millennium developments along Washington Street or head-quartering them in Back Bay office towers. These "one-percenters" are increasingly gravitating to cities such as Boston, and developers are

FIGURE 14. Protest against Power One manufacturing, a call for workers' severance rights, July 2001. Courtesy of Northeastern University Libraries, Archives and Special Collections.

scrambling to serve them. With world-class medical centers and universities, an established public transit system, cultural venues, high-end restaurants, and luxury housing, Boston is well positioned to serve all of their lifestyle needs. Thus, successive waves of construction keep pressing on Boston Chinatown, and the neighborhood's prospects look uncertain. A recent article in *New York Magazine* dismissed it, like other small East Coast Chinatowns, as nothing more than "an ethnic theme park."[4]

Activists such as CPA's new executive director, Karen Chen, and Angie Liou of ACDC believe that the Walsh administration is genuinely supportive of Chinatown. But this patronage is limited. On the whole, market forces and the development policies of Boston's growth coalition have failed Chinatown and other poor and working-class neighborhoods. Briefly, in the mid-1980s, the institution of a linkage policy came close to offering real support for the neighborhood, but that aid was still woefully inadequate and its net effect questionable. The funds were haphazardly collected from developers; and Chinatown, which has faced the most intense development pressures in the city, has never received more than a small percentage of them.[5] Policy implementation was conditional on the whims of the business cycle, mayoral political calculations, relations between neighborhood elites and city hall, and shifting efforts to mobilize the neighborhood. Meanwhile, constant development continued to damage Chinatown via rapidly rising rents and loss of land for housing.

Growth and the ever-intensifying development of urban space are, according to the scholar David Harvey, "repeated bouts of . . . 'creative destruction.' This nearly always has a class dimension, since it is usually the poor, the underprivileged, and those marginalized from political power that suffer first and foremost from this process." As a result, "[the] quality of urban life has become a commodity for those with money, as has the city itself in a world where consumerism, tourism, cultural and knowledge-based industries, as well as the perpetual resort to the economy of the spectacle, have become major aspects of the urban political economy."[6] So whom does local governance serve? If it is supposed to serve the city's residents and the communities that endure the process of growth, then it has failed, and Chinatown is a signal example.

Thus, community agency is crucial and fundamental. In response to structural and policy shortcomings, Chinatown strengthened its capacity to organize, drawing on neighborhood history, social relationships, and culture. The neighborhood's methods moved from appeals, to protests, to multipronged resistance, to building alliances for greater power. Its outlook shifted from parochial, to citywide, to metropolitan, to national. Its goals changed from preservation to redistribution. Yet even though the neighborhood's mobilization abilities evolved, city administrations remained unable or unwilling to address its most crucial issues. So as a further step toward community agency, Chinatown has worked to create a vision for the neighborhood, an alternative strategy for growth that is organized internally. In this way, it is looking forward and defining the community for itself. To address the core issues of community life, it is searching for solutions in organizing rather than in city policy.[7]

While Boston Chinatown is under tremendous pressure, it has assets that sustain it. The construction of several low-income neighborhood housing projects over the years have supported the community's working- and lower-middle-class base.[8] In Lydia Lowe's assessment, CPA's organizing work has stabilized existing low-income housing projects such as Tai Tung, Mass Pike Towers, and Chauncy House. New mixed-use developments partially offset the increasing gentrification of the community's historic rowhouses. There are also several elder housing projects in the area, and the elderly now number more than a fifth of the neighborhood population. The availability of elder housing has not kept other Chinatowns vital. But in Boston the elderly have played an active role in mobilizations, while contributing in numerous ways to community life. In addition, a flow of working-class Chinese immigrants sustains the high demand for housing in Chinatown. Since the 1965 Immigration Reform Act, the volume of Chinese immigration has increased steadily. Though working-class immigrants form a decreasing proportion of that overall flow, their numbers remain high, and some feel a need to live in the neighborhood.

The growing activism and leadership of this immigrant working-class population are among Chinatown's greatest strengths. Thanks to a decades-long focus on workers' issues and the establishment of CPA's

Workers' Center, immigrant workers of color are part of a rising tide of labor activism. In the face of extreme inequality and marginalization, they have courageously stepped up to fight for better conditions—resulting, most recently, with the 2015 breakthrough unionization of home care workers and a series of historic victories for hotel and food service workers. In these workplace struggles, workers are increasingly the organizers, strategists, and decision makers. Chinatown's multiple areas of organizing solidify the their central role in the future of the community.

Boston Chinatown also has other advantages. Over the decades, the traditional associations have bought numerous properties in the neighborhood, often using them to house members in need of shelter. These associations own two dozen area properties, mostly among the remaining rowhouses. Because of a collective decision-making process and local accountability, any decision to sell to developers is protracted and complicated. In addition, several social service organizations, also dependent on local and community constituents, own significant properties in the neighborhood.

FIGURE 15. Residents at a Chinatown street-fair booth supporting neighborhood preservation, July 2019. Courtesy of the Chinese Progressive Association.

While most Chinese Americans in the region no longer live or work in Chinatown, many continue to participate in its activities and remain strongly attached it as the center of the area's Chinese American population. Thus, the community continues to draw on financial, political, and civic resources beyond the geographic neighborhood. Few former residents can recall the intrusions of the Combat Zone, the highway arteries, and T–NEMC without expressing a sense of injustice. One, who has held various government positions, even told me that he believes that Chinatown could justifiably ask for reparations.[9]

Most significantly, Chinatown's capacity to mobilize has grown. Since its naïve and ineffectual protests against Lafayette Place, it has gained the skills to succeed against large development stakeholders. Activists now work effectively through media, regulatory channels, elections, legislation, planning, grassroots mobilization, and lobbying. Community residents are battle-tested and knowledgeable, and the neighborhood has developed effective ties among its various factions, allowing for more effective coalition building. Organizers have constructed citywide networks around a common agenda to support a larger urban social movement through which they can make more significant claims on the city.

Signs of those networks are evident in the spillover of Chinese businesses into adjacent neighborhoods such as the South End and the spread of social services into other areas of the city. CPA works with labor groups on citywide labor issues, the Workshop cultivates ties with other Asian Americans in the city, ACDC serves as a leading CDC in the region, and BCNC is prominent in advocating for statewide policies for adult education and other social services. Through its voter mobilization and involvement in the Right to the City Coalition, CPA has influenced the civic dialogue and fostered unprecedented access to political elites. These new friends in city and state government have given Chinatown more arenas in which to operate and have resulted in some minor victories.

In the future, Chinatown will have difficult decisions to make. Will community members push for the changes that they see as necessary or for the degree of change that political elites can accept? Will these inhabitants who contribute so much to the city have the power to shape it using the values of social, environmental, and economic justice? Chinatown's resilience and its community's ability to grow and learn give it hope. While identity and social values connect many of its younger leaders, material interests bind many of the older ones. A number of younger activists, often children of the neighborhood, have foregone professional careers, choosing instead to undertake the protracted process of sustaining an ever-changing area that still plays a vital role in their ethnic identity. Others have come from the greater Asian American community with the goal to bring recognition to a population that they feel is exploited or taken for granted. Siu Man Luie, a young agency staffperson, expressed a common sentiment: "I don't care about Quincy. I really don't. . . . Even though I live there. Maybe because Chinatown is so small right now. I care about Chinatown."[10] For older leaders and those in business, being active in the neighborhood gives them the leverage to succeed in the political or economic arena—leverage that is not available outside the community. While residents' roles have expanded over the decades, what they can contribute to neighborhood growth has not yet been completely realized. If they can fully mobilize, they will be a new source of community optimism.

The community has already transformed its image from a marginal, reactive actor to a leading one. Time will tell if it can build on these accumulated strengths to overcome the incessant demands of development. Chinatown has tried every available tool—protest politics, community-based planning and development, master plans, negotiations for community benefits, political mobilization, and policy initiatives. It is rapidly exhausting its supply of available parcels to use in negotiations with developers. The question increasingly converges on whether more structural solutions to development are necessary. Boston Chinatown's challenges represent the extreme of development pressures that most of the city's neighborhoods now face. How it resolves them will help determine which populations belong to the city. The history of Boston Chinatown shows that the residents and the larger community will fight hard to keep their place. Organizing has been and will continue to be essential.

NOTES

INTRODUCTION: A CHINATOWN WALK

1. U.S. Census Bureau, "American Community Survey," 2014–18, five-year estimates, tabs. B17001 and B17001D. Because the neighborhood is relatively small, no single census tract captures Chinatown. The residential portion of the neighborhood comprises most of tract 702, where Asian Americans, overwhelmingly Chinese, have an estimated poverty rate of more than 26 percent. Tract 701.01, which overlaps most of the commercial portion of Chinatown but also a large section of downtown Boston, has an Asian American poverty rate of 30 percent. The city's overall poverty rate is estimated at 20 percent. Population density calculations come from an analysis of 1990 census information in Chinatown Initiative, "Chinatown Masterplan 2000: Agenda for a Sustainable Neighborhood" (Boston, 2000), 7. Since that time, new apartment construction has only increased density.

2. Daniel Patrick Moynihan, "Patterns of Ethnic Succession: Blacks and Hispanics in New York City," *Political Science Quarterly* 94, no. 1 (1979): 1–14.

3. Stephan Thernstrom, *The Other Bostonians: Poverty and Progress in the American Metropolis, 1880–1970* (Cambridge, MA: Harvard University Press, 1973); Peter Kwong, *The New Chinatown* (New York: Hill and Wang, 1996), 202–3; Marilynn S. Johnson, *The New Bostonians* (Amherst: University of Massachusetts Press, 2015), 26.

4. Author interview with a former neighborhood resident and activist, Boston, March 9, 1997. All interviews were confidential unless otherwise authorized. The names of the interviewees were withheld by mutual agreement.

5. Deborah A. Oriola and Gregory W. Perkins, *Chinatown User Survey* (Boston: Boston Redevelopment Authority, 1988).

6. With the large wave of Asian American immigration, new types of enclaves have developed. Planned enclaves such as Chinatowns in Los Vegas and majority-Chinese cities such as Cupertino and Monterey Park are distinct socioeconomically from the historic Chinatowns. In Seattle and Cleveland, new Asia-towns (areas with people from multiple countries in Asia) have appeared.

7. Arthur Krim, *Chinatown–South Cove Comprehensive Survey Project: Final Survey Report* (Boston: City of Boston Landmarks Commission, 1997); Rhoads Murphey, "Boston's Chinatown," *Economic Geography* 28, no. 3 (1952): 244–45.

8. A major highway project in Boston, known as the "Big Dig," completed in 2007, shifted the highways sufficiently to allow the construction of the One Greenway complex in 2015. Part of the wall separating Chinatown from the highways was replaced by concrete barriers, though further down Hudson Street the remaining wall is visible.

9. Chinatown Initiative, "Chinatown Masterplan 2000," 43–44.

10. Emily Cohen, Amy Justin Mattlage, Matthew Reardon, and Chia-Hui Shen, "Housing in Chinatown: Yesterday, Today, and Tomorrow" (class report, Tufts University, Department of Urban and Environmental Planning and Policy, 2007).

11. Demographics, of course, vary with neighborhood boundaries, which individual organizations and residents view differently. Moreover, exact data for small geographic areas are difficult to obtain. I refer to the population within the borders of Chinatown as defined by Chinatown Coalition, *The Chinatown Community Assessment Report* (Boston: Chinatown Coalition, 1994). Other documents, such as the community's various master plans, have used changing and different boundaries. For this book, my references are to census block groups 1 and 2 of tract 702 and census block group 7 of tract 701.1 (U.S. Census Bureau, *2010 Census—Census Block Map: Boston City*, MA, 2011, https://www2.census.gov).

12. U.S. Census Bureau, "American Community Survey," 2014–18.

13. Chinatown Master Plan 2010 Oversight Committee, "Chinatown Master Plan 2010: Community Vision for the Future" (Boston, 2010). A campaign in 1998–99 by the Chinese Progressive Association tried to get local business owners to pledge to local laws regarding sick time, minimum wage, and overtime. Only a handful signed the pledge. Over the decades, the group took up a variety of such workers' issues. See Chinese Progressive Association, "Pledge for Community Labor Standards," Boston History Collection, Archives and Special Collections, Northeastern University Library, Boston; and Robert O'Malley, "Setting New Workplace Standards," *Sampan*, June 5, 1998, 3–4. Please note that the issue-date format of *Sampan* varies over time. As a community newspaper with limited resources, it has been inconsistent in its issue dates, which have changed under different editors. Some years, it was published weekly; at other times biweekly, monthly, and even bimonthly.

14. Suzanne Lee, interview by the author, Brookline, MA, February 1, 1997.

15. See Jack Beatty, *The Rascal King: The Life and Times of James Michael Curley, 1874–1958* (Boston: Addison-Wesley, 1992); and Thomas H. O'Connor, *The Boston Irish: A Political History* (Boston: Northeastern University Press, 1995).

16. John H. Mollenkopf, *The Contested City* (Princeton, NJ: Princeton University Press, 1983); Manuel Castells, *The City and the Grassroots: A Cross-Cultural Theory of Urban Social Movements* (Berkeley: University of California Press, 1983).

17. A rich depiction of the evolution of streetscapes in the commercial area of Boston Chinatown is available at http://chinatownatlas.org.

18. Neighborhood resident and leader, interview with the author, Boston, May 14, 1997.

CHAPTER 1: BANDS OF BROTHERS BUILD COMMUNITY, 1880–1941

1. "The Largest Merchandize Depot in the United States," *Christian Watchman*, August 20, 1841.

2. In 1845, a second railroad line, the Old Colony, established depots in South Cove. All of these depots and lines were eventually consolidated into today's South Station terminal.

3. Some earlier buildings were built for Yankee craftsmen and were of better quality. See Neil Larson and Kathryn Grover, "National Register of Historic Places Multiple Property Documentation Form: Historic Resources Associated with Chinese Immigrants and Chinese Americans in the City of Boston," application to the

National Park Service, May 4, 2017, available at the Chinese Historical Society of New England.

4. See Rhoads Murphey, "Boston's Chinatown," *Economic Geography* 28, no. 3 (1952): 245. The South Cove Corporation had also made a large investment in the grand United States Hotel, one of the first major hotels in the country, sited on Beach and Lincoln streets. That investment helped bring the company close to insolvency.

5. Sam Bass Warner, Jr., *Streetcar Suburbs: The Process of Growth in Boston (1870–1900)*, 2nd ed. (Cambridge, MA: Harvard University Press, 1978); Joshua L. Rosenbloom, "The Challenges of Economic Maturity: New England, 1880–1940," in *Engines of Enterprise: An Economic History of New England*, ed. Peter Temin (Cambridge, MA: Harvard University Press, 2000), 177; Charles D. Underhill, "Public Health," in *The City Wilderness: A Settlement Study*, ed. Robert A. Woods (Boston: Houghton Mifflin, 1898), 60. For a brief explanation of attitudes toward areas created by landfill, see Murphey, "Boston's Chinatown."

6. Murphey, "Boston's Chinatown," 247.

7. Jean Gibran and Kahlil Gibran, *Kahlil Gibran: His Life and World* (New York: Interlink, 1991), 25–38; "Boston Chinese Mourn Dr. Sun: City Headquarters of Revolt," *Boston Herald*, March 15, 1925. Ho Chi Minh mentioned his employment in a 1912 letter to a friend in France, and many Vietnamese visiting Boston make a pilgrimage to the hotel kitchen to see the marble table where he worked. See William J. Duiker, *Ho Chi Minh: A Life* (New York: Hyperion, 2000), 50–51.

8. Polly Welts Kaufman, Bonnie Hurd Smith, Mary Howland Smoyer, and Susan Wilson, *Boston Women's Heritage Trail: Four Centuries of Boston Women*, 2nd ed. (Gloucester, MA: Curious Traveller, 1999), 47; Doris L. Rich, *Amelia Earhart: A Biography* (Washington, DC: Smithsonian Institution Press, 1989), 43.

9. Thomas C. Chen, "Remaking Boston's Chinatown: Race, Space, and Urban Development, 1943–1994," (PhD diss., Brown University, 2014), 14.

10. Mae M. Ngai, *Impossible Subjects: Illegal Aliens and the Making of Modern America* (Princeton, NJ: Princeton University Press, 2004), 202.

11. Stephan Thernstrom, *The Other Bostonians: Poverty and Progress in the American Metropolis, 1880–1970* (Cambridge, MA: Harvard University Press, 1973), 15–20, 228–29.

12. "Influx of Chinese," *Boston Globe*, March 13, 1884. Several years earlier, the same paper (under a different name) had reported that no Chinatown yet existed ("The Heathen Chinee," *Boston Daily*, December 23, 1877).

13. The Ping On reference appears to stem from the city of Boston's bicentennial publications about its neighborhoods. The one concerning Chinatown claimed that Chinese laborers pitched tents on Ping On Alley. Arthur Krim convincingly questions this claim and suggests that the intersection of Harrison Avenue and Oxford Place was the more likely site. See Katie Kenneally, *Chinatown: Boston 200 Neighborhood History Series* (Boston: Boston 200 Corporation, 1976); and Arthur Krim, "Chinatown–South Cove Comprehensive Survey Project: Final Survey Report" (Boston: City of Boston Landmarks Commission, 1997), 29–32.

14. H. Jerome, "Boston's Chinese Quarter," *Boston Globe*, February 20, 1893.

15. Bernard Wong estimates that 80 percent of the early Chinese immigrants were from Toisan, with the remainder from surrounding areas (*Patronage, Brokerage,*

Entrepreneurship, and the Chinese Community of New York [New York: AMS Press, 1988], 37). Also see Him Mark Lai, *Becoming Chinese American: A History of Communities and Institutions* (Walnut Creek CA: AltaMira, 2004).

16. Peter Kwong, *The New Chinatown,* 2nd ed. (New York: Hill and Wang, 1996), 19.

17. Michael Liu and Shauna Lo, *Insights into Early Chinese American Community Development in Massachusetts through the U.S. Census* (Boston: Institute for Asian American Studies, 2014).

18. Stephen E. Ambrose, *Nothing Like It in the World: The Men Who Built the Transcontinental Railroad, 1863–1869* (New York: Simon and Schuster, 2000).

19. Ronald Takaki, *Strangers from a Distant Shore: A History of Asian Americans* (New York: Penguin, 1990), 80–92.

20. There were other Chinese inhabitants. For a short period, the Chinese government sent a significant number of Chinese male students to study in the western Massachusetts education system. The program ended in 1895, and most of the students returned to China.

21. Xiao-huang Yin, "The Population Pattern and Occupational Structure of Boston's Chinese Community in 1940," *Maryland Historian* 20, no. 1 (1989): 59–69.

22. Sampson, Davenport, and Company, *Boston Directory* (Boston: Franklin, 1880); Sampson, Murdock, and Company, *Boston Directory* (Boston: Franklin, 1892).

23. Neil Chin, "Occupation: Laundryman," in *A Chinatown Banquet,* dir. Mike Blockstein (Boston: Asian Community Development Corporation, 2006), DVD.

24. Thernstrom, *Other Bostonians,* 250–56.

25. Sucheng Chan, "The Exclusion of Chinese Women, 1870–1943," in *Entry Denied: Exclusion and the Chinese Community in America, 1882–1943,* ed. Sucheng Chan (Philadelphia: Temple University Press, 1991).

26. "Do Not Evade the Law," *Boston Herald,* November 17, 1883.

27. In other census research, Shauna Lo and I found that a number of Chinese were misclassified as white or colored. We identified 312 Chinese; nineteen were female, of whom twelve were wives and seven were daughters. The 96 percent calculation is based on our count.

28. Angelo Ancheta, "The Chinese Exclusion Act," in *A Chinatown Banquet.*

29. On the structure and role of CCBA and huigans, see Lai, *Becoming Chinese American,* 39–76.

30. In the early years, the *Boston Herald* claimed that the Moy clan dominated and vied with the Yee clan, another large extended family. This could not be verified through discussions with members of the Moy family association. Smaller surname groups did form multifamily associations to attain critical membership size.

31. CCBA of New England lists its founding year as 1923, which may have been its incorporation date. Him Mark Lai, based on his review of several sources, puts the date at 1912 (Lai, *Becoming Chinese American,* 61–62).

32. Lai, *Becoming Chinese American,* 47–49.

33. K. Scott Wong, "'The Eagle Seeks a Helpless Quarry': Chinatown, the Police, and the Press. The 1903 Boston Chinatown Raid Revisited," *Amerasia Journal* 22, no. 3 (1996): 81–103; neighborhood resident and leader, interview with the author, Boston, March 28, 1997. Tong battles were reported in the English-language press as

late as 1925; see "Court Thronged for Tong Trial," *Boston Daily Globe,* November 5, 1925; and "The Struggle over Illegal Activities," http://chinatownatlas.org.

34. Lai, *Becoming Chinese American,* 64.

35. Wong, *Patronage, Brokerage, Entrepreneurship,* 270.

36. Thomas H. O'Connor, *The Boston Irish: A Political History* (Boston: Northeastern University Press, 1995), 60.

37. Lawrence W. Kennedy, *Planning the City upon a Hill: Boston Since 1630* (Amherst: University of Massachusetts Press, 1992), 58; Thernstrom, *Other Bostonians,* 113. Figures from 1930–50 were not available.

38. Frederick A. Bushbee, "Population," in Woods, *The City Wilderness, 39–48;* O'Connor, *Boston Irish,* 153. A newspaper article reported that the first house to be leased by Chinese was on Oxford Place ("Chinatown Moguls," *Boston Sunday Globe,* May 7, 1893).

39. Neil Swidey, "Trump's Wall and Prescott Hall," *Boston Globe Magazine,* February 5, 2017, 16–25.

40. Marilynn S. Johnson, *The New Bostonians* (Amherst: University of Massachusetts Press, 2015), 29–31.

41. Bushbee, "Population," 47; Larson and Grover, "National Register . . . Multiple Property," 27–31.

42. Mae M. Ngai, "Birthright Citizenship and the Alien Citizen," *Fordham Law Review* 75, no. 5 (2007): 2521.

43. Bushbee, "Population," 46.

44. "Chinese," *Boston Herald,* March 15, 1886; Sing Yee, conversation with the author, Boston, summer 1975.

45. Larson and Grover, "National Register . . . Multiple Property," 24; "In the New Chinatown," *Boston Daily Globe,* July 13, 1894.

46. See, for example "Dark Ways," *Boston Daily Globe,* January 5, 1895; "Court Notes," *Boston Daily Globe,* April 9, 1895; "Sorrow in Chinatown," *Boston Daily Globe,* May 14, 1895; "Opium Smoking," *Boston Daily Globe,* August 21, 1895; Larson and Grover, "National Register . . . Multiple Property," 34–41.

47. Wong, "The Eagle," 94–95.

48. Sari Roboff, *Boston's Labor Movement: An Oral History of Work and Union Organizing* (Boston: Boston 200 Corporation, 1977), 24.

49. "Girl Teachers Not Wanted: Marriages between Celestials and Their Young and Pretty Instructors Condemned by Majority of Those Interested in Labors among Orientals," *Boston Daily Globe,* September 13, 1903. The article "Bride of a Celestial: Miss Nellie White Becomes Mrs. Moy Dong" (*Boston Daily Globe,* April 28, 1893) reported that there were twenty white-Chinese married couples in Chinatown.

50. Shauna Lo and Laura Wai Ng, "Beyond Bachelorhood: Chinese American Interracial Marriage in Massachusetts during the Exclusion Era," *Chinese America* (2013): 29–37. Lo and Ng found that husbands were often laundrymen, cooks, and merchants who had married domestics, waitresses, and seamstresses. The wives tended to be in their early twenties, while the husbands were several years older.

51. Albert B. Southwick, "White Women Were Backbone of Chinese Laundries," *[Worcester] Sunday Telegram,* September 15, 2002. Interestingly, Huping Ling found

that Chinese laundries in Chicago employed Black and "Mexican" labor. Chicago Chinatown differed from Boston's in its proximity to predominately African American neighborhoods (*Chinese Chicago: Race, Transnational Migration, and Community Since 1870* [Stanford, CA: Stanford University Press, 2012], 80).

52. Mary Chapman, "Notes on the Chinese in Boston," *Journal of American Folklore* 5, no. 19 (1892): 321–324; "Chinese Restaurants," *Boston Globe,* June 23, 1889. The location of Chinese restaurants on the second floor can be verified in contemporary photographs in Wing-kai To and Chinese Historical Society of New England, *Chinese in Boston, 1870–1965* (Portsmouth, NH: Arcadia, 2008), 27, 31.

53. "A Dinner in Chinatown," *Boston Herald,* March 1, 1891; "With Contempt," *Boston Daily Globe,* August 30, 1895; "Saw the Odd Things: Lieut Gov. Wolcott Went Slumming Last Night," *Boston Sunday Globe,* February 16, 1896; "Parties for Chinatown," *Boston Sunday Globe,* May 6, 1894; Herbert Heywood, "China in New England," *New England Magazine* 28 (June 1903): 481; "A Trip to Chinatown," *Boston Sunday Globe,* September 10, 1893.

54. Interview, March 28, 1997.

55. Hop Yuen Company, *Chinese Directory of New England* (Boston, 1931); Todd Stevens, "Dinner at the Den: Chinese Restaurants in Boston, 1900–1950" (unpublished manuscript, 1998); Neil Chin, "Bootlegging," in *A Chinatown Banquet.*

56. Tunney Lee, conversations with the author, February–April 2016.

57. "Goon Dong's First," *Boston Daily Globe,* July 17, 1895.

58. Neil Larson and Kathryn Grover, "National Register of Historic Places Registration Form: Quincy Grammar School," application submitted to the National Park Service, May 4, 2017, available at the Chinese Historical Society of New England.

59. Nine-man volleyball is a form of the sport popular in Toisan (Taishan). See To and Chinese Historical Society, *Chinese in Boston,* 72–73; Larson and Grover, "National Register . . . Multiple Property," 57; "Kew Sing Music Company," *Chinese Historical Society of New England Newsletter* (Summer 1998): 3–5; Carlton Sagara, "A Short History of Volleyball in Chinatown and the Annual North American Invitational Volleyball Tournament," in *50th Annual Chinese Invitational Volleyball Tournament* (Boston: Chinese Consolidated Benevolent Association, 1994), n.p. Please note that the issue-date format of community organization newsletters and publications may not meet accepted publication standards and may vary over time. As is true for Sampan, these publications, with limited resources, are sometimes inconsistent in their issue-dates and issue-date formats, depending on their staff.

60. Hop Yuen, *Chinese Directory.* In 2014, a chapter of the alliance re-formed and has remained active.

61. Chen, "Remaking Boston's Chinatown," 19.

62. Horace Greeley, *An Overland Journey from New York to San Francisco in the Summer of 1859* (New York: Saxton, Barker, 1860), 289.

63. Murphey, "Boston's Chinatown," 245.

64. For more on this enclave, see Olivia Waishek, "Syriantown," in *A Chinatown Banquet;* and "Syrians, Lebanese, and Other Arab Americans," Boston College, Department of History, https://globalboston.bc.edu.

65. Kathryn E. Wilson, *Ethnic Renewal in Philadelphia's Chinatown: Space, Place, and Struggle* (Philadelphia: Temple University Press, 2015), 12.
66. Chen, "Remaking Boston's Chinatown," 3.
67. Larson and Grover, "National Register . . . Multiple Property," 64; To and Chinese Historical Society, *Chinese in Boston*, 56–58.
68. Larson and Grover, "National Register . . . Multiple Property," 64–66; To and Chinese Historical Society, *Chinese in Boston*, 86–87, 97–101.

CHAPTER 2: A NEIGHBORHOOD MOVES THROUGH UNFAMILIAR TIMES, 1942–1974

1. Thomas C. Chen, "Remaking Boston's Chinatown: Race, Space, and Urban Development, 1943–1994," (PhD diss., Brown University, 2014), 52.
2. Thomas H. O'Connor, *Building a New Boston: Politics and Urban Renewal, 1950 to 1970* (Boston: Northeastern University Press, 1993), 8–36.
3. Lawrence W. Kennedy, *Planning the City upon a Hill: Boston Since 1630* (Amherst: University of Massachusetts Press, 1992), 129–55.
4. John H. Mollenkopf, *The Contested City* (Princeton, NJ: Princeton University Press, 1983), 149; Scott Greenberger, "In Fight for Funds, Menino's Hands Tied by History," *Boston Globe*, April 29, 2003; Kennedy, *Planning the City*, 135.
5. Mollenkopf, *Contested City*, 143.
6. Barry Bluestone and Mary Huff Stevenson, *The Boston Renaissance: Race, Space, and Economic Change in an American Metropolis* (New York: Russell Sage Foundation, 2000), 101; O'Connor, *Building a New Boston*, 147.
7. Mollenkopf, *Contested City*, 142.
8. Katie Kenneally, *Chinatown: Boston 200 Neighborhood History Series* (Boston: Boston 200 Corporation, 1976), 9. Segregation and discrimination still affected many Chinese after the war. As Rhoads Murphey noted, Chinese with college degrees still had trouble finding employment and housing outside of Chinatown ("Boston's Chinatown," *Economic Geography* 28, no. 3 [1952]: 252).]
9. "Boston, Wellesley Greet Madam Chiang Kai-Shek," *Boston Herald*, March 7, 1943.
10. Gloria Negri, "Neil Chin, 90, Founder, Guide to Many Chinatown Community Organizations," *Boston Sunday Globe*, October 18, 2009.
11. Bill Ong Hing, *Making and Remaking Asian America through Immigration Policy, 1850–1990* (Stanford, CA: Stanford University Press, 1993) 36.
12. The 1950 census grouped "Chinese" under the racial category "Other." It is possible that Japanese American and Native American populations accounted for a small fraction of this number (U.S. Census Bureau, U.S. Census of Population, 1950, vol. 3, Census Tract Statistics [Washington, DC: U.S. Government Printing Office, 1952], 2, 9). Also see Charles D. Underhill, "Public Health," in *The City Wilderness: A Settlement Study*, ed. Robert A. Woods (Boston: Houghton Mifflin, 1898), 61–66; Charles Sullivan and Kathlyn Hatch, *The Chinese in Boston, 1970* (Boston: Action for Boston Community Development, 1970), 67–69.
13. Sullivan and Hatch, *Chinese in Boston, 1970*, 70.

14. Cynthia Yee, conversation with the author, May 2009; Betty Hok-Ming Lam, "Old Quincy School Reopens Its Doors as New Community Center," *Sampan* (February–March 1984): 1, 10.

15. Caroline Chang, "The Original Settlers Are Now the Strangers," in *A Chinatown Banquet*, dir. Mike Blockstein (Boston: Asian Community Development Corporation, 2006), DVD.

16. Hing, *Making and Remaking*, 81.

17. Massachusetts Department of Labor and Industries, Division of Statistics, *A Directory of Massachusetts Manufacturers Employing Fifty or More Production Workers, 1951* (Boston, 1951), 6–14. This listing includes only larger shops; there were probably numerous smaller garment enterprises.

18. John R. Logan and Harvey L. Molotch, *Urban Fortunes: The Political Economy of Place* (Berkeley: University of California Press, 1987).

19. Hynes became acting mayor after Curley was imprisoned in 1947. He was elected in his own right in 1949 (O'Connor, *Building a New Boston*, 20–32).

20. Mollenkopf, *Contested City*, 157.

21. Boston City Planning Board, *General Plan for Boston: Preliminary Report* (Boston: City of Boston Printing Department, 1950).

22. Charles Abrams, *Forbidden Neighbors: A Study of Prejudice in Housing* (1955; reprint, Port Washington, NY: Kennikat, 1971), 245; Derrick Jackson, "Out of Rubble, Resolve," *Boston Globe Magazine*, March 2, 1997, 39; Herbert J. Gans, *The Urban Villagers: Group and Class in the Life of Italian-Americans*, 2nd ed. (New York: Free Press, 1982), 370.

23. Kennedy, *Planning the City*, 159.

24. Mel King, *Chain of Change: Struggles for Black Community Development* (Boston: South End Press, 1981), 20–21.

25. Ibid., 22.

26. Peter Canellos, "Old Boston Grievances Die Hard," *Boston Globe*, November 25, 1997; Anthony J. Yudis, "Boston's Pieces Coming Together," *New England Magazine of the Boston Sunday Globe*, November 23, 1975, 18.

27. Mollenkopf, *Contested City*, 166. For more about Logue's and Collins's effect on the Boston landscape, see ibid., 163–79; Kennedy, *Planning the City*, 159–92; and O'Connor, *Building a New Boston*, 172–240.

28. Canellos, "Old Boston Grievances"; J. Anthony Lukas, *Common Ground: A Turbulent Decade in the Lives of Three American Families* (New York: Vintage, 1986), 153–54; King, *Chain of Change*.

29. Mollenkopf, *Contested City*, 165–67.

30. Lukas, *Common Ground*, 201.

31. Sullivan and Hatch, *Chinese in Boston, 1970*, 18.

32. Richard Soo Hoo, "Hudson Street Stories," in *A Chinatown Banquet*.

33. "Saving Chinatown," *Boston Traveler*, October 21, 1953, 42.

34. Yanni Tsipis, "Hudson Street Stories," in *A Chinatown Banquet*.

35. Mark Hall and Frank Ling, *Chinatown Planning Project, 1971* (Boston: Harvard Urban Field Service, 1971).

36. David Moy, interview by the author, Boston, December 13, 1996.
37. Tufts–New England Medical Center changed its name to Tufts Medical Center in 2008.
38. Chen, "Remaking Boston's Chinatown," 108–19; Kevin Lynch, *New England Medical Center in the South Cove: A Study for the Development of the New England Medical Center and Its Neighborhood* (Boston: New England Medical Center, 1955).
39. Gans, *Urban Villagers,* xiii–xiv; Jackson, "Out of Rubble, Resolve"; Boston Redevelopment Authority, *Urban Renewal Plan: South Cove Urban Renewal Area* (Boston, June 8, 1965 [with amendments through January 1969]).
40. Zenobia Lai, Andrew Leong, and Chi Chi Wu, "The Lessons of the Parcel C Struggle: Reflections on Community Lawyering," *Asian Pacific American Law Journal* 6, no. 1 (2000): 9.
41. For more detail about the local opposition to the Central Artery, see Chen, "Remaking Boston's Chinatown," 80–90.
42. Reggie Wong, "The Chinese Merchants Building," in *A Chinatown Banquet.*
43. Tunney Lee, personal communication, July 2012.
44. Ibid.
45. Karilyn Crockett, *People before Highways: Boston Activists, Urban Planners, and a New Movement for City Making* (Amherst: University of Massachusetts Press, 2018).
46. Hall and Ling, *Chinatown Planning Project,* 57; Sullivan and Hatch, *The Chinese in Boston, 1970,* 38–42.
47. Hing, *Making and Remaking,* 80–88.
48. Zenobia Lai, interview by the author, Brookline, MA, March 2, 1997.
49. Chinese American Civic Association, *The Future of Chinatown* (Boston, March 1972), 34.
50. Sullivan and Hatch, *Chinese in Boston, 1970,* iii–iv.
51. Neil Larson and Kathryn Grover, "National Register of Historic Places Multiple Property Documentation Form: Historic Resources Associated with Chinese Immigrants and Chinese Americans in the City of Boston," application to the National Park Service, June 1, 2016, available at the Chinese Historical Society of New England, 71–72; Sullivan and Hatch, *Chinese in Boston, 1970,* 56–58; Murphey, "Boston's Chinatown," 252–53.
52. "With Little Translation, 1100 Chinese Garment Workers Kept in the Dark by the Local ILGWU," *Sampan* (April 1980): 1; "In the Garment Shops, Under-the-Table Work Benefits the Boss, Not the Worker," *Sampan* (May 1980): 2.
53. Suzanne Lee, interview by the author, Boston, November 8, 2019; Shiree Teng, "Women, Community, and Equality," *East Wind* 2, no. 1 (Spring–Summer 1983): 20–23.
54. Sullivan and Hatch, *Chinese in Boston, 1970,* 12.
55. Richard Farrell, "The White Peril Threatening Chinatown," *B.A.D.,* October 19, 1971.
56. Asian American Civic Association, "Mission," https://AACA-boston.org; Stephanie Wong Fan, "QSCC's Beginnings—25 Years Ago," *Quincy School Community Council Newsletter* (March 1995): 2, 4.

57. For a fuller history of the Asian American movement's activism, see Michael Liu, Kim Geron, and Tracy Lai, *Snake Dance of Asian American Activism* (Lanham, MD: Lexington, 2008).

58. Free Chinatown Committee, "Stop Tufts!!" [flyer] (Boston, 1971).

59. Tufts–New England Medical Center, "Open Letter to the Community" (Boston, June 6, 1971).

60. For a partial list of voluntary, civic, and activist organizations in this period, see Hall and Ling, *Chinatown Planning Project*, 23–40. In addition to those mentioned in this chapter, they include voluntary groups such as the Chinese Drop-In Center, Chinese Americans for Tomorrow, and the Free Chinatown Committee. Also see Chinatown Housing and Development Task Force, "Chinatown Housing and Land Development Task Force: Goals and Principles" (Boston, ca. 1979); "A Quarter Century of Change for Boston's Asian Community," *Sampan*, October 17, 1997, 5; and Alan LaRue, "Pacific Asian Coalition: Teaching People to Use Political Action to Solve Problems," *Sampan* (October 1976): 2.

61. Don Clark, "Disputes Shatter Chinatown Unity," *Boston Herald Traveler,* October 24, 1971; Richard Farrell, "FBI Recruiting Informers in Chinatown," *B.A.D.,* November 2–8, 1971. Traditional leaders also invited conservative non-neighborhood groups into Chinatown; for instance, they paraded alongside Young Americans for Freedom in October 1971.

62. Betsy Q. M. Tong, "In Step with the Chin Bros.: After Years of Politicking, Two Players Reflect on the Game," *Boston Globe,* September 5, 1993; Frank Chin, interview, December 3, 1996, in Gene Koo, "Representing Chinatown" (undergraduate paper, Harvard University, March 1997).

63. Min Zhou, *Chinatown: The Socioeconomic Potential of an Urban Enclave* (Philadelphia: Temple University Press 1992).

64. Hall and Ling, *Chinatown Planning Project,* 57, 60.

CHAPTER 3: THE NEIGHBORHOOD IN A WORLD-CLASS CITY, 1974–1983

1. Lawrence W. Kennedy, *Planning the City upon a Hill: Boston Since 1630* (Amherst: University of Massachusetts Press, 1992), 193–215; J. Anthony Lukas, *Common Ground: A Turbulent Decade in the Lives of Three American Families* (New York: Vintage, 1986), 196–215.

2. Richard Martin, "300 Tenants at Boston Rally Urge Rent Control Extension," *Boston Evening Globe,* December 31, 1975; David Rogers, "Hub Rent Control Law Enacted for Four Years," *Boston Evening Globe,* January 2, 1976.

3. Lukas, *Common Ground,* 616.

4. Kennedy, *Planning the City,* 209.

5. Ibid., 204; George V. Higgins, *Style versus Substance: Boston, Kevin White, and the Politics of Illusion* (New York: Macmillan, 1984), 143.

6. Thomas H. O'Connor, *The Boston Irish: A Political History* (Boston: Northeastern University Press, 1995), 250.

7. Kennedy, *Planning the City,* 211.

8. John Avault and Mark Johnson, "A Survey of Commercial and Institutional Development in Boston's Neighborhoods, 1975–1989" (Boston: Boston Redevelopment Authority, 1987).

9. "Chinatown—Deterioration and Dilapidation," *Chinese American Civic Association Newsletter,* September 8, 1970, 6.

10. South Cove Community Health Center, "Celebrating 25 Years of Community Service" (Boston, October 1997), 1–9; "Grant Sought to Aid Local Economic Development," *Sampan* (December 1974): 1.

11. Chinese Progressive Association, "About Us," https://CPAboston.org; "October 1st Celebration a Success," *Getting Together* (November 1976): 3; "Third World Construction Workers Fight Inequalities," *Getting Together* (June–July 1976): 5; Marian Hwang, "Confrontation with Union Sparks City Hall Rally: Chinese Hardhats Unite!," *Sampan* (June 1976): 5. More moderate groups such as the Chinese American Civic Association also worked with Third World Jobs Clearinghouse but weren't active in protests at job sites.

12. John Wang, "The Kuomingtang Here," *New York Times,* January 20, 1979; "ROC [Republic of China] Consulate Closes Doors in Boston," *Sampan* (March 1979): 1. Numerous individuals from traditional Chinatown organizations held honorific positions in bodies established by the Republic of China. For example, while Shih-hing Lee was president of CCBA, he was also elected to the republic's legislature ("ROC Names Shih-Hing Lee to its Legislative Yuan," *Sampan* [January 1976]: 5). Some of these individuals received economic support from the republic, and almost all traditional organizations in Boston continue to support it.

13. May Lee Tom, "Remembering Hudson Street," *CHSNE Newsletter* 2 (Spring 1996): 3.

14. Gloria Chun, "Mayor White Meets with Chinese Leaders," *Sampan* (March 1975): 1.

15. Ibid.

16. Mark Hall and Frank Ling, *Chinatown Planning Project, 1971* (Boston: Harvard Urban Field Service, 1971), 65.

17. Steve Bailey, "Which Way, Chinatown?," *Boston Globe,* January 22, 2003.

18. Neighborhood resident and leader, interview with the author, Boston, March 28, 1997.

19. "CCBA Opposes Proposed Life Ctr. Elderly Housing," *Sampan* (April 1976): 6; Gloria Chun, "Elderly Housing Project Nears Deadline," *Sampan* (June 1976): 3.

20. "Chinatown—Deterioration and Dilapidation," 6.

21. Fred C. Doolittle, George S. Masnick, Phillip L. Clay, and Gregory A. Jackson, *Future Boston: Patterns and Perspectives* (Cambridge, MA: Massachusetts Institute of Technology and Harvard University, Joint Center for Urban Studies, 1982), 71.

22. Why the area became known as the Combat Zone is unclear. One theory is that the frequenters of such businesses historically came from the local military bases, though this was more accurate when these businesses were in Scollay Square. Some attribute the name to the frequent brawls in the area, and others say that local newspaper reporters popularized the designation in their writing (Jonathan Kaufman, "From Scollay Square Tattoo Parlors to Combat Zone Porno Films," *Boston Globe,* December 27, 1984; Ian Smith, "Interesting Photos Glimpse into

the Everyday Life of the Combat Zone, Boston in the 1970s," December 25, 2015, https://www.thevintagenews.com).

23. Salvatore M. Giorlandino, "The Origin, Development, and Decline of Boston's Adult Entertainment District: The Combat Zone" (master's thesis, Massachusetts Institute of Technology, 1986).

24. J. Larocca, letter to the editor, *Boston Globe*, October 18, 1974.

25. "Combat Zone 'Containment' Proposal Passes," *Sampan* (November 1974): 1–2.

26. Tom Lee, "The Combat Zone," in *A Chinatown Banquet,* dir. Mike Blockstein (Boston: Asian Community Development Corporation, 2006), DVD.

27. Neil Chin, "Hudson Street Stories," in ibid.

28. Much of the following narrative about busing in Chinatown derives from interviews with May Yu and Suzanne Lee in Lorrayne Shen, "The Chinese American Experience during Desegregation Busing in Boston" (thesis, Tufts University, 2012); Thomas Chen, "Remaking Boston's Chinatown: Race, Space, and Urban Development, 1943–1994" (PhD diss., Brown University, 2014); and Suzanne Lee, interview by the author, Boston, November 8, 2019.

29. *An Act Providing for the Elimination of Racial Imbalance in the Public Schools,* 1965 Mass. acts 414, August 18, 1965.

30. Mel King, *Chain of Change: Struggles for Black Community Development* (Boston: South End Press, 1981), 158–59.

31. Ronald P. Formisano, *Boston against Busing: Race, Class, and Ethnicity in the 1960s and 1970s* (Chapel Hill: University of North Carolina Press, 1991), 69.

32. Chen, "Remaking Boston's Chinatown," 88–89; King, *Chain of Change,* 30–46.

33. Jeanne Theoharis cites spending figures of $340 for white students and $240 for Black students ("'We Saved the City': Black Struggles for Educational Equality in Boston, 1960–1976," Radical History Review 81 [October 2001]: 66).

34. Formisano, *Boston against Busing,* 44.

35. Ibid., 47.

36. King, *Chain of Change,* 45.

37. Jim Vrabel, *A People's History of the New Boston* (Amherst: University of Massachusetts Press, 2014), 170–71.

38. King, *Chain of Change,* 157–58.

39. Corinne Zaczek Bermon, "Selected Resources Documenting School Desegregation," Healey Library at University of Massachusetts Boston, https://umb.libguides.com; Lukas, *Common Ground,* 616; Formisano, *Boston against Busing,* 70.

40. Chen, "Remaking Boston's Chinatown," 180–81.

41. Deanna Wong, the first Chinese teacher in the Quincy School, remembered being left out of meetings and generally shunned. Lee experienced similar treatment at the Harvard Kent School in Charlestown and went to union meetings at which white teachers accused teachers of color of "taking their jobs" (Suzanne Lee, interview, November 8. 2019; Deanna Wong, personal communication, Brookline, October 1, 2019). Under the court desegregation order, one Black teacher had to be hired for every white teacher. The U.S. Supreme Court, in *Lau v. Nichols,* had also recently required supplemental educational programs for non-English-speaking

students. This decision led to the hiring of bilingual teachers for Chinese- and Spanish-speaking students in the Boston system (*Morgan v. Hennigan,* 379 F. Supp. 410 [D.C. Mass., June 21, 1974]; *Lau v. Nichols,* 414 U.S. 563 [1973]).

42. James Tam and George Tam were involved in a nighttime melee with a large group of white youth. Patrice Borden, who was among that group, died in the fight, and the Tam brothers faced trial, one for manslaughter. Though all of the participants lived in Charlestown, the Chinatown community began a defense committee and fundraised for the brothers.

43. Karen Lindsey, "Pride and Promise," *Boston Herald Sunday Magazine,* May 12, 1985, 12.

44. Shen, "The Chinese American Experience," 21.

45. Ibid., 20–21.

46. Lee, interview, November 8. 2019.

47. Manli Ho and Carmen Fields, "Chinatown, South End Have Same Thought: Education," *Boston Globe,* September 2, 1975.

48. Boston Chinese Parents Association (BCPA), "For Immediate Release," September 3, 1975.

49. Ibid. There had been an intervening meeting with Associate Superintendent Charles Leftwich that produced inadequate commitments for safety.

50. Shen, "The Chinese American Experience," 25; Lee, interview, November 8, 2019.

51. Chen, "Remaking Boston's Chinatown," 194; "Bulletin," *Sampan* (September 1975): 1.

52. The service had been created under the Civil Rights Act of 1964 to provide technical assistance in racial discrimination issues (U.S. Department of Justice, "Community Relations Service Annual Report 2011" [Washington D.C., 2011], ii).

53. Shen, "The Chinese American Experience," 26.

54. Chen, "Remaking Boston's Chinatown," 190–91.

55. Ibid., 197.

56. Ibid., 195.

57. Tufts University, "New England Medical Center Timeline: 1665–1992," https://dl.tufts.edu; "Tufts Plans Major Chinatown Construction," *Sampan* (October–November 1978): 2.

58. "Chinatown Tenants Fight Eviction, Tufts' Plans," *Sampan* (April 1979): 1–2; Chinatown Housing and Land Development Task Force, minutes, April 20, 1979.

59. Boston Redevelopment Authority, letter to Chinatown Housing and Land Development Task Force, January 22, 1979; Chinatown Housing and Land Development Task Force, "Bradford Towers Housing for the Elderly" [letter to Stanley Chen, Thomas Cornu, and Richard Sayre], August 1, 1979.

60. Anthony J. Yudis, "Chen Gets Deadline on Plan for Elderly," *Boston Sunday Globe,* January 14, 1979; Community Task Force on Housing and Land Development in Chinatown, minutes, October 27, 1978.

61. Boston Redevelopment Authority, "South Cove Urban Renewal Plan" (Boston, 1965).

62. Chinatown Housing and Land Development Task Force, "Come Rally in Support of Chinatown" [leaflet], November 1978.

63. Anthony J. Yudis, "Downtown Development Gets under Way," *Boston Sunday Globe,* April 5, 1981.

64. "Community Protests Tufts Expansion Plans," "Public Hearing Ignored by TNEMC," *Sampan* (December 1978): 1–2.

65. Chinatown Housing and Land Development Task Force, "Why We Are Marching: Preserve Chinatown" [leaflet], ca. 1980; "Demonstration at Tufts," *Chinatown Housing Newsletter,* February–March 1980): 1.

66. Robert Jordan, "Chinatown Hits Lease of 2 Buildings," *Boston Globe,* April 23, 1981; Edward McInnis, "Tufts' Lease on Two Kneeland Street Buildings Threatens over 600 Jobs in Chinatown," *Sampan* (May 1981): 1, 7; Joan Axelrod, "Hanging by a Thread: Chinatown Garment Trade Threatened by Tufts Expansion," *Boston Ledger,* May 15–22, 1981, 1, 3; "Stitchers Cling to Chinatown Lifestyle," *Boston Sunday Globe,* July 19, 1981.

67. Doris Sue Wong, "New Tufts Master Plan Could Have 'Substantial Impact' on Community," *Sampan* (December 1982): 1–2.

68. Doris Sue Wong, "Tufts-Chinatown Negotiations for Joint Housing at a Standstill," *Sampan* (March–April 1983): 1, 4; Steve Marantz, "Five Take a Firm Stance for Chinatown," *Boston Globe,* March 15, 1983; Doris Sue Wong, "Coalition Calls for Tufts Building Moratorium, Proposes More Housing and Jobs for Chinatown," *Sampan* (May 1983): 1, 8–9.

69. Gene Koo, "Representing Chinatown" (undergraduate paper, Harvard University, March 1997), 37; Joanne Ball, "Chinatown Agrees to Tufts–Medical Center Pact," *Boston Globe,* September 13, 1983.

70. Nearly half a century later, a mixed-use project is now proposed for the site.

71. Caroline Chang, Richard Chin, Florence Soo Hoo, Richard Soo Hoo, Tunney Lee, Jeffrey Wong, and Reggie Wong, "The Original Settlers Are Now the Strangers," in *A Chinatown Banquet.*

72. John H. Mollenkopf, *The Contested City* (Princeton, NJ: Princeton University Press, 1983), 176.

73. Ibid., 180–90, 289. Mollenkopf quotes from the National Commission on Neighborhoods, "The Case for Neighborhoods: A Progress Report" (Washington, DC, 1978), 11.

CHAPTER 4: CHINATOWN JOINS THE REVOLT OF THE NEIGHBORHOODS, 1975–1983

1. The events described in this chapter overlap those in chapter 3. My hope is that focusing on the particular issues' development will help readers follow the complex narrative. Similar chronological transitions will occur in later chapters.

2. Boston Redevelopment Authority (BRA), "Jordan Marsh/Lafayette Place" (Boston, 1975).

3. Anthony J. Yudis, "Boston's Pieces Coming Together," *Boston Sunday Globe,* November 23, 1975.

4. Boston Finance Commission, "Report on the Lafayette Place Development Project" (Boston, April 26, 1979).

5. The U.S. General Accounting Office later called the grant award "highly questionable." It concluded that the grant was used primarily to relieve tax burdens on the developers rather than address economic and physical redevelopment needs. See Chris Black, "Lafayette Pl. Grant Questioned," *Boston Globe,* May 8, 1979.

6. White contributed to Lafayette Place's difficulties by diverting a major project, a million-square-foot federal office building, away from the area. See Lawrence W. Kennedy, *Planning the City upon a Hill: Boston Since 1630* (Amherst: University of Massachusetts Press, 1992), 207; and Jean Gogolin, "Kevin's Gospel," *Boston Magazine* 72, no. 7 (1980), 70–73, 94–108.

7. BRA, "Jordan Marsh/Lafayette Place," 16; Boston Redevelopment Authority (BRA), "Lafayette Place Final Environmental Impact Statement" (Boston, 1978), 232–36.

8. City of Boston, "Lafayette Place: Urban Development Action Grant" (Boston, January 1978).

9. "Chinatown Seeks Job Commitments from Lafayette Place Developers," *Sampan* (July 1979).

10. Douglas Simmons, "Lafayette Passes, Chinatown Promised Housing," *Sampan* (October–November 1978): 1.

11. "Looking for Jobs on Lafayette Place, Chinatown Group Is Making Headway," *Sampan* (August 1980); Chinatown Citizens Advisory Committee, "A Request to the City" (Boston, 1980).

12. "Preliminary Mayoral Election, Vote! Tuesday, Sept. 25: Sampan Interviews Mayoral Candidates," *Sampan* (September 1979): 3.

13. David Moy, interview by the author, Boston, December 13, 1996.

14. Kenneth Chung-keung Yee, "What Lafayette Place Will Mean for Chinatown," *Sampan* (January 1984): 13.

15. Lawrence Cheng, interview by the author, Cambridge, MA, July 22, 1997.

16. Robert Campbell, "Boston's Worst Buildings," *Boston Globe,* December 23, 1984.

17. Suzanne Lee, personal communication, March 15, 1998.

18. Scott Cummings, "Private Enterprise and Public Policy," in *Business Elites and Urban Development,* ed. Scott Cummings (Albany: State University of New York Press, 1988), 11–12.

19. "The Future of Kevin White" [editorial], *Boston Globe,* July 14, 1982.

20. Kirk Scharfenberg, "Image Could Help, Hurt Finnegan," *Boston Sunday Globe,* July 24, 1983; Donald A. Gillis, "The Sociology of a City in Transition: Boston, 1980–2000" (PhD diss., Boston University 2015), 60; Ed Quill, "Campaign 1983: The Ungluing of White's Organization," *Boston Globe,* August 22, 1983.

21. Robert L. Turner, "Some Warning Signs for Finnegan," *Boston Sunday Globe,* August 19, 1983. The source of the linkage idea is not entirely clear. The concept was instituted formally in San Francisco before it was brought to Boston. Kirk Scharfenberg, a columnist for the *Boston Globe,* was the first to publicly propose it as an urban policy issue appropriate for Boston. Subsequently, Bruce Bolling proposed a linkage ordinance to the city council. The council passed the ordinance, and White vetoed it. Massachusetts Fair Share collected sufficient signatures to put the plan to a referendum vote in 1983. During that year's campaign, Mel King was the first candidate to propose a linkage policy.

22. Charles Kenney, "2 Referendum Questions Will Be on Tuesday's Ballot," *Boston Globe*, November 12, 1983.

23. James Green, "The Making of Mel King's Rainbow Coalition: Political Changes in Boston, 1963–1983," *Radical America*, 17, no. 6/18, no. 1 (1983–84): 129.

24. Joan Vennochi and Charles Kenney, "It's Coming to a Boil: Finnegan, Flynn Clash," *Boston Globe*, October 7, 1983.

25. Green, "Making of Mel King's Rainbow Coalition"; Pierre Clavel, *Activists in City Hall: The Progressive Response to the Reagan Era in Boston and Chicago* (Ithaca, NY: Cornell University Press, 2010), 55–58; Kennedy, *Planning the City*, 217–18.

26. Mike Liu, "Grassroots Politics and Boston's Asian Community," *Radical America*, 17, no. 6/18, no. 1 (1983–84): 80–82; "CPPA Endorses Mel King for Mayor," *Sampan* (August 1983): 7.

27. Liu, "Grassroots Politics," 82; Betty Hok-Ming Lam, "Harassment, Violence against Indochinese Refugees," *Sampan* (August1983): 1, 5; Doris Sue Wong, "Judge Denies Resentencing in Vincent Chin Case; U.S. Dept. of Justice Gives Case Priority Status," *Sampan* (July 1983): 2, 12; Betty Hok-Ming Lam, "Boston Chinese Organizations Support Re-opening of Vincent Chin Case," *Sampan* (July 1983): 2.

28. Ellen Herman, "Ain't No Stopping Us Now: Notes from the Community," *Radical America*, 17, no. 6/18, no. 1 (1983–84): 62–64.

29. Doris Sue Wong, "Chinatown Perspectives on Politics," *Sampan*, May 1, 1984, 5.

30. Liu, "Grassroots Politics," 82–84.

31. Wong, "Chinatown Perspectives on Politics," 1.

32. David Nyhan, "Populism Was the Big Victor in This Election," *Boston Globe*, October 13, 1983.

33. Michael K. Frisby, "Only Sporadic Problems at the Polls," *Boston Globe*, November 16, 1983.

34. Bruce A. Mohl, "The Day After, Business Appears Conciliatory," *Boston Globe*, October 13, 1983.

35. John H. Mollenkopf, *The Contested City* (Princeton, NJ: Princeton University Press, 1983), 289–94; Susan S. Fainstein, "Local Mobilization and Economic Discontent," in *The Capitalist City*, ed. Michael Peter Smith and Joe R. Feagin (Cambridge, MA: Blackwell, 1987), 323–42.

36. Doris Sue Wong, "Rainbow Leader Says Vandalizing May Be Response to Stance on Arabs," *Boston Globe*, January 11, 1988; Judith Evans, "Hub Blacks Support Asians in Beating Case," *Boston Sunday Globe*, June 9, 1985; Sheila D. Collins, *The Rainbow Challenge: The Jackson Campaign and the Future of U.S. Politics* (New York: Monthly Review Press, 1986), 200–202; Elizabeth O. Colton, *The Jackson Phenomenon: The Man, the Power, the Message* (New York: Doubleday, 1989), 16, 27.

CHAPTER 5: LIMITS OF THE POPULIST GROWTH COALITION, 1984–1989

1. Pierre Clavel, *Activists in City Hall: The Progressive Response to the Reagan Era in Boston and Chicago* (Ithaca, NY: Cornell University Press, 2010), 65–66.

2. Lawrence W. Kennedy, *Planning the City upon a Hill: Boston Since 1630* (Amherst: University of Massachusetts Press, 1992), 219–28.

3. Clavel, *Activists in City Hall*, 65.

4. Campbell Gibson and Kay Jung, *Historical Census Statistics on Population Totals by Race, 1790 to 1990, and by Hispanic Origin, 1970 to 1990, for Large Cities and Other Urban Places in the United States* (Washington, DC: U.S. Bureau of the Census, February 2005), tab. 22.

5. While my research could not determine the percentage of the electorate who were people of color, the *Boston Globe* reported in 1993 that 35 percent of city residents of voting age were people of color. Because of lower citizenship status among Asians and Latinos, their voter eligibility rate is lower, and historically people of color have registered at rates below those of whites.

6. Marie Kennedy, Mauricio Gaston, and Chris Tilly, "Roxbury Capital Investment or Community Development?," in *Fire in the Hearth: The Radical Politics of Place in America,* ed. Mike Davis, Steven Hiatt, Marie Kennedy, Susan Ruddick, and Michael Sprinker (London: Verso, 1990), 123–34; Joanne Ball, "Secession Supporters to Push New Campaign," *Boston Globe,* April 22, 1987.

7. Boston Municipal Research Bureau, "Boston's Linkage Program: A New Approach to Managing Linkage Funds for Housing and Job Training" (Boston, 1998).

8. Peter Medoff and Holly Sklar, *Streets of Hope: The Fall and Rise of an Urban Neighborhood* (Boston: South End Press, 1994), 64.

9. Kennedy, *Planning the City,* 222–28; Todd Swanstrom, "Urban Populism, Uneven Development, and the Space for Reform," in *Business Elites and Urban Development,* ed. Scott Cummings (Albany: State University of New York Press, 1988), 141.

10. Swanstrom, "Urban Populism," 142.

11. Hillel Levine and Lawrence Harmon, *The Death of an American Jewish Community: A Tragedy of Good Intentions* (New York: Free Press, 1992), 108.

12. Medoff and Sklar, *Streets of Hope,* 115–44, 141.

13. Former neighborhood resident and activist, interview with the author, Boston, March 9, 1997.

14. Robert O'Malley, "A Quarter Century of Change for Boston's Asian Community," *Sampan,* October 17, 1997, 5–6.

15. Howard Wong, interview by the author, Milton, MA, July 19, 2015.

16. Betty Hok-Ming Lam, "Lee-Tom Sees Activist's Role," *Sampan,* June 19, 1985, 1–2; Betty Hok-Ming Lam, "Frank Chin Resigns from City Post," *Sampan,* August 15, 1984, 1, 8; Anna Wong Yee, "Nursing Home to Open in May, Serve Old Folks from All Races," *Sampan* (February 1985): 33, 43; "New Bylaws Approved by CCBA," *Sampan,* July 2, 1986, 1.

17. Asian American Resource Workshop, *Long Road to Justice: The Case of Long Guang Huang* (Boston, 1985), VHS; Betty Hok-Ming Lam, "Committee Lists Demands: Unity Perhaps Unprecedented," *Sampan,* May 22, 1985, 1–2.

18. Doris Sue Wong, "Chinatown Shows New Unity in Huang Assault Case," *Boston Globe,* May 18, 1985; Gary McMillan, "Suit Eyed against Hub Officer," *Boston Globe,* May 4, 1985; Doris Sue Wong, "200 March to City Hall Plaza to Protest Alleged Police Brutality against Chinese Immigrant," *Boston Globe,* June 19, 1985.

19. Kevin Cullen, "No Winners in Chinatown Case; Detective Kelly's Suspension for Punching Huang Leaves No One Fully Satisfied," *Boston Globe,* June 8, 1986.

20. During this period, hate crimes had victimized many Southeast Asians living in Dorchester and East Boston and in the North Shore suburbs. The Asian American Resource Workshop formed support committees during the related trials and

worked with the victims. See Thomas Palmer, "Marine Gets Life Term in Stabbing," *Boston Globe,* May 2, 1985.

21. Asian American Resource Workshop, *Against the Zone* (Boston, 1986), VHS; "Chinatown on the March," *Boston Globe,* October 19, 1985.

22. Chinese Progressive Association Workers' Center, "Garment Workers Struggle in Boston: Chronology of Events (Draft IV)" (February 1987); Doris Sue Wong, "Workers Charge Jobs Program Dragging," *Boston Globe,* April 3, 1986.

23. Peter N. Kiang and Man Chak Ng, "Through Strength and Struggle: Boston's Asian American Student/Community/Labor Solidarity," *Amerasia Journal* 15, no. 1 (1989): 285–93; Garment Workers Support Committee, "Overall Objectives" and "Subcommittee Goals and Duties" (June 18, 1986).

24. P&L Workers, "Unite to Fight! For Our Rights! Our Survival!" [leaflet] (March 1986).

25. Therese Feng and Shirley Mark Yuen, "A Victory for Garment Workers in Boston," *U.S.-China Review* 11, no. 2 (1987): 19–20.

26. Doris Sue Wong, "Garment Workers Broaden Horizons," *Boston Globe,* July 17, 1987; Lydia Lowe, "Chinese Immigrant Workers and Community-Based Labor Organizing in Boston: Paving the Way," *Amerasia Journal* 18, no. 1 (1992): 39–48.

27. Robert O'Malley, "NEMC Files Suit to Take Oak Street Building: Mayor and BRA Back Chinatown," *Sampan,* July 6, 1988, 1, 7; Robert O'Malley, "Future of Oak Street Building Still Uncertain," *Sampan,* July 20, 1988, 1, 8; Robert O'Malley, "St. Margaret's Withdraws Plan to Move Facility to Chinatown," *Sampan,* March 2, 1988, 1–2.

28. Betty Hok-Ming Lam, "Community's Decision to Set Up Neighborhood Council Differs," *Sampan,* November 21, 1984, 1, 4; Betty Hok-Ming Lam, "Chinatown Agencies Disturbed by CCBA Statement on Neighborhood Council; Meeting Scheduled to Resolve Differences," *Sampan,* December 19, 1984, 1–2; L. Kim Tan, "Flynn Appoints 21 to 1st C-T Neighborhood Council," *Sampan,* November 6, 1985, 1, 3.

29. L. Kim Tan, "Council Includes Activists, Business Owners & Residents," *Sampan,* November 6, 1985, 2; Chinatown/South Cove Neighborhood Council, "By-Laws of the Chinatown/South Cove Neighborhood Council" (January 21, 1986).

30. Marilyn Lee-Tom, personal communication, February 16, 2019; Chinatown Neighborhood Council, "Statement of Purpose" (ca. 1985), 1.

31. John Avault and Mark Johnson, "A Survey of Commercial and Institutional Development in Boston's Neighborhoods, 1975–1989" (Boston: Boston Redevelopment Authority, April 1987).

32. Maureen Dezell, "Turning Midtown Around: The Unveiling of Coyle's Dream City," *Boston Phoenix,* May 6–12, 1988.

33. Boston Municipal Research Bureau, "Boston's Linkage Program," EX3.

34. Carol Lee, interview by the author, Boston, September 2, 1997.

35. Peter Bagley, "City Memo on Parking Garage Indicates Growing Support of Chinatown in BRA," *Sampan,* July 1, 1987, 1.

36. Lawrence Cheng, interview by the author, Cambridge, MA, July 22, 1997; Chinatown/ South Cove Neighborhood Council, City of Boston, and Boston Redevelopment Authority (BRA), "Chinatown Community Plan: A Plan to Manage Growth" (Boston: Boston Redevelopment Authority, March 1990).

37. Jeffrey P. Brown, "Profile of Boston's Chinatown Neighborhood" (Boston: Boston Redevelopment Authority, June 1987); Boston Redevelopment Authority, "A Summary of Neighborhood Characteristics, Chinatown" (Boston, ca. 1987); Chinatown/South Cove Neighborhood Council et al., "Chinatown Community Plan," 31, 34.

38. Sally Jacobs, "Dreams Crowded Out in Chinatown," *Boston Sunday Globe,* August 12, 1990.

39. Tufts University, "New England Medical Center Timeline: 1665–1992," https:// dl.tufts.edu/.

40. Irene Sege, "Tufts, Hospital Agree to Swap Properties," *Boston Globe,* December 16, 1988.

41. Dezell, "Turning Midtown Around"; Boston Redevelopment Authority and Boston Office of Arts and the Humanities, "Midtown Cultural District Plan" (Boston, 1988).

42. Chinatown/South Cove Neighborhood Council et al., "Chinatown Community Plan," 32.

43. Gregory W. Perkins and Deborah A. Oriola, "Chinatown Housing Survey" (Boston: Boston Redevelopment Authority, December 1987).

44. Brown, "Profile of Boston's Chinatown Neighborhood," n.p.

45. Ibid.; Perkins and Oriola, "Chinatown Housing Survey," tab. 2.

46. Perkins and Oriola, "Chinatown Housing Survey," 12; Brown, "Profile of Boston's Chinatown Neighborhood," tab. 3.

47. Boston Redevelopment Authority, "Parcel to Parcel Linkage Program: Interim Report. Project 1: Kingston-Bedford Study" (Boston, 1986), 3.

48. John Powers, "A Linkage Proposal with Downtown Lure," *Boston Sunday Globe,* March 30, 1986; Boston Redevelopment Authority, "Development Prospectus for Southwest Corridor Parcel 18 and Kingston-Bedford Garage Site" (Boston, 1985).

49. According to the 1980 census, the median family income in Chinatown was $10,553 (Brown, "Profile of Boston's Chinatown Neighborhood," n.p.). The median family income in Roxbury was $10,773 (Margaret C. O'Brien, "Diversity and Change in Boston's Neighborhoods: A Comparison of Demographic, Social, and Economic Characteristics of Population and Housing, 1970–1980 [Boston: Boston Redevelopment Authority, October 1985], 154).

50. BRA, "Parcel to Parcel Linkage Program: Interim Report," 10–18; Tarry Hum, "Parcel to Parcel Linkage: Who Benefits from the Redistribution of Wealth" (master's thesis, Massachusetts Institute of Technology, 1987), 32–33.

51. BRA, "Parcel to Parcel Linkage Program: Interim Report," 45.

52. "Roxbury Unlinked" [editorial], *Boston Globe,* April 1, 1986.

53. Boston Redevelopment Authority, "Linkage" (Boston, 1988).

54. BRA, "Parcel to Parcel Linkage Program: Interim Report"; Charles A. Radin, "Minority Teams Strong in Bid for Hub Development Sites," *Boston Globe*, March 14, 1987.
55. Michael Frisby, "Partnership Seeks Piece of Major Developments," *Boston Globe*, September 19, 1986; Michael Frisby, "Minority Developers' Bid Receive Praise from Flynn," *Boston Globe*, September 20, 1986; Peter Howe, "Developers Make Pitch to Roxbury," *Boston Globe*, March 29, 1987.
56. BRA, "Parcel to Parcel Linkage Program: Interim Report," 10–37.
57. Boston Redevelopment Authority, "Kingston–Bedford–Essex Street Development: Draft Environmental Impact Report" (Boston, January 1988).
58. Cheng, interview.
59. Jerry Chu, interview by the author, Boston, August 28, 1997.
60. C. Lee, interview.
61. Suzanne Lee, interview by the author, Brookline, MA, February 1, 1997; Anthony J. Yudis, "BRA Chief Proposes Minority Firm for Parcel Plan," *Boston Globe*, June 19, 1987.
62. John King, "New Projects Tie Downtown to Roxbury," *Boston Globe*, January 8, 1989.
63. Jerry Ackerman, "Commercial: Have Ideas and Hopes, but Need Some Tenants," *Boston Sunday Globe*, December 31, 1989; Steve Marantz, "Linkage Revision Is Said to Be under Consideration," *Boston Globe*, January 2, 1991.
64. The Massachusetts Registry of Motor Vehicles became Parcel 18's sole tenant, but "sick building syndrome" soon forced the registry to vacate the building. Also see Paul Chan, interview by the author, Boston, October 22, 1997.
65. Edward Wong, "Parcel 18 Benefits Coming to Chinatown," *Sampan*, December 20, 1991, 1, 3.
66. Robert O'Malley, "ACDC Housing Still Needs More Financing," *Sampan*, April 2, 1993, 1–2; Robert O'Malley, "Construction Begins on Chinatown Housing," *Sampan*, October 1, 1993, 1, 6.
67. David Polochanin, "1,000 Wait in Chinatown for Hours for New Housing," *Boston Sunday Globe*, August 28, 1994.
68. Robert O'Malley, "Allegations Mar First Chinatown Election," *Sampan*, May 4, 1988, 1, 6; M. E. Malone, "2 Members, Director Resign from Chinatown Council," *Boston Globe*, May 26, 1988; Claire Ambrosini et al., letter to the editor, *Sampan*, June 1, 1988, 6.
69. Robert Campbell, "Learning the Lessons of the '80s Boom," *Boston Globe*, September 17, 1989; Swanstrom, "Urban Populism," 137.
70. Clavel, *Activists in City Hall*, 178.

CHAPTER 6: "TO BE OR NOT TO BE" FOR THE PARCEL C GARAGE, 1990–1993

1. Jerry Ackerman, "Commercial: Have Ideas and Hopes, but Need Some Tenants," *Boston Sunday Globe*, December 31, 1989; Jerry Ackerman, "Little Credit, Few

Tenants," *Boston Sunday Globe,* December 30, 1990; Jerry Ackerman, "Vacancies Up and Up," *Boston Globe,* February 11, 1991; Federal Deposit Insurance Corporation, *History of the Eighties: Lessons for the Future,* vol. 1, *An Examination of the Banking Crises of the 1980s and Early 1990s* (Washington, DC, 1997).

2. Jerry Ackerman, "Boston according to Coyle: A Q&A with the City's Chief Planner," *Boston Globe,* January 27, 1991.

3. Michael Rezendes and Dan Aucoin, "BRA Chief Coyle to End 7-Year Role: Accepts AFL-CIO Post," *Boston Globe,* December 20, 1991; Peter S. Canellos, "Flynn Slow to Fill City Hall Vacancies," *Boston Globe,* February 6, 1993; Adrian Walker, "Flynn Says Yes to Vatican Post," *Boston Globe,* March 17, 1993.

4. Steve Bailey, "What Next, Mr. Mayor?," *Boston Globe,* December 13, 2006; Thomas M. Menino and Jack Beatty, *Mayor for a New America,* (New York: Houghton Mifflin Harcourt, 2014), 14.

5. Bryan Marquard and Jim O'Sullivan, "Thomas Menino, Boston's Traditional and Transformative Mayor, Dead at 71," *Boston Globe,* October 31, 2014.

6. Adrian Walker, "Menino Burnishes Links to Business: Development Agencies Get Overhaul," *Boston Globe,* March 6, 1994. Other than Kingston-Bedford/Parcel 18, only one other parcel-to-parcel linkage package has ever been proposed.

7. Maureen Dezell, "Build-Down: Recession, Angry Residents Dog BRA Head Paul Barrett," *Boston Phoenix,* August 20, 1993, 12.

8. Dezell, "Build-Down," 12–17.

9. Campbell Gibson and Kay Jung, "Historical Census Statistics on Population Totals by Race, 1790 to 1990, and by Hispanic Origin, 1970 to 1990, for Large Cities and Other Urban Places in the United States," U.S. Census Working Paper 76, February 2005, https://www.census.gov; Chinatown Initiative, "Chinatown Masterplan 2000: Agenda for a Sustainable Neighborhood" (Boston, 2000); Chinatown Coalition, "The Chinatown Community Assessment Report" (Boston, 1994), 3.

10. Robert O'Malley, "South Cove Health Center Buys Building in the Leather District," *Sampan,* March 4, 1994, 1; Chinatown Coalition, "Community Assessment," 1–2: Robert O'Malley, "Board Members Help CEDC Pay Consultant," *Sampan,* March 15, 1989, 1, 8.

11. Michael Liu, "AARW's Annual Report to the Membership," *The Newsletter* (December 1993–January/February 1994): 1, 8–9; Lydia Lowe, personal communication, March 21, 1998.

12. Robert O'Malley, "Trouble at Gee How Oak Tin: Some Members Question One Group's Control of the Association and Its Property," Sampan, July 4, 1997, 5–6; Catherine Carlock, "Nearly 800 Residential Units Approved in Boston's South End," *Boston Business Journal,* July 13, 2018.

13. Boston Evangelical Church, "Ministry Summary" [flier] (Boston, 1996).

14. Boston Chinatown Neighborhood Center, "History and Awards," http://BCNC.net; May Louie, "CPA Celebrates 20 Years of Community Work," *Sampan,* September 5, 1997, 3.

15. Zenobia Lai, interview by the author, Brookline, MA, March 2, 1997.

16. Paul Chan, interview by the author, Boston, October 22, 1997.
17. Robert O'Malley, "What Is the Community and Who Represents It?" *Sampan*, June 4, 1993, 1–2.
18. Robert O'Malley, "Future of Oak Street Building Still Uncertain," *Sampan*, July 20, 1988, 1, 8.
19. Bill Moy, presentation to Boston Chinatown community forum, July 23, 1997.
20. John Avault, Mark Johnson, Shelagh Taber, Roger Dunlop, Colin Walsh, Charles Welch, et al., "Survey of Boston's Health Services Economy: Interim Report" (Boston: Boston Redevelopment Authority, 1987).
21. New England Medical Center, "Master Plan, 1990–2000" (Boston, 1990).
22. Linda Bourque, Gerard Kavanaugh, and William McCarthy, letter to Stephen Coyle, July 20, 1990.
23. Lawrence Cheng, interview by the author, Cambridge, MA, July 22, 1997; Robert O'Malley, "Pan Says He Was Unjustly Accused by US Government," *Sampan*, August 17, 1988, 1, 9.
24. Cheng, interview.
25. Boston Redevelopment Authority, "Grant Agreement by and between the Chinatown Community Center, Inc., and Boston Redevelopment Authority" (Boston, February 28, 1990).
26. T. Daugherty, "Chinatown Community Center" (Boston: Brown, Rudnick, Freed, and Gessmer, 1990); David Moy, interview by the author, Boston, December 13, 1996.
27. Zenobia Lai, Andrew Leong, and Chi Chi Wu, "The Lessons of the Parcel C Struggle: Reflections on Community Lawyering," *Asian Pacific American Law Journal* 9, no. 1 (2000): 10–11.
28. As early as the spring of 1991, the BRA had suggested the option of building a garage for the medical complex in conjunction with the community center, but this was never formally presented to the CCC principals. See Boston Redevelopment Authority, "Parcel C/Chinatown Community Center (CCC) Project: Interim Project Update" (Boston, May 1991).
29. Robert O'Malley, "Chinatown to Weigh Community Center Offer," *Sampan*, March 19, 1993, 1–2; Tina Cassidy, "Chinatown to Vote on Garage Proposal," *Boston Globe*, May 15, 1993.
30. An adjoining homeowner and activist, interview with the author, Boston, June 25, 1997.
31. New England Medical Center, "Parcel C Garage: Draft Project Impact Report/Draft Environmental Impact Report" (Boston, 1994); Lydia Lowe, "Six Agencies, the People, and Parcel C," *Sampan*, May 21, 1993, 3.
32. Lydia Lowe, "Center Commitments Should Be Honored," *Sampan*, March 19, 1993, 7; Vivian Wu Wong, letter to the editor, *Boston Herald*, June 4, 1993.
33. Betsy Q. M. Tong, "Chinatown Neighborhood Council Approves Controversial Garage Plan," *Boston Globe*, May 23, 1993; Kevin Kempskie, "Neighborhood Split over Parcel C," *Boston Tab*, July 20, 1993.
34. Lowe, "Six Agencies"; Robert O'Malley, "Coalition Forms to Oppose Garage," *Sampan*, June 4, 1993, 1–2.

CHAPTER 7: LEADING AGAINST THE GROWTH MACHINE, 1993–1998

1. Members of the Parcel C legal group have written extensively about the campaign. See Zenobia Lai, Andrew Leong, and Chi Chi Wu, "The Lessons of the Parcel C Struggle: Reflections on Community Lawyering," *Asian Pacific American Law Journal* 9 no. 1 (2000): 1–43; and Andrew Leong, *The Struggle over Parcel C: How Boston's Chinatown Won a Victory in the Fight against Institutional Expansion and Environmental Racism* (Boston: University of Massachusetts, Institute for Asian American Studies, 1995).

2. Howard Wong, "A Resident's Concern for Chinatown's Future," *Sampan*, July 16, 1993, 4.

3. Recent deep divisions within CCBA also contributed to its leaders' decision to join the Parcel C Coalition. Their opposition to the influence of the Chin faction may have been related to a struggle for control between the Wong clan and the Chin and Lee clans. See Julie Paik, "The Mediating Effects of Leadership on Social Movements: The Struggle over Parcel C in Boston's Chinatown" (thesis, Harvard University, 1999), 77.

4. Zenobia Lai, interview by the author, Brookline, MA, March 2, 1997.

5. Neighborhood resident and leader, interview, Boston, May 14, 1997.

6. Long-time neighborhood resident and leader, interview, Boston, March 28, 1997.

7. Robert O'Malley, "Council Approves Garage/Center Plan," *Sampan*, May 21, 1993, 1–2; Betsy Q. M. Tong, "N.E. Medical Garage Still on Table," *Boston Globe*, June 18, 1993; Robert O'Malley, "Council Discusses Parcel C Reaction," *Sampan*, July 2, 1993, 1–3.

8. David Moy, interview by the author, Boston, December 13, 1996; Lai, interview.

9. Lydia Lowe, "Lessons from the Struggle for Parcel C," *Unity Boston* (December 1993): 1, 4–5.

10. Betsy Q. M. Tong, "Chinatown Garage Plan Highlights Political Strife," *Boston Globe*, June 20, 1993.

11. Lai et al., "The Lessons of the Parcel C Struggle," 20.

12. Marie Gendron, "BRA OKs Plans for Chinatown Garage," *Boston Herald*, June 11, 1993; David Moy, "BRA Garage Decision: What Happens Next?" *Sampan*, June 18, 1993, 7.

13. Marla R. Van Schuyer, "State Hears Opposition to Chinatown Garage Plan," *Boston Globe*, September 1, 1993; "Chinatown Garage Needs Environmental Review," *Boston Tab*, September 14, 1993; Leong, *The Struggle over Parcel C*, 10–11.

14. Robert O'Malley, "Mayoral Candidates Discuss Chinatown," *Sampan*, August 20, 1993, 1, 13–14.

15. Coalition to Protect Parcel C for Chinatown, "Parcel C Voting Guidelines Released," *Sampan*, August 20, 1993, 9.

16. Betsy Q. M. Tong, "Chinatown Residents to Vote on Land Offer," *Boston Globe*, July 30, 1993; Marie Gendron, "Chinatown Group Rejects BRA Plan," *Boston Herald*, August 5, 1993.

17. Marie Gendron, "Chinatown Vote Says No to Garage," *Boston Herald*, September 15, 1993.

18. Marie Gendron, "Chinatown Calls for Garage Vote," *Boston Herald,* July 16, 1993.
19. Peter Gelzinis, "Turf War in Chinatown Reveals the Soul of the City," *Boston Sunday Herald,* September 12, 1993.
20. Robert O'Malley, "Council Supporters Sweep to Victory over Garage Opponents," *Sampan,* December 3, 1993, 1–2.
21. Coalition to Protect Parcel C for Chinatown and Chia-Ming Sze, Architect, "A New Chinatown Community Center on Parcel C: South Cove Urban Renewal Center Area, Boston MA" (Boston, April 12, 1994).
22. Lai et al., "The Lessons of the Parcel C Struggle," 21.
23. Traci Grant, "Chinatown Residents Rally for Parcel C," *Boston Globe,* August 21, 1994.
24. Leong, *The Struggle over Parcel C.*
25. Marie Gendron, "Neighbors Revolt against BRA," *Boston Herald,* July 20, 1993; Maureen Dezell, "Build-Down: Recession, Angry Residents Dog BRA Head Paul Barrett," *Boston Phoenix,* August 20, 1993; Kevin Kempskie, "Bashing the BRA: Citywide Criticism over Development," *Boston Tab,* August 31, 1993.
26. Lai et al., "The Lessons of the Parcel C Struggle," 21; Robert O'Malley, "State Rejects NEMC Environmental Report," *Sampan,* May 20, 1994, 1–2.
27. Robert O'Malley, "Menino," *Sampan,* October 15, 1993, 1, 6.
28. Joan Vennochi, "Menino Plays Favorites, Boston Loses," *Boston Globe,* October 6, 2011.
29. Lai, interview.
30. Lydia Lowe, interview by the author, Boston, November 18, 2011.
31. Adrian Walker, "Chinatown Community Group Wins Say on Development of Parcel," *Boston Globe,* October 22, 1994.
32. CPC was unable to sustain itself in the long run and later became a project under CPA.
33. Robert O'Malley, "Tufts Plan Questioned at Chinatown Meeting," *Sampan,* August 5, 1994, 1–2; Robert O'Malley, "Council Approves Tufts Plan," *Sampan,* November 4, 1994, 1–2.
34. Elena Choy, personal communication, September 1997.
35. Mary Hurley, "Parcel C's Future Still Uncertain," *Boston Sunday Globe,* April 12, 1998. The revival of downtown development had created possibilities for linkage funds. The city retrieved responsibility over Parcel C from the CCBA.
36. Asian Community Development Corporation, "ACDC Designated to Develop Parcel C for the Community," ACDC *Newsletter* (Winter 1999): 2.
37. The Boston Chinatown Neighborhood Center and Asian Youth Essential Services also gained space in the Metropolitan complex. Their new facilities came from agreements to yield their existing spaces, which were not originally part of Parcel C, for the Metropolitan. The developers found the project easier to build if they had all the space on the block.
38. Lai, interview.
39. Thomas Palmer, Jr., "200 Protest Plan for Turnpike Ramp into Chinatown," *Boston Globe,* April 30, 1996; Chinatown Central Artery/Tunnel Taskforce, newsletter (August 1996); Thomas Palmer, Jr., "Plans for Chinatown Offramp Are Dead," *Boston Globe,* June 25, 1997.

40. Lai, interview.

41. Tom O'Malley, "Parcel C," in *A Chinatown Banquet*, dir. Mike Blockstein (Boston: Asian Community Development Corporation, 2006), DVD.

42. Lowe, interview.

43. Manuel Castells, *The City and the Grassroots: A Cross-Cultural Theory of Urban Social Movements* (Berkeley: University of California Press, 1983), 318–27.

44. Suzanne Lee, interview by the author, Brookline, MA, February 1, 1997.

CHAPTER 8: BUILDING NEW ALLIANCES, 1999–2007

1. Richard Kindleberger, "A Taste for Boston," *Boston Sunday Globe,* February 6, 2000; "Billion Dollar Boom: Major Building Projects in Boston" [map], *Boston Globe Magazine,* February 15, 1998, 16.

2. Timothy Leland and Thomas J. Piper, "Plotting the Course," *Boston Globe Magazine,* October 25, 1998, 4; Anthony Flint, "The Hot Spot: The New Seaport District Could Be the Centerpiece of the Harbor Revival—or Just Another Skirmish in the City's Tribal Wars," *Boston Globe Magazine,* October 25, 1998, 6–10; "At the Right Price, Tiny Apartments Could Fuel Big Hopes in Boston" [editorial], Boston Globe, December 22, 2011.

3. Stephanie Ebbert, "Activists Back Bill on Low-Cost Housing," *Boston Globe,* April 24, 1999; "Boston: 'We Are at a Crisis Point, Really,'" *Boston Sunday Globe,* May 9, 1999; Tom Mashberg, "Unaffordable Housing," *Boston Sunday Herald,* August 8, 1999; Bruce Butterfield, "Urgent Need for State Housing Aid Cited," *Boston Globe,* December 23, 1999.

4. Andrew Spano, "The New Face of Chinatown," *Improper Bostonian* 8, no. 15 (1999): 16–22.

5. Racial demographic counts are not straightforward. The white-only population includes those who identify themselves solely as white in responding to the federal census and is a minimal count of those who are typically considered white. Because racial designations are self-selected and defined, non-white-only populations include "two or more races" and "other race" respondents who may be partially white or whom others may consider white. Some Latinos/Hispanics also consider themselves racially white.

6. Scott S. Greenberger, "Menino Rebuffed on Rent Curbs: City Council Rejects Plan as Ineffectual," *Boston Globe,* November 21, 2002; Andrea Estes and Heather Allen, "Council Shuts Down Rent Control, *Boston Globe,* December 9, 2004.

7. Michael Rosenwald, "Downtown Hotel Project Moves Ahead," *Boston Globe,* August 3, 2001; Thomas C. Palmer, Jr., "New Development: Six Buildings Reflect Shift in Hub's Commercial Real Estate Market," *Boston Globe,* February 28, 2002; Thomas C. Palmer, Jr., "Office Plan Wins Hayward Place Bid: Housing Proposals Lose to Millennium," *Boston Globe,* January 17, 2003.

8. Chinatown Initiative, "Chinatown Masterplan 2000: Agenda for a Sustainable Neighborhood" (Boston, 2000).

9. Robert O'Malley, "Vying for Influence in Chinatown," *Sampan,* January 16, 1998, 6A–7A.

10. Karen Eschbacher, "Chinese Neighbors Divided on Parade," *Boston Globe*, February 5, 2000.

11. Eric William Schramm, "Kwong Kow Vacates 90 Tyler Street," *Sampan*, July 21, 2000, 3–4; "A Not-So-Benevolent Action: The Benevolent Association Puts a Social Service Agency on the Street," *Sampan*, November 20, 1998, 3–4.

12. Tatiana With Ribadeneira, "Chinatown Set to Give Its New Y a Workout," *Boston Sunday Globe*, February 13, 2000 1.

13. Chris Reidy, "Street Fight: Activist Raps Developer's Use of Public Ways to Set Project Boundaries in Bid to Skirt Height Rules," *Boston Globe*, July 2, 2003; Thomas C. Palmer, Jr., and Chris Reidy, "Elastic Zoning in Boston, Negotiation Matters More Than Written Rules," *Boston Globe*, July 13, 2003.

14. Kristen Lombardi, "To Hell with Everyone," *Boston Phoenix*, October 15–21, 2004; *Overshadowed: Boston's Chinatown* (Boston: Emerson College, Journalism Department, 2005), compact disc.

15. Steve Bailey, "Build 'Em High," *Boston Globe*, December 17, 2003.

16. Martha Tai, "Liberty Plaza: 26 Stories . . . 426 Parking Spaces . . . 274 Hotel Rooms . . . 291,750 s.f. of Office: What Happened to the Chinatown Community Plan?," *Campaign to Protect Chinatown* 3, no. 2 (2000): 1, 4; Thomas C. Palmer, Jr., "Neighborhood Rising: 10-Acre Project Would Include Housing, Library Annex, Supermarket," *Boston Globe*, December 11, 2004; Thomas C. Palmer, Jr., "Developer Buys Historic Hub Textile Building for $9M, Plans Residences" *Boston Globe*, November 7, 2006.

17. Scott Greenberger, "Chinatown Activists Seek to Control Artery Parcel," *Boston Globe*, April 29, 2003.

18. "Reclaiming a Lost Chinatown: Hudson Street and Parcel 24," *Chinese Progressive Association Newsletter* (May 2003): 1–2; Jeremy Schwab, "Chinatown Activists Eyeing Pike Parcel," *Bay State Banner*, May 13, 2004; Adam Smith, "Chinatown Council Leader Questions Parcel 24 Campaign," *Sampan*, May 21, 2004, 3; Asian Community Development Corporation, "ACDC Presents Vision for Parcel 24," ACDC *Newsletter* (Summer 2005): 1–4.

19. Robert A. Brown and J. P. Shadley, "The Chinatown–Leather District Park," *Boston Globe*, June 14, 2003.

20. Campaign to Protect Chinatown, newsletter *2, no. 6* (1999): 1.

21. Mah Wah, interview by the author, Boston, July 16, 2016.

22. Helen Liu, "First Chinatown Resident Association Founded," *Chinese Progressive Association Newsletter* (August 1999): 1.

23. Chinatown/South Cove Neighborhood Council, City of Boston, and Boston Redevelopment Authority, "Chinatown Community Plan: A Plan to Manage Growth" (Boston, March 1990).

24. Corey Dade, "Rift in Chinatown: Residents Want More Say in Development Decisions," *Boston Sunday Globe*, August 11, 2002.

25. Zenobia Lai and Daniel S. Manning, letter to Boston Redevelopment Authority, comments on "Draft Project Impact Report—Liberty Place," February 20, 2002, 20.

26. Adam Smith, "BRA Presents Scaled-Down Liberty Place; Critics Not Happy," *Sampan*, July 5–19, 2002, 2, 8; Adam Smith, "Zoning Board of Appeal Unanimously Approves Liberty Place Building 28-Stories," *Sampan*, August 16–September 6,

2002, 2, 6. Data from the 2000 U.S. census list the median income for Asian residents in Chinatown as $14,670.

27. "Change in Chinatown" [editorial], *Boston Globe*, December 19, 2002.

28. Cindy Rodriguez, "Minority Areas Show Biggest Hub Jump in Voters: Gap in Participation Still Remains, Though," *Boston Globe*, November 7, 2002.

29. Donovan Slack, "Coercion of Voters Reported in Chinatown," *Boston Globe*, September 26, 2003; Donovan Slack, "City Election Was Flawed, State Finds," *Boston Globe*, October 21, 2003; Yvonne Abraham, "Justice Department Accuses City of Voting Rights Violations," *Boston Globe*, July 30, 2005; Andrea Estes, "City Agrees to Accept Election Monitoring," *Boston Globe*, September 16, 2005.

30. Anand Vaishnav, "A Unified Agenda for Minorities Eyed," *Boston Sunday Globe*, October 19, 2003. At the time, the University of Massachusetts Boston was the home of the Institute for Asian American Studies, the Mauricio Gaston Institute for Latino Community Development and Public Policy, and the William Monroe Trotter Institute, which focused on African American issues.

31. "Calendar: Candidate Forum," *Boston Sunday Globe*, October 2, 2005.

32. Alliance of Boston Neighborhoods, bylaws (Boston, 1999).

33. Lisa Wangsness, "Now Yoon Faces the Spotlight," *Boston Globe*, November 10, 2005; Yvonne Abraham, "Chinatown Voter Awareness Helped Propel Yoon's Win," *Boston Globe*, November 10, 2005.

CHAPTER 9: BUBBLE, TROUBLE, AND TESTING A NEW VISION, 2008–2014

1. Donovan Slack, "Rushing to a Standstill," *Boston Globe*, March 26, 2009; Casey Ross, "Chinatown Tower Plan Moves Ahead," *Boston Globe*, November 10, 2010; Jeffrey Krasner and Casey Ross, "Hospitals Freeze Big-Ticket Plans," *Boston Sunday Globe*, December 14, 2008.

2. Robert Gavin, "Pace of Job Cuts Quicken in Mass.," *Boston Globe*, January 23, 2009; Ross Kerber, "Putnam to Shed 260 People as Industry Slides," *Boston Globe*, February 12, 2009; Jay Fitzgerald, "2008: A Year to Forget," *Boston Herald*, December 30, 2008.

3. "Restaurant Workers Struggle for Back Pay," "Jin Workers Win $110,000 Class Action Lawsuit," and "C-Mart Complaint Brings Company-Wide Settlement," *Chinese Progressive Association Newsletter* (Spring 2008): 7–8.

4. Bill Moyers, "Steve Meacham and City Life/Vida Urbana," https://billmoyers .com, May 1, 2009; City of Boston, "A Report on Boston's Housing Strategy for 2009–2012" (Boston, March 2009).

5. Matt Viser and Michael Kranish, "Mass. Could Get $11.7b from Stimulus," *Boston Globe*, February 14, 2009. Local banks and financial firms also benefited from other federal bail-out initiatives; see Maria Sacchetti, "Mass. Buoyed in Recession, Data Indicate," *Boston Globe*, September 29, 2010.

6. Megan Woolhouse, "Developers Tap into Demand for Apartments: Thousands of Units Planned," *Boston Globe*, October 25, 2010.

7. Victoria Cheng, "Moving in, Moving Out," *Boston Globe*, July 6, 2008; Casey Ross, "A Bigger, Bolder Plan for Herald Site," *Boston Globe*, February 2, 2012;

Jay Fitzgerald, "South End Landscape Getting a Rapid Makeover," *Boston Globe,* March 13, 2012; Paul McMorrow, "A Boston for Rich and Poor, with No Middle Class," *Boston Globe,* October 15, 2013.

8. The BRA counted 4,444 residents but excluded Castle Square, technically part of the South End but usually included in Chinatown community plans; see Chinatown Master Plan 2010 Oversight Committee, "Chinatown Master Plan 2010: Community Vision for the Future" (Boston, 2010).

9. Lydia Lowe, personal communication, June 2015.

10. Angie Liou, interview by the author, Boston, April 17, 2018.

11. Inclusionary development mandated either the inclusion of affordable housing in a proposed development or the creation of affordable housing offsite; see Casey Ross, "Construction Begins on Chinatown Tower, *Boston Globe,* September 22, 2012.

12. Lisette Le, "City Begins Chinatown Library Feasibility Study," *Chinese Progressive Association Newsletter* (Winter 2007): 6; Meghan E. Irons, "For Chinatown, a New Chapter," *Boston Globe,* September 21, 2009. A temporary branch library finally opened in 2017. More importantly, a permanent location was identified in an upcoming development on Washington Street near the Quincy Elementary School.

13. AARW moved its offices to Dorchester in 2015, where it worked out of the Vietnamese American Community Center.

14. Asian American Resource Workshop, https://aarw.org; "Chinatown Should Get Housing That It's Been Promised," *Boston Globe,* April 4, 2012.

15. In the summer of 2015, Quinzani's announced its closing and sale to an anonymous developer. The bean-sprout factory also announced its closing.

16. "Organizing for Jobs at Whole Foods & Roche Bros.," *Chinese Progressive Association Newsletter* 1 (2015): 7.

17. Liou, interview.

18. "Our Right to Remain," *Chinese Progressive Association Newsletter* 1 (2015): 3–4.

19. Matt Carroll, "Tenants to Own Cooperative," *Boston Globe,* June 1, 1990.

20. Chinese Progressive Association, "Year of the Tiger Celebration" (Boston, 2010).

21. Andrew Ryan, "A Changing Geography Lesson," *Boston Globe,* October 19, 2011; Andrew Ryan, "District 2 Race Recount Likely," *Boston Globe,* November 16, 2011.

22. Andrea Estes, "City Agrees to Accept Elections Monitoring," *Boston Globe,* September 16, 2005; Lydia Lowe and Glenn Magpantay, "Boston Asian American Voters Win Bilingual Ballots," *Chinese Progressive Association Newsletter* (Winter 2015): 1–2.

23. Maria Sacchetti, "Fresh Fight over Bilingual Ballots," *Boston Globe,* May 14, 2008; "Victory for Asian American Voting Rights," *Chinese Progressive Association Newsletter* (Summer 2010): 2.

24. "In Boston Redistricting, Don't Split Up Chinatown," *Boston Globe,* November 28, 2011; Andrew Ryan, "A Changing Geography Lesson," *Boston Globe,* October 19, 2011.

25. Lydia Lowe, "A Year for Growing Political Power," *Chinese Progressive Association Newsletter* (Winter 2012): 1, 6–8; Lisette Le, interview by the author, Boston, November 19, 2014.

26. Right to the City, http://righttothecity.org.

27. Henri Lefebvre, "The Right to the City, Henri Lefebvre," http://atlasofplaces.com; David Harvey, *Rebel Cities: From the Right to the City to the Urban Revolution* (London: Verso, 2013).

28. Both locally and nationally, RTTC has allied itself with legal aid, grassroots media, environmental, alternative economic development groups, and other issue advocates.

29. Le, interview; Right to the City Boston, "Bad Day for B of A! 1,500 Rally & 20 Arrested as Foreclosed Families #Occupy Boston Bank of America," http://righttothecity.org; Mel King, "A New Rainbow Coalition Backs Walsh," *Boston Sunday Globe,* November 17, 2013.

30. "Temporary Workers' Rights Bill Becomes Law," *Chinese Progressive Association Newsletter* (Fall 2012): 5; "City Halls Must Join Battle against Restaurant Wage Theft," *Boston Globe,* December 24, 2014.

31. Peter Medoff and Holly Sklar, *Streets of Hope: The Fall and Rise of an Urban Neighborhood* (Boston: South End Press, 1994), 119–21.

32. Chinese Progressive Association, "What's New: Chinatown Community Land Trust," *2014 Annual Report* (Boston, 2014), 3.

33. Felix Arroyo, Jr., was the son of Felix Arroyo, Sr., who was part of Team Unity in 2005. The younger Arroyo was first elected to his seat in 2010.

34. Wesley Lowery, "Historic Diversity in Mayor's Race, *Boston Globe,* July 29, 2013.

35. Akilah Johnson, "Community Group Supports Barros," *Boston Globe,* September 7, 2013.

36. Adrian Walker, "Dinosaur Politics Afoot in a Strategy for Mayor's Race," *Boston Globe,* September 6, 2013.

37. Akilah Johnson, "Minority Voters Were Key in Victory," *Boston Globe,* November 7, 2013; David Scharfenberg, "Majority-Minority Boston Asks: Was Mayoral Election a Victory or a Defeat?" *WBUR News,* http://www.wbur.org.

38. Wu served as city council president in 2016–18. Sam Yoon left the council in 2009.

39. Deirdre Fernandes, "Luxury Condos Soar in the City," *Boston Globe,* April 21, 2014; Yvonne Abraham, "Lost in the Building Boom," *Boston Globe,* February 6, 2014. As of 2020, Walsh has taken some steps to support the community—for instance, blocking various hotel proposals within Chinatown boundaries.

40. Casey Ross, "Luxury Units Up, So Too Concerns," *Boston Globe,* March 25, 2014.

41. Sean Murphy, "As City Booms, BRA Runs Almost without Scrutiny: Answerable Only to Mayor, City Development Agency Has Bent Rules in Some Cases, Diverted Housing Funds," *Boston Globe,* December 22, 2013.

42. KPMG, "Report on Applying Agreed-Upon Procedures: Boston Redevelopment Authority/Economic Development Industrial Corporation" (Boston, July 11, 2014).

CHAPTER 10: CHINATOWNS AND ETHNIC SURVIVAL IN A GLOBALIZED WORLD

1. Fred C. Doolittle, George S. Masnick, Phillip C. Clay, and Gregory A. Jackson, *Future Boston: Patterns and Perspectives* (Cambridge, MA: Massachusetts Institute of Technology and Harvard University, Joint Center for Urban Studies, 1982), 71.

2. Alan Ehrenhalt, *The Great Inversion and the Future of the American City* (New York: Vintage, 2012); Bernadette Hanlon, John Rennie Short, and Thomas J. Vicino, *Cities and Suburbs: New Metropolitan Realities in the U.S.* (New York: Routledge, 2010); Loretta Lees, Hyun Bang Shin, and Ernesto López-Morales, *Planetary Gentrification* (Cambridge, UK: Polity, 2016).

3. Alissa Walker, "Why U.S. Cities Need More Multi-Racial, Mixed-Income Neighborhoods," August 21, 2018, https://www.curbed.com.

4. Bonnie Tsui, "Chinatown Revisited," *New York Times,* January 24, 2014.

5. Rose Hum Lee, "The Decline of Chinatowns in the United States," *American Journal of Sociology* 54, no. 5 (1949): 422–32.

6. The construction of the Dan Ryan and then the Stevenson expressways, part of the interstate highway system, demolished part of Chicago's new Chinatown in the 1960s.

7. Chuo Li, "Chinatown and Urban Redevelopment: A Spatial Narrative of Race, Identity, and Urban Politics, 1950–2000" (PhD diss., University of Illinois at Urbana-Champaign, 2011); Huping Ling, *Chinese Chicago: Race, Transnational Migration, and Community Since 1870* (Stanford, CA: Stanford University Press, 2012).

8. Jan Lin, *Reconstructing Chinatown: Ethnic Enclave, Global Change* (Minneapolis: University of Minnesota Press, 1998), 31.

9. Bernard Wong, *Patronage, Brokerage, Entrepreneurship, and the Chinese Community of New York* (New York: AMS Press, 1988), 78–97.

10. Bethany Y. Li, Andrew Leong, Domenic Vitiello, and Arthur Acoca, *Chinatown Then and Now: Gentrification in Boston, New York, and Philadelphia* (New York: Asian American Legal Defense and Education Fund, 2013), 23–31. The business count by this study includes only ground-floor businesses.

11. Helen Stapinski, "Essex Crossing: A Renewal Project 60 Years in the Making," *New York Times,* June 15, 2017; Asian American Federation of New York, "Chinatown: One Year after September 11th. An Economic Impact Study" (New York, 2002); Li et al., *Chinatown Then and Now.*

12. The most comprehensive source for information about Philadelphia Chinatown is Kathryn E. Wilson, *Ethnic Renewal in Philadelphia's Chinatown: Space, Place, and Struggle* (Philadelphia: Temple University Press, 2015).

13. Lena Sze, *Chinatown Lives: Oral Histories from Philadelphia Chinatown* (Philadelphia: Asian Arts Initiative, 2004), 28.

14. Wilson, *Ethnic Renewal,* 31–39.

15. Mary Yee, "The Save Chinatown Movement: Surviving against All Odds," *Philadelphia Legacies,* May 4, 2012, 24–31.

16. Mary Yee, phone interview by the author, Philadelphia, May 10, 2018.

17. Yee, "The Save Chinatown Movement," 27.

18. An outside consultant developed the "Chinatown I Urban Renewal Plan," working closely with PCDC and the Philadelphia City Planning Commission. PCDC had petitioned the planning commission for the study.

19. Daryl Joji Maeda, *Rethinking the Asian American Movement* (New York: Routledge, 2012), 77–79.

20. Yee, interview.
21. Wilson, *Ethnic Renewal,* 140–54.
22. Li et al., *Chinatown Then and Now,* 32–40.
23. Wilson, *Ethnic Renewal,* 75.
24. In Philadelphia, city planning and the redevelopment authority were in separate divisions. The BRA, as I have noted, was unique in consolidating both functions.
25. Li et al., *Chinatown Then and Now,* 2–3.

CONCLUSION: MAKING THE ROAD BY WALKING

1. City of Boston, "Housing a Changing City: Boston 2030" (Boston, 2014).
2. Casey Ross, "A New Age for An Old Town," *Boston Sunday Globe,* March 1, 2015.
3. Daniel Hartley, "Gentrification and Financial Health," *Federal Reserve Bank of Cleveland,* November, 2013, https://www.clevelandfed.org; Katie Johnston, "A Troubling Look at Homelessness in Boston," *Boston Globe,* December 12, 2014; Katie Johnston, "Homeless Numbers Soar in Massachusetts," *Boston Globe,* October 31, 2014; Natalie Holmes and Alan Berube, "City and Metropolitan Inequality on the Rise, Driven by Declining Incomes" (Washington, DC: Brookings Institute, January 2016); Kathleen Conti, "Tenants Aim at Higher Rents," *Boston Globe,* September 23, 2016; Milton J. Valencia and Tim Logan, "Plan Seeks High-End Real Estate Fees," *Boston Globe,* January 14, 2019.
4. Tabor, Nick, "How Has Chinatown Stayed Chinatown?" *New York Magazine,* September 24, 2015.
5. Boston Municipal Research Bureau, "Boston's Linkage Program: A New Approach to Managing Linkage Funds for Housing and Job Training" (Boston, 1998); "A Nudge for Affordable Housing in the Hottest Markets," *Boston Globe,* December 25, 2015.
6. David Harvey, *Rebel Cities: From the Right to the City to the Urban Revolution* (London: Verso, 2013), 16, 14. Also see John R. Logan and Harvey L. Molotch, *Urban Fortunes: The Political Economy of Place* (Berkeley: University of California Press, 1987).
7. There has been new energy, primarily through the formation of a regional coalition called APIs CAN!, which is focused on civic engagement. Both the AARW and ACDC have also increased their organizing efforts around development issues, while the growing population has supported organized Asian American activity in electoral politics.
8. Tunney Lee, personal communications, February–April 2016.
9. Long-time neighborhood resident and leader, interview, Boston, March 28, 1997.
10. Siu Man Luie, interview, Boston, October 7, 1997.

INDEX

Page numbers in *italics* indicate figures.

INDEX

INDEX

War Brides Act (1945), 36

White, Kevin, and White administration: Chinatown relationship, 63–64; Chin brothers support, 56, 105; Combat Zone and, 66; downtown development focus, 60–61; downtown focus, 92, 97; growth coalition policies, 90; Lafayette Place and, 88–89, 223n6; land swap, 82; mayoralty race (1968), 59; scandal and corruption, 91; school desegregation, 70; traditional organizations and, 83; urban development plans, 86

Whose Boston, 181

Wilson, Kathryn, 31, 195, 198

Wing, Beverly, 128

women, Chinese: employment of, 131; garment industry and, 38, 50; immigration of, 36; interracial marriage, 27; laundry workers, 27; men to women ratio, 29; protests against Japanese, 36

Wong, Ann, 128–29

Wong, Bernard, 23, 211–12n15

Wong, David, 106, 110, 117

Wong, Deanna, 21, 220–21n41

Wong, Fanny, 72

Wong, Howard, 105, 142

Wong, Reggie, 47

Wong family, 193

Woo, Davis, 117, 143–44

World War II, effect on Chinatown, 33–36

Wu, Chi Chi, 46, 141

Wu, Michelle, 185, 237n38

Xiao-huang Yin, 29

Yancey, Charles, 171

Yee, Henry, 142, 152, 168

Yee, Ken, 89

Yee, Mary, 196, 198

Yee clan, 212n30

Yellow Seeds, 195–96, 198

Yep, Cecilia Moy, 195–96

Yin, Xiao-Huang, 11, 29

YMCA (Wang), 162

YMCA, Chinatown, 6, 52, 63, 130, 135, 137, 145, 147

YMCA, South Cove, 135, 151, 162

Yoon, Sam, 171, 237n38

Yu, Lai Miu (May), 72–73

Zhou, Min, 56

zoning and land use: building height restrictions, 112, 152, 162; construction moratorium, 82; downtown construction, 60; Park Plaza project, 60. *See also* Chinatown master plan; Combat Zone; Tufts–New England Medical Center

Zoning Board of Appeals, 168

Zuckerman, Mort, 61